Perspectives

A radical examination of the alien abduction phenomenon

Also by John Spencer from Macdonald

PHENOMENON
(edited by Hilary Evans and John Spencer)

Perspectives

A radical examination of the alien abduction phenomenon

JOHN SPENCER

Macdonald

A Macdonald Book

First published in Great Britain in 1990
by Macdonald & Co (Publishers) Ltd
London & Sydney

British Library Cataloguing in Publication Data
Spencer, John *1954–*
Perspectives
1. Kidnapping by extraterrestrial beings
I. Title
001.942

ISBN 0-356-186776

Typeset in Plantin by Leaper & Gard Ltd,
Bristol, England

Printed and bound in Great Britain by
Biddles Ltd, Guildford and King's Lynn

Macdonald & Co (Publishers) Ltd
Orbit House
1 New Fetter Lane
London EC4A 1AR
A member of Maxwell Pergamon Publishing Corporation plc

ACKNOWLEDGEMENTS

No book written by one person is the result of only that person's efforts. Thanks are due to many who have assisted me; some are named in the narrative, some are specifically not named at their request, some do not form part of the story. In addition to these people, special thanks are due to:

— Bob Digby, who gave me information and copies of material from congresses I was unable to attend.

— Walt Andrus for assistance with 'Gulf Breeze' and other material.

— Bertil Kuhlemann and his family, for their hospitality and help during my stay in Sweden.

— Hilary Evans and the Mary Evans Picture Library for general assistance and inspiration.

— John Shaw (photography) for assistance with the photographic material.

— Birgitta, my secretary, for typing and translation of Swedish material.

— Lena, Clive, Christian and Maria, for helping to arrange quiet moments when I needed them.

— my parents, for giving up Christmas so that I could complete the work I was doing.

and especially to:

— Anne, Katie and Jenny, for putting up with the disruption.

Organisations exist in most countries investigating UFO and abduction reports.

For those in the U.K. interested in serious scientific research of the UFO phenomenon BUFORA, the British UFO Research Association Limited, can be contacted at the following address:

16 Southway, Burgess Hill,
Sussex RH15 9ST, United Kingdom

BUFORA will be pleased to supply a list of organisations operating in other countries.

The United States, with its high incidence of UFO reports, must be regarded as a special case. Despite doubts stated in the text of the book about techniques applied in that country (and other countries, including the UK) to investigations the American investigators named in the book appear to me to be sincere in their desire to seek the truth and to help witnesses. The same applies to MUFON and to it's International Director, Walt Andrus.

The reader must decide for himself whether such techniques are appropriate to his situation.

MUFON, the Mutual UFO Network, can be contacted at the following address:

MUFON, 103 Oldtowne Road, Seguin, Texas 78155, United States of America (International Director: Walt Andrus)

ICUR, the International Committee for UFO Research, exists to co-ordinate research across national boundaries and to facilitate compatible computer data exchange.

Organisations interested in international co-operation should contact ICUR at the following address:

PO Box 314, Penn, High Wycombe, Bucks, HP10 8PB,
United Kingdom

CONTENTS

INTRODUCTION

Reaching ahead of your car, beyond the range of its headlights, a long road lies ahead. It is dark and late at night, and you are returning from a long business meeting, or a family outing, or a casual social call. The radio in the car is playing; either softly just as company or maybe very loudly in an attempt to keep you awake so that you can complete the journey without having to lay up for a time en route.

You're not dangerously sleepy, but perhaps you're drowsy, the road is monotonous, most of the scenery is shrouded in the night; there are few cars passing you, and even fewer travelling with you.

Perhaps suddenly, but more probably slowly, you become aware that in fact there are no cars around you, and there haven't been for some time. The atmosphere seems heavier than it did, and an unusual stillness — even silence — is all around you. Your own car seems quieter than it should. Perhaps it feels warmer and you loosen your tie, but the gesture serves only to prove that the uncomfortable warmth is *in* you, not around you.

Then you become aware that some light is shining on your car. For a while this pulls you out of your drowsiness, and you sit more upright, maybe wind down a window, try to concentrate that bit harder. The light becomes stronger.

At this time perhaps you look around the road and the skies for the source of the light, and there above you, somewhere away from the car, you see a bright light that just couldn't be an aeroplane, and is certainly too bright for a planet or star. You check on it every now and again, keeping one eye on the road, and it seems to be pacing you. If you've read about them in the papers perhaps you even think that it might be one of those UFO things; if you do, it will probably bring a wry smile to your face. At this stage.

For a time you watch while the object changes its apparent position relative to the car; earlier you were sure that this was due to the bends in the road changing your position, but now you're not so sure. Could it actually be following the car? By now perhaps you wish that another car would appear, ahead, behind or even passing you. Company seems desirable.

You might check your watch or the car clock, and regret that it's still another hour before you get home; when you do you can sink into your armchair and watch that late programme you wanted to see and laugh off your apprehensions; because that's certainly what they've become now.

And then, to your relief, the light goes and you cannot see the object anywhere. Already you're passing it off as just one of those things — a story to eat out on.

And then you turn a bend in the road.

Sometime later it's as if you've just woken up; you shake your head to clear it and you feel better, if even more tired. Cars are passing you, perhaps there is one on the road ahead and you inch up to be that bit closer; you're glad of the company. Maybe you remember the light, but only as a vague feeling of unease that you cannot quite define. And then the signpost ahead says you are near home, and soon you are pulling up outside your house and the journey is over.

When you get inside you might be a bit surprised that the family have already retired to bed, but it's late and so Good luck to them, you think. You'll have a quick drink, catch that television programme and then join them. You settle into the armchair and turn on the TV. All you get is static and you flick through the stations, but they're all blank. Perhaps you curse the TV for a time, check to see what time your programme is on, then check the time on your watch.

That's when you realise it's later than you think, perhaps two or three hours later, and the TV stations have shut down some time ago. It doesn't make sense, you try to work out how you could have taken maybe five hours on a two or three hour journey. By now, you can't think straight and you just need sleep, so you go to bed.

The events of the night before may irk you somewhat the

next morning, but it's doubtful you'll have time to concentrate on them. The family is having breakfast, your spouse wants to know how last night went with so-and-so, the children are getting ready for school. And you have to be at work so you check your briefcase, make some notes, or whatever. And anyway, the cold light of morning has washed away all those spooky fears of the night before; you're beginning to dismiss the whole thing.

It might be years before the next relevant events occur. During that time you haven't been 'quite your old self', more irritable and less able to concentrate. Perhaps you've been having nightmares that have been leaving you exhausted and somehow ill at ease during the day. Somewhere, at some level of consciousness, you associate your moods with those lights you sighted in the car. Perhaps you find that you are uneasy at nights alone in the car, not actually afraid but less comfortable. Or perhaps that particular stretch of road causes you some apprehensions; even visiting those people you were with makes you recall more than you would wish. Eventually, for many this can lead to a doctor, and then to a psychiatrist or psychologist.

In your sessions with him, the events of that night come out, as do your nightmares and your other fears. He suggests a technique called regression hypnosis to take you back in time, in your memory, to the night that seems to be the stem from which all your troubles are sprouting.

Once 'under' the hypnosis, the doctor instructs you to feel your way back in time to your drive that night. And you're back on that road, in your car, and you can feel that unexpected warmth, you notice again that there are no cars around you, and you can see the light, and that object pacing the car.

And, again, you turn that bend in the road.

This time, your memory is unsprung; ahead of you on the road a large, seemingly metallic object sits astride the carriageway. You can see, can describe, its landing legs and aerials, and the flashing lights. And in the windows you can see faces such as you have never seen before. Almost featureless, expressionless faces, with small, lipless mouths, compressed noses, no hair. And you notice the eyes; huge disproportionate black eyes that wrap around half the face.

You notice them particularly because there is no doubt that they are watching you.

(Your fears will become manifest now, and the doctor may well be physically holding you down as you gesture violently.) Your car stops, and will not respond to your frantic efforts to re-start it. The radio is dead. The lights have gone out. Only by the eerie light of the object ahead can you see the misshapen forms that are walking towards you. Your mind is flooded with fear, yet you are unable to resist; the creatures remove you from the car and support you as they take you away from your car, along the road, towards — and into — their alien craft. Inside the craft you are led through a series of corridors, and into a room stark by ordinary standards; just some machinery.

And the platform bed that they are now strapping you down onto.

During the course of the next hour or so you relate the story of what happens; of being stripped naked, of being examined — often painfully — by the creatures who insert long metallic instruments into your nose, your navel, who take semen and ovary contents for examination; who burn your eyes and genitals with lights that actually hurt.

Perhaps they communicate with you, in words or by telepathy, even with musical sounds. They offer platitudes of comfort but they don't seem really to care, just want you to be easier to handle.

Eventually it comes to an end; they lift you off the table, return your clothes to you. Perhaps they let you walk around parts of the craft, touch some of the machinery. Never — though you desperately try — will they let you remove any of its artifacts that might have helped you confirm what is happening to you. Soon, they remove you from the ship into the cold air. It has been hours, but the craft is still straddling the road. Still no cars pass by, let alone stop. They return you to your car, re-seat you. You remember their most forceful command; that you will *not* remember, that you *will forget* what has happened. You watch, immobilised, as the craft takes off, and without your conscious control you restart the car and drive on.

Sometime later it's as if you've just woken up; you shake

your head to clear it and you feel better, if even more tired. Cars are passing you, perhaps there is one on the road ahead and you inch up to be that bit closer; you're glad of the company. Maybe you remember the light, but only as a vague feeling of unease that you cannot quite define. And then the signpost ahead says you are near home, and soon you are pulling up outside your house and the journey is over.

And you leave the doctor's couch feeling drained, but this time a new journey — a search for understanding — is just beginning.

This is a stereotypical abduction, reported by people from many parts of the world, and research into these events has produced a most curious paradox;

We *know* these events are *real*...
... *But do they actually happen*?

To understand this paradox it is necessary to first study the context in which the abduction reports began to occur ...

PART ONE

The Pre-Abduction Years

The diversity of the phenomenon of Nature is so great, and the treasures hidden in the heavens so rich, precisely in order that the human mind shall never be lacking in fresh nourishment.

JOHANNES KEPLER

ARNOLD GIVES BIRTH - BUT TO WHAT?

Somewhere amidst the Cascade mountains of the Pacific coastal state of Washington lay the wreckage of a C-46 Marine Transport plane.

Less than ten thousand feet above, on a course between Chehalis and Yakima, a light airplane tramped through the clear blue skies. It was a Callair aircraft, a special three seater, single engine 'mountain plane' modified for the atmospheric and weather problems of mountain search and rescue, and capable of high altitude take-offs and rough field landings. Its lone pilot was not formally engaged in a search for the Transport, but having just completed his work for the day — installing fire fighting equipment for the Central Air Service at Chehalis — he had decided to undertake a private search, spurred on by both humanitarian and financial reasons. The relatives of the lost victims had put up a $5000 reward for discovery of the plane.

He was not to find it.

Although the flight was to prove uneventful in most respects, the pilot — Kenneth Arnold — was to be distracted for just two or three minutes by a distant and unclear sighting that would not only claim his attention for the remainder of the time he was in the air, but would go on to change the social perceptions of the human race forever.

He had taken off at around two o'clock and flow directly towards Mount Ranier, at an altitude of around nine to ten thousand feet. He dropped down and searched the high plateau to the west, then the nearby canyon. Above Mineral, he swept in a 300 degree arc back towards Mount Ranier, climbing again to a little over 9000 feet. The air was smooth, the flying pleasurable and easy, and Arnold coasted along watching the scenery pass by.

5000 feet above and behind him to his left, a DC-4 shared the sky.

Suddenly a flash of light alarmed Arnold. Could he be too close to another aircraft? He searched quickly for the source of the flash and saw to the left and north of Mount Ranier what appeared to be a formation of objects in flight. He assumed at first that they were jet planes, but noticed that they moved in a curious way, flipping up and down sufficiently for the sun to catch them, causing the reflections that had attracted his attention. When he came to describe this later he used a phrase the consequence of which he could hardly have foreseen — he described them as moving 'like a saucer would if you skipped it across the water'.

Being an experienced pilot he made as careful an observation as possible of the objects, even opening his window to get a clear view; they were flying almost at right angles to him, between Mount Ranier and Mount Adams, which gave him the chance to estimate their speed; somewhere between 1300 and 1700 miles per hour; faster than any plane of the day could fly. He estimated their distance from him to be around 23 miles, the length of their formation some five miles. Using a Zeus bonnet fastener as a guide, and the DC-4 off his left shoulder for comparison, he was able to estimate their individual size as about two-thirds the size of the DC-4.

All of these estimates have been called into question in the forty-odd years since this sighting of Tuesday, 24th June 1947; as we shall see, the accuracy of the observations was to prove relatively unimportant.

What *was* to prove important was a reporter's use of Arnold's phrase 'like a saucer would if you skipped it across the water.' In a short time the expression 'flying saucer' was born.

Arnold went on to continue the search for the plane but later admitted that the $5000 had somehow become less important, he wanted to get onto the ground and to tell someone of his sighting. His mind was no longer on the job, he did not locate the plane despite a further twenty or so minutes of flight and a last search of the Tieton Reservoir, and at around four o'clock he flew into Yakima and history.

So why was this sighting so important? It was not the most important sighting of its kind, not the first, not the closest or the best observed. It was not corroborated by anyone else, it had been distant, indistinct and of very short duration.

But it had one distinction. It attracted the attention of the media, and gave to the phenomenon a name that the public found it could identify with — Flying Saucer. It was just the right term for the mood of the moment; it was in fact the birth of the best and most enduring advertising slogan in the world — despite doubts about the product, it is still being bought world-wide forty-odd years later!

Despite the now-household familiarity of the name, it was the cause of the first and one of the greatest misunderstandings of the UFO-era. Were Arnold's 'saucers' in fact saucer-shaped? Certainly that is the general impression given in many books and articles since that date, but in fact Arnold's own sketches of the objects show them as rounded boomerangs. I even tested this theory with a group of UFO investigators and researchers; all but one thought that Arnold's saucers *were* saucer-shaped and even the one who thought otherwise got the description wrong. Arnold's description using the word saucer was of their *flight movements*, not their *shape* ('Like a saucer would [move] if you skipped it across the water').

Scarcely born, the UFO legends were distorting already as the media took hold.

Let me, then, state at the outset of this book my concern as to the media's influence in this subject. Saucer shapes had not been *described*, but they had been *named*. Almost immediately, saucer *shapes* were to be reported and this has continued to be one of the main descriptions of what are now generically referred to as UFOs to the present day. In this birth of the modern era of UFOs we are already looking at either an exceptional coincidence, or impressive media influence.

Subsequent public perception of the phenomenon has been no less shaped and distorted by the media. This does not mean that UFOs are a media creation, after all Arnold saw *something*, but how much of what the media would have us believe to be true is in fact true? And to what extent have the media influenced — deliberately or otherwise — what people report even when they too have seen, or experienced, *something*?

THE EARLIEST REPORTS?

If Arnold's UFO sighting of June 1947 was not the first, then what was? Clearly, no answer will ever be forthcoming. UFO merely means Unidentified Flying Object, limiting though even this phrase is. At some distant point in prehistory a creature that would one day become Man may have observed the Moon, or a Planet on the horizon, or some curious weather effect, and his primitive mind would have registered it as a UFO. He may had been unable to report his 'sighting', but his descendants were better off. Whatever they saw they could report down the ages to us; there are those who believe that some cave paintings show early UFO reports.

As Man became more sophisticated so he was better able to communicate. Writings that have survived to the present time include ancient literature from China, Egypt, Japan, Greece, Rome and the Americas; all are held by some to include possible UFO reports. As the 'sightings' are described in the language of the time, these 'reports' are ambiguous, but they are also thought-provoking.

The early Bibles of many religions contain references that are taken by some to be UFO reports; Ezekiel in the Old Testament of the Christian Bible, the vimanas of the ancient Sanscrit Ramayana and Mahahbarata.

We have to come into the early 1700s to find the first clear UFO report, even then without any suggestion as to *what* was actually observed. In 1717 the astronomer Halley — more famous for his discovery of the comet named after him — reportedly watched unknown objects for two hours. Forty-five years later astronomers Croste and DeRostan reported an unknown object. In 1777 astronomer Messier reported an unknown disc shape.

From this date onwards reports have continued to the present day. There have been periods of special interest; the Foo fighter sightings, the Airship waves, and the Ghost Rocket sightings in particular, but few periods pass without some sort of UFO report or another. Whatever the reason, Man's fascination for the skies is undeniable.

The first major concentration of UFO reports occurred in 1896, through to 1897. Across parts of the United States thousands of witnesses were reporting the flight of a huge 'airship'. Descriptions varied, of course, but basically it appears to have been a large cigar-shaped object possibly with a 'pilot's cabin' attached, often apparently using propellors for movement. Since the first accepted flight of an airship is taken to be 1901, when Santos-Dumont rounded the Eiffel Tower, it is presently suggested that this vehicle seen in America cannot have been of terrestrial origin. If it were not so, then alien technology has been keeping a consistent pace with our own. Four years after 'they' were using propellor-driven airships we were doing so; by curious coincidence it would be four years after Arnold reported his 'saucers' moving at over 2000 km per hour that the Douglas D558-11 sky rocket research aircraft did so with a man at the controls. This question of 'cultural tracking' — their technology matching ours — is one that we shall examine much later.

However, a reasonable case has been made to show that the airship might well have been the brainchild of one E J Pennington. The airship was seen resting on the ground in Brown County, Indiana by two farmers, Jerimah Collier and William York. Pennington admitted it was his, and said it was undergoing repairs. This airship had been developed at Mount Carmel, Illinois in 1891 and clearly matched many of the witness descriptions given. If Santos-Dumont could do a ten-mile lap of the Eiffel Tower in 1901 then it is highly probable that more primitive craft had flown earlier. That a later event is credited with being 'the first' is not uncommon in the history of science; almost every major invention which every schoolboy 'knows' was invented by such-and-such usually has a less lucky claimant to an earlier prototype; for example the invention of the television, or the hovercraft.

What is important about the airship waves is not the dates

involved; four years between reports of a type of vehicle and proof that we are able to achieve the same level of technology is too little time for the assumption to be made that the original reports are extra-terrestrial. What is important is that the airships were perceived to be 'unknowns' and as such caused much media attention at the time, and of even more importance that we have a clear example of 'cultural tracking' which suggests that UFOs are — *at least in part* — a developing modern mythology.

In fact, a second airship wave of reports occurred in Europe between 1909 and 1913, and many of these reports have a slightly more sinister and 'alien' tone to them. Given that Europe was undergoing the enormous political and military pressures that would shortly erupt in The Great War of Civilisation the background to these events was quite different. That these airships were forerunners of the military vehicles used in that war seems highly probable; since the later extra-terrestrial theory seems to stem almost entirely from the 'alien' language of the pilots, it seems reasonable to assume that foreign terrestrial languages would serve as easily as any other explanation of this belief.

Between the first and second World Wars, the UFO flap was concentrated mainly in Sweden; and is known generally as the 'ghost rocket' sightings. They started in 1933 in the Swedish county of Vasterbotten, near the Arctic Circle. Strange distant lights were seen in the valleys, apparently behaving like airplane lights. Later reports included one in 1946 where the object crashed into Lake Kilmjarv, again in the north of Sweden. It apparently detonated on impact. There have been many suggestions as to what lay behind this unsolved period of events; both Russia and Germany have been suggested as likely candidates for the origin of these objects; testing some early form of cruise missile perhaps. It has been pointed out that such technology is not known to have existed at the time, and inevitably extra-terrestrials have been suggested as the cause. Again, we see the myth develop. 'Their' technology is not far off our own of the time — Germany during World War Two was launching its V2 rocket across Europe — and why would extra-terrestrials suddenly begin testing 'rocket-bombs' on Earth? When searching for an explanation, a literally down-to-Earth possibility is available; we should not seek to reach for the more exotic until we have eliminated that more likely possibility. And yet many do.

While the 'ghost rockets' were flying in extreme northern Europe, a different UFO wave was building up in the combat arena of the second World War. Fighter planes were reporting what became known as 'Foo fighters'. Generally speaking they were luminous balls of light that seemed to pace the aircraft, though one report was of small, three inch, discs showering around a plane. Although very much a part of the UFO development there are few conclusions drawn about them and within the scope of this book they have little relevance.

Throughout all of this time various and varied reports were being continuously received, but up to the late Forties there was very little concentrated research effort being made.

Then Kenneth Arnold rolled out his plane ready for that flight . . .

CRASH RETRIEVALS - A CONSPIRACY OF.... WHAT?

One of the modern era of UFO's most resilient legends is that of the crashed saucers. There have been a number of such claims; the stereotype, and the most famous of all such claims, is that of the Roswell Crash of 1947. In fact, as we shall see, there is some reason to consider that this incident may be the only factual case in the question of crash retrievals.

In the month following the Arnold sighting, July 1947, it was reported that a Flying Saucer had exploded in the air above New Mexico, that wreckage from the explosion had crashed to the ground and was reported to be scattered across part of a ranch owned by one William (Mac) Brazel. Brazel reported this to the local Chaves County sheriff's office; Sheriff George Wilcox contacted Major Jesse A Marcel at Roswell Army Air Base and also sent Brazel to the military. The response Brazel received was perhaps not what he expected — they kept him locked up for several days! During this time he was encouraged not to talk about the incident, since it was a matter of National Security. His son later noted that he would have taken this very seriously as he was strongly patriotic.

While Brazel 'rested' at the Government's expense, Major Marcel and others were ferreting about at the ranch, collecting the debris. They filled a bag, then the boot of the car they were driving, a Buick, and finally loaded more onto the back seats, taking the haul back to Roswell. The following afternoon they loaded this onto a B-29 aircraft on orders from the base's commanding officer, Colonel William H Blanchard. It was flown to Wright-Patterson. Marcel reports that he was to have accompanied it all the way but that he was diverted at Fort Worth by his superiors and the wreckage went the rest of the way without him.

Marcel does not indicate that he retrieved substantial 'chunks' of flying saucer, but other reports indicate that these *were* retrieved from the crash site. Details are confusing, with many of the witness's stories being contradictory; this has led to speculation that the whole thing was fabricated in some way — which is unlikely — or that more than one crashed saucer incident occurred.

Details of what was recovered have been equally confused, including claims that humanoid aliens were taken from the site; one of the more exotic claims was that when recovered one of these was alive, but died later.

It is alleged that the Roswell commanding officer, Blanchard, authorised the release of the following press announcement confirming that wreckage of a flying disc had in fact been recovered:

> Roswell Army Air Base, Roswell, N.M.
> 8 July 1947, a.m.
> The many rumours regarding the flying disc became a reality yesterday when the intelligence office of the 509th Bomb Group of the Eighth Air Force, Roswell Army Air Field, was fortunate enough to gain possession of a disc through the co-operation of one of the local ranchers and the sheriff's office of Chaves County.
> The flying object landed on a ranch near Roswell some time last week. Not having phone facilities, the rancher stored the disc until such time as he was able to contact the sheriff's office, who in turn notified Major Jesse A Marcel of the 509th Bomb Group Intelligence Office.
> Action was immediately taken and the disc was picked up at the rancher's home. It was inspected at the Roswell Army Air Field and subsequently loaned by Major Marcel to higher headquarters.

A local radio station in Roswell, KSWS, picked up the news and attempted to put it on the ABC wire service. The reporter for the station claimed to have seen a more or less complete, but damaged saucer in a farmer's shed before the Army picked it up. While the station's teletype operator was transmitting the information the machine apparently stopped; and then a message came *in* through the teletype:

> Attention Albuquerque. Do not transmit. Repeat. Do not transmit this message. Stop communication immediately.

The controversy continues about what exactly was recovered; we have some reports of humanoids, some of debris and some of a complete but damaged saucer. Marcel makes clear that he never saw any aliens, only wreckage, though he is quite clear that the wreckage was like none he had ever seen before. What is taken to be a cover story was put out, that the wreckage was of a Rawin sonde or Rawin target balloon and appropriate such material was paraded before the press. Marcel seems certain that this was not 'his' wreckage.

There were other reports that some of the 'real' wreckage had indecipherable hieroglyphics imprinted onto it, that there was thin foil like metal that would not dent even if it was hit by a hammer, that material resembling balsa wood would not burn when a lighter was applied directly to it.

This is a very shortened summary of the Roswell crash; it has been exhaustively examined by many people over the last few years and continues to be the main work of several present-day investigators. For a more detailed analysis of their work to date the reader might consult various papers and publications by Leonard H Stringfield, those by William Moore, the book 'The Roswell Incident' by Charles Berlitz and Moore, and Tim Good's book 'Above Top Secret'.

In summary then, we appear to have two separate claims being made; one, which is quite certain of the recovery of debris and material of no particular shape, and one claim of an intact saucer and recovered aliens, which is unsubstantiated by the same degree of hard evidence the former offers.

But Roswell was not to provide the only evidence; Leonard H Stringfield, an experienced and conscientious investigator has made this type of study his personal quest and reports many such incidents; a crash in Mexico in the early 1950s, another in New Mexico in 1962. He has had conversations with army personnel and medical experts who claim to have seen the bodies of several different types of aliens. One very important description he has been offered is that in most of these cases the humanoids recovered are small in height, with heads larger than would be normal on an equivalent human. One drawing by Stringfield based on a witness description shows an alien that will become very familiar to us later in this book, as we examine the claims of the abductees.

It is not necessary to go further into an analysis of specific crash retrievals. The purpose of this chapter is to 'set the scene for' — and to put into perspective — the subject of alien abductions. But to this end, crash retrievals produce some very interesting contradictions which we must now consider.

Firstly, although the aliens seem to have been dropping UFOs clumsily out of the sky for many years, and with alarming frequency, they have invariably done so over remote desert areas; they have yet to drop one in a reasonably well populated area. Does this mean that in fact they tend to avoid such centres of population and operate only in remote locations? The answer here is a clear *no.* American researcher Budd Hopkins reports accounts which show that they are quite content to appear even in city centres, near apartment blocks and the like. Yet they apparently need their craft to transport them; Hopkins has shown in his cases that often those who recall abductions may also recall some UFO incident; or where they do not remember it as such, it can be brought to recall by regression hypnosis. His are some of the most documented abduction cases in the world, and UFOs form an important part of them. So they have to operate — and apparently *do* operate — where there are large groupings of people. Have they just been remarkably lucky, or unlucky depending on your point of view, in that they haven't sent a craft crashing through a skyscraper?

Secondly, Hopkins' cases show that the alien entities seem to have an almost metaphysical control over their physical form, and other examples have suggested a similar control over their craft. If we accept this, then it seems to contradict their very physical clumsiness in crashing their saucers. This may not be a contradiction; they may well be advanced but not all powerful. But beings which can materialise through walls, UFOs that can perform incredible feats of manoeuvrability, even sudden appearances and disappearances, surely should not be so vulnerable as to be struck by lightning (which was suggested in the Roswell Case) and then be rendered as mortal as an everyday car crash.

Thirdly, the aliens make a point of trying to maintain secrecy in their activities; 'switching off' people they do not want to be involved in their activities. They seem to be able to do this with some ease. Why then, in the many tales of crashed saucers being retrieved and removed to Air Force bases, have they never made a successful attempt to recover their craft and colleagues by simply 'switching off' the base personnel for a couple of hours? In the one case on record of a suspected attempt at recovery in 1978 (from Leonard Stringfield's case A3, from his Status Report III as detailed in 'The chase for proof in a squirrel's cage' in UFOs 1947–1987 edited by Hilary Evans and myself) they not only failed but it seems to have ended like a re-make of 'Gunfight at the O K Corral', with the intruding alien 'shot and wounded by an MP'. This hardly seems to fit in with the abilities they demonstrate on other occasions, and the fact that it sounds more like the plot of a poor 1950s science fiction film may be less than a coincidence.

Fourthly, a lot of people have spoken to UFO researchers and others making claims of seeing the aliens or the saucers, or of knowing someone else who has; some have offered photographs which have either been discredited or are unclear, some have offered physical artifacts as proof, none have delivered. The fact is that if Roswell *alone* is the story of a true crash retrieval of a saucer and occupants, then in the forty-odd years since a great number of people have successfully conspired to keep the secret, and those who have tried to 'break' the secret have been unsuccessful. How many doctors and scientists must have had access to the material if any worthwhile study was to have been conducted? How many military personnel had to be used to guard this enormous secret, all of whom would have had some firsthand knowledge of the material? And how many top government officials — and not a few Presidents — would have insisted on some involvement? Yet not one of these people ever took an unambiguous photograph or clandestinely removed an unambiguous artifact despite the obvious fact that whoever did so would be on the gravy train for life. Contrast this massive and successful *forty-year* cover-up with the fact that between June 1972 and August 1974, just *two years*, the then President was unable to contain a cover-up to keep himself in the highest office in the Western World, despite the fact that essentially only a handful of top White House aides had to be 'controlled'. Whatever the somewhat dubious facts of crash retrievals may suggest, is such a cover-up even credible?

Fifthly, in recent years we have seen that top 'spy agencies' officials, such as Peter Wright (a former senior official of the British Intelligence Service), have decided to show little regard for the Government's interpretation of the Official Secrets Act. They have 'kissed and told all' for reasons of their own. The documents involved in the crash retrieval cover-ups indicate that it is these agencies such as the CIA that have had the most access to the material. Yet not one of these candid revelations even hints at UFOs in any form at all. Peter Wright's 'Spycatcher' reveals a good deal of information regarding his own involvement with the CIA in the early 1950s, *and he was a scientist*; yet he mentions nothing of this subject. Not out of regard for secrecy one presumes, more likely because there was nothing there to tell.

So what should our conclusions be, bearing in mind that we know for sure that some material was recovered from the Roswell Crash since the military paraded their balloon remains as an 'explanation'.

We might consider that the one real crash of the time — the one that Marcel recovered debris from — was of a structured vehicle; and one about which the Government and the military did not want the public to have information. Does that suggest an extra-terrestrial explanation? Or is there literally a more down-to-earth possibility? In 1947, the state of New Mexico was the testing ground for the most highly secret military work the United States has ever undertaken; at Los Alamos the Manhatten Project had recently developed the atomic bomb under Dr Robert J Oppenheimer. (Curiously one of the latest myths about the crash retrievals of UFOs includes documents allegedly released by a US Government group called MJ12, apparently a highly secret project to learn from the retrieved saucers; Dr Oppenheimer appears on the list of members of that panel.) White Sands Missile Range and Proving Grounds is in much the same area as our reported retrievals, at Almagordo; which was where the US Government was experimenting with captured German V2 rockets and, of course, was also one of the cradles of the American Space Programme.

It is held by many that this concentration of highly important projects would be a reason for the aliens to be keeping an eye on our development; could it not be more easily explained that if any of the experiments they were conducting went wrong then the Government would want to retrieve the highly classified material without the public and the press crawling all over it? Could that not be the reason for the clampdown on such as farmer Brazel? Would that not adequately explain their contention that he should remain silent about the details of what he saw for reasons of National Security? But what, then, of the statement apparently issued by Roswell Base that a saucer had indeed been recovered? How can this be contested?

In fact this is the key to what probably lies behind the crash retrieval stories. UFOs had been reported for some time, speculation that they were extra-terrestrial was already popular in the press, Kenneth Arnold's sighting having made the whole subject a matter for public debate, not to mention the extra-terrestrial theory being quoted as a possibility just the day after the sighting. And whole groups of amateurs were coming together as UFO researchers, to discover — in those days — just how strong this extra-terrestrial theory was. Could the Government have decided that here was the perfect set-up for retrieving their own failed experiments? Use the UFO stories as their own cover-up in the knowledge that they could easily make the UFO investigators look foolish not by starving them of information *but by feeding it to them*?

Scientist and 'Spycatcher' Peter Wright may have been silent on the subject of UFOs but he was very clear on the subject of disinformation; putting out false stories to lead others off of the trail they might be on. It is a known fact that all intelligence agencies utilise such methods. And would

UFOs from other worlds be too ridiculous to consider? Not a bit of it. It would keep the public's mind on something very serious, and away from something else very serious, for a good time. The controversy rages even now after more than forty years. It would probably help, in fact, if lower ranking military personnel *believed* the rumours and helped to spread the word; this would certainly explain the 'leaks' and their lack of substance. As for being ridiculous, when you are in a corner looking for a way out any route will do; I recall hearing the astronomer Patrick Moore saying, whilst telling of his war service days, that a suggestion was made (never enacted!) to confuse German bombing raids on Britain by floating a life-sized raft of the British Isles in the North Sea! UFOs from other worlds seems unimaginative by comparison.

A UK researcher, Andy Roberts, the editor of the British based magazine 'UFO Brigantia', related to me the story of receiving highly confidential information. He had asked for some copy documents from a person in the United States but received also other material naming recent members of MJ12. This material was 'very hot stuff' and the informant, who claimed information from high ranking members of the Government and Military, stressed that Andy must keep the information to himself. He did not know Andy, all he knew of him was that he had written to him as the editor of a magazine! And he was given classified material and then told to tell no-one. Why? Not for security reasons surely!

If we accept the suggestion of disinformation as a working hypothesis then we can make a further observation; it is highly unlikely that when starting these rumours the Government could have foreseen just how long UFOs would run, and it has certainly 'gone the distance'. But if they were clever they would see that here was a subject where they could almost permanently try out their new disinformation techniques because in the so-called UFO community there would always be people prepared to listen, and to spread the stories. In times of war particularly it is important for Governments to know the effect of propaganda — witness the many messages to citizens during the second World War of the 'walls have ears' variety. Here is the perfect testing ground; a subject that perhaps has little basis in hard fact, with a world-wide network of 'believers' and — equally important — non-believers, and a subject generally accepted but barely understood.

When looking for an explanation to anything it is reasonable to look first at the mundane, likely explanations and move on to the more exotic only when you have disproved the rest; perhaps UFOs *do* come from other worlds, but we don't have to believe that to understand crash retrievals — there is a more down-to-earth possibility to eliminate first.

And what of the remaining stories of crash retrievals; they could be the disinformation of governments, planting false documentation for posterity, they could be the distortions of known facts as a modern myth develops, they could be the wishful thinking of devotees.

It must be borne in mind here that I am not suggesting a long-term UFO cover up by Government is the result of their successful ability to keep this — or anything else- secret for long. Quite the opposite: it is their clear failure to do so that gives the lie to this aspect of UFOs. Perhaps the only reason that Governments have succeeded in keeping this one 'secret' is because they are guarding a truth that does not exist.

So whereas in the Arnold sighting we had the distortions by the media, now we have accidental (and deliberate) distortions by the media possibly combined with deliberate distortions of Governments.

None of this says that there is no UFO phenomenon to study, I am quite certain that there is and I believe that this book will demonstrate that, but we can see already the potential for *unreliable evidence.*

And if we accept that the modern era of UFOs started with Arnold in June 1947 then we are less than a month into our 40-odd year examination!

CONTACTEES AND THE FIRST ALIENS

Although we are only just into our review of the early UFO phenomenon we must recap on what we have examined so far, because only in perspective will the principal subject of the book — abductions — be understood.

Firstly, we had the Arnold sighting of June 1947 where he inadvertently coined the phrase 'Flying Saucer' and brought a phenomenon to the public's eager attention. This has since fuelled a review of earlier sightings right back through history, and even pre-history, but as a media phenomenon 1947 is the birth date.

Then, within a very short time, we have the claims of crash retrievals featuring dead aliens and crashed saucers.

Already we have a pattern forming. Firstly some unidentified objects are seen and it immediately becomes the popular theory that these are extra-terrestrial vehicles. Bear in mind that no-one has yet claimed to have met an alien associated with these sightings, or communicated with them, and therefore any suggestion that they are extra-terrestrial is *certainly* at this date an earthly, human speculation. But just as Arnold described saucer-like movements which were wrongly interpreted as saucer-like *shapes*, which were then reported, so here we have demonstrably human claims that flying saucers are alien *immediately proven* because the claims abound that they have been found crashed and that these unfortunate dead aliens have been recovered.

If we assume that this is a human — principally media — creation then what would logically be the next step?

Inevitably, if they are alien spacecraft then they have pilots, if they crash and dead pilots are recovered then they must — ipso facto — have living pilots. Sooner or later someone was going to come forward to say, in effect, 'I've spoken to one of the aliens'.

And sure enough . . .

In 1953, after six years of 'flying saucer' sightings, George Adamski published a book revealing that he had made frequent contact with beings from another world. His recall of events went back to 1946, the year before Arnold, but in examining the development of the UFO phenomenon over the past 40 years it must be made clear that it is the dates when matters are *reported* that are important, rather than when they were *claimed* to have taken place.

An important point to note immediately is that the UFO phenomenon here apparently takes a slight, and temporary, diversion. The little humanoids with oversized heads that were reported in the Roswell incident do not occur again for a number of years, though they do in fact reappear true to description when abductions begin being reported. In the meantime, Adamski and others were reporting very human-like, attractive beings. A point of caution on dates is needed here though; investigation into crash retrievals is more recent than some of the literature would indicate. Stories of interviews given and documents raised in the forties and fifties in fact surface in later years, notably the seventies. Just as before, we must be cautious in remembering when a report is made, not when it purports to have occurred. If it is demonstrated that media and other influences have shaped the UFO phenomenon then it may also follow that the similarities of reports are less than coincidental.

For the time being however, our humanoids are of a very different breed. And their social manners are a good deal better than those who will follow later, since they seem to talk to their contactees on a one-to-one basis rather than treating them as laboratory rats. They appear also to have quite different motives to their successors; they exhibit concern for our world and the way we are running it, they rarely threaten, though some of their warnings are rather pointed. And they select particular individuals for whatever reason, appointing them their messengers on Earth with a mission to spread their word amongst us.

As the aliens appear to set so much store by their contactees, let us look at some of the people they selected for this mission. Mentioned already was the first, and certainly the most famous, of these: George Adamski. Born in 1891, he was 62 when he published his story. He appears to have had little formal education but seems to have exhibited that indefinable characteristic that can be best summed up as 'charisma'. From the outset of his contacts he was associated with the largest telescope in the world, the 200-inch reflector at Mount Palomar. He seems not to have minded the association in the early years and it certainly did no harm to his credibility, in much the same way as his adopting the title of Professor. His qualifications as a professor are not clear, but his position on Mount Palomar is; he apparently served hamburgers in a small cafe on the slopes. In his book, with co-author Desmond Leslie, he makes clear that he never was part of the staff of the observatory. By now though, his fame overrode any disadvantage such a revelation would raise.

Adamski met his first alien on Thursday, November 20th 1952 at about 12.30 in the afternoon, in the California desert 10 miles from Desert Centre, towards Arizona. The alien arrived in a small flying saucer which was described by its occupant as a Scout Ship. Presumably we are encouraged to infer certain motives from this title. This first meeting was, to a slight extent, witnessed. Two families, the Baileys and the Williamsons, accompanied him having expressed the desire to be with him next time he felt he would see a saucer. To that date he had reported many sightings. However, by the time the encounter with the alien occurred, Adamski was on his own; the others watching from some distance through binoculars. While he was photographing the saucer Adamski noticed a man beckoning to him. He was about five feet six inches in height, appeared to be about 135 pounds weight, and roughly the human equivalent of 28 years old. His mouth was average with beautiful white teeth, his eyes a calm grey-green, his hair long, flowing and blonde, his skin tanned. His features apparently tended slightly towards Oriental. He wore a one piece chocolate-brown outfit.

By a combination of sign language and telepathy, which Adamski knew would work because he had been 'teaching this as fact for 30 years' the alien indicated that he came from Venus. Adamski refers to Venus as Earth's sister, a belief held in these early pre-spaceflight days; in fact of course no planet ever had a less likely sister — subsequent probes to the planet show it to be a world totally unsuited to our form of life. Other contactees we shall look at shortly have indicated Venus as the home world of the aliens, some of their claims persisting to this day in face of the evidence, though current claims are usually modified by hinting that perhaps a different dimension is involved as well.

When asked what he was doing on Earth, he indicated that his intentions were friendly and there was concern over the atomic radiations being emitted from Earth. Their people believe in God but they follow a more devoted path than we do. Asking why they never landed in populated places, Adamski was told that they would cause widespread fear and that their people would be torn to pieces by us if they appeared. Adamski apparently understood this, though why the appearance of a person looking as they do, living a devoted and 'good' life should cause widespread fear and leave them being ripped to shreds is not made clear. We shall be looking at the influence of science fiction on this subject at a later point in the book; at this point it is perhaps worthy of note that the science fiction films of the time almost invariably had in them what is known as 'the angry villager bit' where, having discovered that aliens are hiding in the hills, or that Baron Frankenstein is recreating his Creature yet again, hordes of angry villagers descend on the aliens, or the Baron's castle, or whatever, and destroy them, him, it etc. In fact this situation is never likely to have been more than a convenient way of ending a film — in reality people do not rise up en masse in this way; consider the reports of muggings and rapes in full daylight in crowded areas, where the victim claims that 'People just walked past me and ignored my screams.'

In any case, it was later revealed that many of the 'space brothers' were walking the Earth unnoticed by the majority of the population, so presumably this fear related only to their method of arrival by flying saucer.

Later conversation made it clear to Adamski that the humanoid form was universal, an interesting point to which we shall return later in the book.

A further point to note is that Adamski's visitor seemed to give the hint — with a nod and a broad smile in response to the question — that his people were abducting human beings. The implication of this part of the 'conversation' seemed to be a somewhat different form of abduction from the type we are going to examine; in this case the permanent removal from the Earth of certain people. This is not made particularly clear.

In the next few years Adamski's adventures became quite remarkable and equal only to the fictional achievements of Flash Gordon and Buck Rogers in earlier decades; he met aliens in the bars and cafes that they frequented in California (when not using telepathy and awkward sign language the aliens talked in an incomprehensible language that sounded to Adamski like a combination of Chinese and something that may have been an ancient Earth language. This did not apparently cause any difficulties in the bars and cafes, though.), he flew with them throughout the Solar System and met a range of Martians, Saturnians and Jovians; the latter two at least from planets now known to be quite unsuitable for our type of life-form. A point to consider is that if any of these contactees had succeeded in stepping out of a spaceship on Jupiter, Saturn or the like, then the effects would have been devastating; a man of average height stepping onto the surface of Jupiter would immediately resemble one of those unfortunate flattened hedgehogs so often seen on motorways.

Adamski was not the only one of us selected for interplanetary contact; just one year after the publication of his first book in 1953, Truman Bethurum published *his* account of alien contact in 'Aboard a Flying Saucer'. His aliens came from Clarion, which is apparently hidden behind our moon. (In 1954 there was of course no space programme, and it must have seemed remarkably unlikely that Man would ever actually do what Flash Gordon could and fly in space, let alone journey around the Moon. However, no American or Russian flights since that date have yet located Clarion.) His aliens were quite different from Adamski's, being a little shorter, up to about five feet. They did however have olive skins, and wore uniforms.

Clarion is more advanced in its studies of Earth than

Venus, because its flight crews spoke perfect English. They didn't use 35-foot Scout Ships either, 300-foot wide scows were their mode of transport.

Bethurum was luckier than Adamski in other ways too; the captain of the ship he met, Aura Rhanes, was a woman 'tops in shapeliness and beauty' and she and Bethurum spent the night swapping 'planet' stories; she occasionally mingled amongst us also. However, Bethurum evidently did not make a lasting impression on her, when he saw her drinking orange juice in a restaurant later, she ignored him.

In the same year, 1954, a third contactee published his story. Daniel Fry met his alien in a desert in New Mexico where he had landed his flying saucer near the top security White Sands Proving Ground. His name was A-Lan and his home planet had gone one further than Venus or Clarion; they had not only progressed past the stage of telepathy and sign language, even past perfect English, but had arrived at the idiomatic language of the period, warning Fry 'Better not touch the hull, pal. It's still hot.' A-Lan did suggest using the name Alan as that would be easier; this seems curious. He could have just used this terrestrial name from the start, so similar was it to his own, and avoided the 'alien' overtones, unless of course he wanted to sound like an extra-terrestrial. Or, more suspiciously, maybe Fry wanted him to sound so. In any case, if A-Lan was his name then it suggests that his development in many ways closely paralleled that of Earthlings. Considering his grasp of the period's slang, either he had done better homework than his slip-up over his name suggests, or his planet had developed not only an American but a beatnik cult as well.

A-Lan asked Fry to write a book that would warn the Earth about impending nuclear war.

Two other principal contactees were to arise in America in the fifties; Orfeo Angelucci, in his 1955 book 'Secret of the Saucers', and Howard Menger, in his 1959 book 'From Outer Space to You'. Angelucci's contacts were rather run of the mill, they warned us of our impending peril if we continued on our path to self-destruction; Angelucci also took what was then becoming a reasonably routine space flight, in this case to Neptune, and discovered he had — in a previous existence —

been one of 'them'. Meetings were as expected by now for alien contacts; they took place in cafes and bus terminals. One up on his predecessors however, Angelucci met Jesus, who was in fact an extra-terrestrial!

Menger's contacts were generally from the same sort of mould, though he seems to have been dogged by a series of beautiful blonde women of obvious physical attributes, one of whom was over 500 years old. Nothing much seems to have been imparted to Menger that others had not claimed, although this group were good enough to give him the secret of their power system, which he built and displayed (non-operational) to the world.

Around the same time, 1954, Marian Keech reported being contacted by entities from planets Cerus and Clarion. It is interesting that the planet Clarion arises again, because that was of course where Bethurum's contactees came from. However, Jesus, now apparently known as Sananda, contacted her; he was from there. Eventually the crux of the messages came; having spotted some faults in the Earth's crust they were able to predict that a great flood was going to wipe out Salt Lake City in Utah. The believers were to group together to save themselves. On the appointed day, 21st December, no spaceship came to take them away, which mattered little since no flood came either. The group dispersed.

Generally speaking these above mentioned people remained sole contactees who passed down their messages to the masses.

Others, more recently, have formed named cult groups; the One World Family formed by Allen-Michael Noonan, who had accepted the position of saviour of the world in a message from one Ashtar; the Institute for Cosmic Research formed after contact with a race on one of the moons of Jupiter; the Human Individual Metamorphosis formed by a couple known as Bo and Peep; the Raelian movement which is devoted to the cause of building an embassy free of Earth's political strictures.

Perhaps the best known is the Aetherius Society founded by George King. This London taxi-driver was alone in his flat in West London when he was informed by a voice that he would become the voice of Interplanetary Parliament. He went on to make several trips to Mars and Venus, saved the Earth by assisting in a fight with a meteor, and took the organisation of the Society to California, where it heads a truly international organisation. Their most well-known achievement is that they keep batteries stored with prayer power, which can be used to relieve suffering throughout the world. Their contactees are quite forthcoming; unlike Adamski's beings who would not appear over populated cities these beings were quite happy to leave an enormous ship hovering over Los Angeles. They protected the fears of the masses however by keeping it invisible.

It has been necessary to review these people and these cults in order to follow the continuing development of the UFO phenomenon; however this is not the place to evaluate the claims made by these groups. Some observations are pertinent though.

Firstly, there may be fraudulent claims included in the above, or other, statements of contactees and cults, but clearly not all of them are fraudulent for an obvious reason. The claims of Mrs Keech, for example, appear to have no motive other than the genuine beliefs of the 'channel' — Mrs Keech — through which the messages are received. This does not mean that claims without apparent ulterior motives are likely to be true, even if they are genuinely held, nor does it mean that those organisations which seem to have rather obvious, materialistic motives need necessarily be false.

Secondly, it is important to recognise that the believers of these cults are rarely given first hand contact with the extraterrestrials involved, rather they have to rely on all their messages through the channels, in other words the only person in actual contact with the aliens is the named leader, the others in fact are following *him*, not the other-worlders. Their belief, in reality, relies on their faith in the (human) contactee. This gives the contactee considerable power and makes the possibility of fraudulent claims more likely than, say, if everyone involved experienced a personal contact, which they could evaluate. The same could be said, of course, of the major 'accepted' religions.

Thirdly, and following from the above, when someone does get a contact they are generally dissimilar to those experienced by previous contactees, which fails to confirm either; rather their experience leads them to start their own following, and the point of most concern about this is that rarely do the claims of different groups even *resemble* each other.

The aliens are different; they come from different planets; they have different motives for their visit.

Fourthly, and again of some concern in evaluating the claims, is that none of these aliens appear to know each other even when they claim to come from the same planet. They never say to Mr X that they should discount the claims of Mr Y because they are untrue, even when they seem to conflict with one another, and they never say anything like 'When we take you to Venus don't worry if you meet some other contactee there, no doubt his alien contacts are taking him for a visit to their headquarters, etc. etc'. In fact they seem *oblivious* of the claims of others.

Fifthly, they appear to vary considerably in their state of the art knowledge of this planet, even though some of them claim to have been coming here for thousands of years. As we have seen, some are unable to use simple English, while others have mastered slang expressions.

Six, and perhaps in summation for this exercise, their claims could be said to reflect the fears of humans, and possibly of the contactee. They worry about exactly the things we worry about; in the early fifties when we were developing the atomic bombs and the CND movement was at its peak, the messages from other worlds concerned that very aspect of society, yet in later times when we had apparently learned 'to live with the Bomb' their fears and their messages took on a new course, as did the fears of the human race. Currently, many claims centre on the Earth's damaged ecological balance.

For the serious researcher of UFOs, these cults and their personalities have been an embarrassment. No other aspect of the subject has done more to feed the tabloid press with what they regard, and publicise, as 'lunatic' stories of UFOs and 'believers'. That may be fair or unfair; as I have already indicated it is beyond the scope of this book to do more evaluation here, but this review has been important for two reasons:

The cults are perceived generally to be a part of the UFO phenomenon, and have certainly influenced its development as well as the media and public perception.

Also, the cults show a striking contrast to the abductee claims where there are rarely 'followings' as such, where messages are rarely imparted in quite the same way, where the claims of various individuals rarely conflict and where the apparent and stated aims of the abducting aliens seldom seem to be following the wishes of the abducted. In fact they show quite different characteristics and we must look now at what may have formed the change, the next stage in UFO development as it were, when this next — and probably only latest — manifestation arises.

It is probable that at least some of the claims of the cults and contactees represented wishful thinking, at best.

On the face of it, the claims of abductees seem to reflect quite the reverse.

PART TWO

Genesis

Myself when young did eagerly frequent
Doctor and saint, and heard great argument
About it and about, but evermore
Came out by the same door as in I went.

OMAR KHAYYAM

THE HILL ABDUCTION

This book begins with an outlined stereotype abduction. In fact there are many forms of stereotypical abduction, including bedroom visitation, the abduction of people in or from their homes, from lone walks and from car driving situations. The stereotype used at the beginning was of a car driving situation, and was very loosely based around the Hill abduction of 1961, which was the true beginning of the abduction phenomenon.

That is not to say that it is the earliest reported abduction, such reports are now being received going back into the forties, and indeed the Villas-Boas case of 1957 is now very well known but it did not come to the attention of even many UFO researchers until much later. But in being released in major book form — in John G Fuller's excellent book 'The Interrupted Journey' the Hill case is the first major public exposure of the material.

In as much as Kenneth Arnold gave birth to the modern era of UFOs, then Betty and Barney Hill can be said to have given birth to the modern era of the abduction phenomenon.

The Hill abduction therefore contained for the first time the details which have become so familiar in studying the abduction phenomenon and which are examined elsewhere in this book. The claims made then have remained largely consistent with current statements, and there is some suspicion that the Hill case may well have helped form the future shape of abduction reports. We shall come to this later. Firstly, let me say that I have no doubts whatsoever that the Hill abduction is real. This is not to suggest that I believe the events actually happened but I have no doubts as to the truthfulness and honesty of the two participants, Betty and Barney Hill. I believe that they actually experienced some events, and genuinely believed they had experienced others. There is no suggestion I can find anywhere in other studies of their case, nor arising through my own studies, which would indicate that they had been other than fully truthful in their relating of events. However, I have made a study of this abduction a key area as it seems to me that there is every reason to believe that *the final unlocking of the abduction mysteries lay within this case.*

September 1961, and a hurricane is cutting up America's east coast. Reports have indicated that it is likely to move across the state of New Hampshire, which was not a threat to be taken lightly. Hurricanes of former years had caused considerable chaos, particularly to road users, by bringing down trees, power cables and other debris, thus blocking many roads. On September 19th, Betty and Barney Hill made the decision that they would therefore drive overnight to avoid difficulties that might arise. They had been holidaying in Canada, and had not funds for an extended emergency stay due to road blockages, and therefore they decided to return immediately to their New Hampshire home. At approximately nine o'clock in the evening of September 19th, they crossed the Canadian border with the United States and stopped at a restaurant in Colebrook for a short break. At approximately five past ten that evening they left the restaurant and resumed their drive down US3 highway. On leaving the restaurant, Barney indicated to his wife that he believed they would be home by two-thirty or three o'clock the following morning. As they drove past the village of Lancaster, Betty noticed a particularly bright light to the left of, and slightly below, the moon. Shortly afterwards, she noticed that another bright light had appeared above the first and she was curious that this second light appeared to be getting bigger and brighter. She pointed this out to her husband who slowed the car and also observed the light. Barney's first reaction was that he believed it to be a satellite 'gone off its course'.

As their journey progressed, they watched the light apparently moving behind trees and mountain tops, reappearing at intervals, but at this stage they were unable to determine whether or not the light was actually moving or if the movement of the car on the winding road was giving it an apparent motion. In the back of the car their dog, Delsey, was shifting in such a way as to indicate some restlessness, which may only have been due to a need to relieve itself. Betty suggested that they should stop the car and give the dog a run while taking advantage of the opportunity to watch the light from a stationary position. Barney pulled the car over at a point where there was reasonably clear vision all around. Barney warned Betty to keep an eye out for bears, which were known to roam the area, but Betty laughed off this suggestion, regarding Barney as a 'worrier'. Betty and Barney walked together along the road with Delsey, and were certain at that point that the light was definitely moving. Betty handed the leash to Barney, went back to the car and picked up their binoculars, with which to see the light better. Through the binoculars a shape could be made out, and Barney was of the opinion that it was some kind of plane. He suggested various types of planes from commercial airliners to small Piper Cubs and military aircraft, indicating that he was not able to identify the object clearly. He also suggested it could be a helicopter. One thing that was clear to both of them was it was exhibiting movements no satellite or star could duplicate, and at one point it crossed the face of the moon.

Looking through the binoculars, Betty reported seeing various coloured flashing lights. Fuller, in his analysis of this event, mentions an interesting point at this juncture. Barney was apparently getting irritated that Betty refused to accept his offer of a natural explanation and he was sure that she was about to refer to Unidentified Flying Objects. Apparently her sister had described seeing a UFO in New Hampshire four years before, in 1957. Betty had believed the story of the sighting but Barney had remained sceptical and he was hoping she was not going to bring up the conversation again. In fact she did not, but this shows immediately the differences, and similarities, in perception of the object between the two observers. *Both* probably had UFOs on their mind, Barney certainly so because he did not want to have to consider this possibility and Betty probably so because she apparently was only too willing to consider the subject. Later events were to bear out this assumption. Their respective characters may be important to consider here; as we noted earlier, Betty regarded Barney as a worrier and here he was in a very wild and open tract of countryside where, for example, bears were known to roam, people were known to freeze to death from exposure in the wide open mountainous area and where private recovery vans would patrol in areas the official rangers could not reach. Betty, on the other hand, was able to laugh off these fears, but nonetheless was a believer in UFOs. On a dark night in such desolate surroundings, their characters and the nature of this sighting may already have been forming some of the facets later to be reported.

They got back in the car and drove on towards the Cannon mountain at a very slow pace, watching the object, convinced that it was circling around them, and causing Barney some anxiety because he could not hear a sound. He also expressed concern because there were no other cars on the road. Although witnesses to UFO abductions have often reported at this stage the onset of a sort of false isolation from the real world, there is no reason here to suppose that Betty and Barney Hill were experiencing this. The fact that there was no sound from the object could easily be a factor of wind speed and direction; the fact that there were no other cars on the road was quite typical for the area for that time of the year. It is interesting to consider, though, that the origin of this idea of 'false isolation' may arise from this description.

As they progressed, the object appeared to pace them and they were watching it through the thickening forest of trees. They passed an open motel and Betty considered pulling in and ending the sighting then and there.

What effect this would have had on the development of ufology we can only speculate!

However, their curiosity was aroused and she was determined to see more of the object, so they did not stop. At this point, and while the car was still moving, Betty put the binoculars to her eyes and saw that the object appeared to be an enormous craft with a double row of windows. She then reported that a red light came out from one side of the object followed by a light on the other side of the object. According to Betty, Barney was at this point actually trying not to look at the object but Betty was encouraging him to do so.

Barney stopped the car in the middle of the road, apparently with less regard for other traffic than he had shown earlier, and took the binoculars. Considering what appears to be his state of mind at this point he then did something rather unusual. Unlike Betty, who had been observing the object through the windshield of the car, he got out of the car leaving the motor running and stepped to one side, looking at the object through the binoculars. Even here his first thought was that he was seeing an airplane and it was determined argument from Betty which made him think again. She challenged his analysis on the basis that planes have one red and one green light rather than two red lights.

Then, Barney did something entirely out of character, something which has arisen in many UFO reports since and something which gives some substance to the possibility, though only the possibility, of an external influence on him. Given his probable state of mind he might have been expected to get back in the car and lock the doors. Certainly, he might well have turned off the car engine which was apparently causing too much vibration to observe the object clearly, and he could have observed the object through an open window in a stationary, quiet car. He did none of these things; having stepped a few feet away and observed that the object did indeed seem to have some unusual characteristics such as the double row of windows, he became 'fully gripped with fear' but for a reason unexplained he walked over the road onto, and across, a field, directly towards the object. This may only have been a desire to confront his fears; certainly he was known to deal with problems in this way, for example as a boy when threatened with attack by a street gang Barney sought out and confronted its leader.

He believed he walked to within fifty feet of the object, which had dropped down to the height of a tree. Betty stayed with the car, now feeling some concern that other traffic on the road might hit them in the poor position that they had 'parked'. It was only after a short while she realised that Barney had disappeared into the night gloom.

Through the binoculars, Barney was now receiving one of his most fearful impressions; through the windows he believed he could see at least a dozen people looking back at him. He believed that they were wearing uniforms but mostly he remembered the eyes of the crew members which were gripping his attention almost hypnotically. He became convinced — for no apparently logical reason — that he was about to be captured. He then screamed back across the field to Betty, who was in fact shouting at *him* to return and move the car. Having run back across the field, he jumped into the car. They drove off down the road with Barney shouting he was sure they were going to be captured. Betty tried to see the light or the craft but could find neither and at this point they heard a beeping noise, felt a tingling drowsiness come over them and apparently drowsed.

Later in the drive they reported a further set of beeping sounds; there was no apparent gap between the two, only an awareness that there were two distinct periods of this sound. Betty made some interesting observations at this point, saying to Barney, 'Now do you believe in flying saucers?' Barney replied that he did not. At the sign indicating 17 miles to Concord, Betty said to Barney that they now knew where they were, which appears to indicate that they had felt some disorientation prior to that.

Betty and Barney reached home in nearly full daylight; both checked their watches to find that they were not working, but the kitchen clock indicated that it was gone 5 o'clock in the morning, which was a couple of hours later than they had earlier expected to arrive home. It is not certain at what point they actually recalled the fact that they seemed to have arrived home late. The initial implication of Fuller's analysis of events is that this occurred to them immediately on their arrival at home. However, it seems from a later part of the narrative that the question arose when Betty and Barney were discussing events with a team of investigators, which was on November 25th, some two months after the event. Present at that meeting was a friend of theirs — a retired Air Force Intelligence Officer, Major MacDonald — and two scientific technicians, Robert Hohman and C D Jackson, who had been inspired to follow up the case by their reading of the NICAP report by investigator Walter Webb. One of them pointed out that the time taken to cover the distance did not seem to add up. Barney Hill reacts to this question 'To think that I realised *for the first time* that at the rate of speed I always travel we should have arrived home at least two hours earlier than we did' (emphasis added). Whether or not the significance of this was created by the investigators, do we here see the birth of the 'missing time' element of abductions?

Going back to the events of September; on the morning following the experience, Betty discovered small circular spots of metallic polishing on the trunk of their car and she seemed considerably excited by these and the results of her subsequent tests with a compass, which was suggested to her through a conversation with her sister. She had telephoned her sister to share the experience with her, as she had had a UFO sighting years before. At this time Barney apparently insisted that it was all her imagination and was not inspired to go and look at the car. However, her own excitement must have been extreme because it attracted the attention of a couple living in the same house as the Hills, who noticed that Betty was quite agitated. Again, this suggests a quite different approach to the experience by the two of them.

Following the suggestion by her sister, Betty called the Air Police at Pease Air Force Base in Portsmouth, a strategic Air Force command installation, who seemed quite interested in the description of the craft. Apparently no description was given of the occupants of the craft, since Barney was reluctant to include these details. We do not know from the narrative whether or not Barney felt he was reluctant to discuss this in hindsight, and therefore we have no knowledge of quite how important this was to Barney *at the time.* We know, of course, that this had become a central part of his fears by the time of his much later reports for publication. Barney apparently held back on discussing the figures on the craft because he feared being regarded as foolish might put him in a position of being doubted. *There is no obvious reason for this.* If Barney truly believed that the craft was a structured vehicle of some kind, then its having a pilot and crew should almost automatically follow and he was quite willing to describe the structural appearance of the craft. This seeming contradiction may reflect Barney's sincere fears about the occupants, but it should also be borne in mind that it could well also reflect an uncertainty on his part that he was describing a craft rather than some other phenomenon. There have been many suggestions that the original stimulus for the experience was a natural object such as the moon, or even a planet seen through the magnifying binoculars, and at this stage that cannot be ruled out as one of the possible originating stimuli which led to the more exotic experience to follow. Dr Jacques Vallee, in his book 'Dimensions', points out however that there appears to be official corroboration of some object in the air that night; it was apparently detected by military radar. This is also pointed out in the 1979 epilog to the revised edition of 'The interrupted journey'.

To try and determine whether there was any hard reality behind their experience, Barney suggested to Betty that each of them draw the object they had seen. The resulting drawings they made are often held out as being very similar. In fact, my own impression of the two sketches is that they are really quite different. Betty's sketch amounts to an undetailed banana shape with two circular balls, representing the lights, attached to the ends of the main body. Barney's sketch shows a circular object seen in an elliptical perspective with rows of windows breaking up the main body (and indeed figures at the windows), but with the two lights to either side much further from the main body and separated by two fins. The sketches are similar enough to indicate that clearly the two of them were drawing the same object and it seems apparent from this that there was a real object of some kind at which they were looking, but the sketches are also dissimilar enough to show that there were differences in perception between the two of them which may have been due to their own personal beliefs and attitude towards what they were seeing. It must be remembered, however, that Barney had a much closer look at the object than Betty, at least according to their conscious recollection at this stage.

Fuller's book relates that Barney was 'worried about his inability to justify what he actually saw with his conviction such a thing could not be'. This question of believability is extremely important, and we shall look more closely at an example of it shortly. Nevertheless, it is important to note that there is good evidence in many prominent UFO reports to suggest that witnesses temper their claims in order that they should be more acceptable to the receiving public, fearing that they may otherwise lose credibility. Let me stress immediately that this is not to suggest that witnesses lie.

Betty's interest in the subject was fired by these events and *two days* after the sighting she went to the library to collect as much information as possible on UFOs. She is known to have read a book by Major Donald Keyhoe, 'The Flying Saucer Conspiracy'. It would seem that she read this at a single sitting, which shows her growing passion for the subject. Keyhoe's book makes clear that of the two hypotheses he considers to be most likely, the one he ranks highest is that people are in fact seeing structured vehicles. Inspired by this book, and presumably other reading, Betty wrote to Major Keyhoe *just one week after the sighting* on September 26th, 1961. Her letter to the Major gives many more details than had previously been outlined by the couple which Fuller explains 'As Betty Hill's confidence increased through her study of the NICAP material so did her willingness to reveal more of the details'. This could well be a product of the question of believability, in that she felt more relaxed about making exotic claims knowing others had made similar reports, but there is every reason to consider the alternative possibility: that she was beginning to subconsciously feed into her own recollections some of the data she had picked up from her reading. This is not at all to suggest that at any time Betty Hill was deliberately prefabricating memories of the events, indeed I am satisfied that everything I have read and studied of her material shows her complete integrity. Other parties close to this couple have also stressed their good character. However, her recollection was certainly unclear, which is after all the basis of the investigation and her manner was excited; further, she had expressed her belief in UFOs and it is certainly possible that what she believed to be her recollections were being amended by the material she was reading.

Just three days after writing the letter to Major Keyhoe and therefore *ten days* after the sighting, Betty had a series of vivid dreams which lasted for five nights never to return again. These dreams were the basic abduction encounter, *i.e.* of being stopped by the landed UFO, of being taken aboard the craft and subjected to medical examination. It is vital to remember, whatever the source of the original stimulus, that these dreams occurred after her fears had possibly been magnified by the reading of NICAP and other material. That these dreams reflected her fears rather than her experiences is one possibility which has to be considered in any objective study.

Betty is held not to have communicated the substance of her dreams to Barney, only the fact of them, in which we are told he was not particularly interested. However, it is clear that before the first hypnotic regression session with Dr Simon, where the abduction material was revealed, she *had* communicated the substance of the dreams to Barney. As Fuller's book reveals 'The reality or non-reality of the dreams was of course foremost in Betty's mind. For nearly two years now, the answer to this question had been gnawing away at her. For Barney, as he had already told Betty, was hoping that for once and for all she would accept the fact that her experience in regard to an abduction was no more than an intensive vivid dream'. In one session with the doctor, Barney says, 'She told me a great many of the details of the dreams' and also 'I would be listening as she told this to Walter Webb'. When it occurred to Betty that the dreams might reflect real events is uncertain, though it appears she discussed it at work. The doctor himself noted after one session with Betty 'there are definite indications that her dreams had been *suggested as a reality* by her supervisor' (my emphasis). There is no doubt that these dreams affected Betty; on a subsequent journey by car when they encountered an automobile breakdown and several people blocking the road, she panicked, forcing Barney to accelerate past the group virtually as an escape. As would be revealed, her dreams were that their car, on the night in question, was halted by a group of humanoids blocking the road, leading to the abduction. This, however, only means that the dreams had become fears that were very real to Betty. Barney was apparently unmoved by the sight of the broken-down automobile and therefore no abduction memories seemed to have been triggered in him at this stage. When I spoke to Betty Hill in late 1988 I asked her about this point; and she told me that this detail had been missed in the original reports, that in fact Barney *had* been affected by this incident but less so than herself.

Let us, then, quickly recap the sequence of the events to this time before the hypnotic regression sessions. On September 19th 1961 Betty and Barney, driving together, sighted a UFO, which appeared throughout the early part of the sighting as a bright star and which seems to have appeared to be some sort of (terrestrial) aircraft of one sort or another. Betty stayed in the car, principally out of concern for the dangerous way in which Barney had 'parked' it, while Barney took binoculars and walked into the neighbouring field to more closely examine the object. He was clearly frightened by what he believed to have been rows of windows containing people looking at him, and returned screaming to the car to rejoin Betty, apparently in some sort of state of shock. The following morning Betty was already excited by the incident and discussed it with her sister because they were apparently sharing the UFO experience. Barney at this stage seemed uninterested or at least apparently unmotivated. Within a couple of days Betty was reading most of the then current UFO material available through NICAP publications and wrote to Major Keyhoe of NICAP giving details of the sighting. Betty then had a series of vivid abduction dreams which contained the substance of the events later to be revealed by regression hypnosis. Barney dismissed these as dreams while Betty became convinced *in conversation with others* that they may not necessarily be so. In an incident with a broken down automobile when they were driving on the road, Betty's actions were clearly coloured by her fears arising from the dreams, while Barney had much less of a reaction to this event. However, by the time they drove to Dr Simon for their first hypnotic regression session it was clear that Betty had discussed in detail the substance of the dreams with her husband who was therefore *now as fully armed with the abduction details as she was.*

Let us look in some more detail at the respective characters of Betty and Barney. Betty appears to be less of a worrier than her husband, taking things pretty much as they come and in a fairly light vein. For example, when they stopped the car in the White Mountains, Barney fears an attack by a bear while Betty dismisses it with levity. Betty is known to believe in UFOs, accepting the report her sister made some years previously. Her character seems to change momentarily at the time of the broken down automobile incident, when *she* is expressing anxiety, rather than her husband. However, it should be remembered that she had suffered very frightening dreams which must certainly have taken on the characteristics of reality, as often dreams do. Throughout the two years leading up to the regression hypnosis it seems to be Betty who is pursuing the need for an explanation to the sighting, and she appears to be pursuing it along determined UFO lines expressing considerable interest in detailed UFO material.

Barney, however, is distinctly the worrier. It was he who was concerned about being attacked by a bear on a deserted road which, while possible, must have been a statistical improbability. He points out that whenever he stopped at a motel he feared being turned away, presumably because he was a negro, although he admits that this never actually happened. Clearly he was one of those people who was prepared to worry in advance of problems. He also appears to be highly suggestible: he described the feeling he got when he watched the late show by himself at night as 'I get chilled as the ghost walks around the old haunted house'. It is perhaps significant that Barney also had ulcers which were aggravated by stress.

Factors that might be relevant in the case, relating to the stresses on the couple, include the fact that Betty had had a hysterectomy, and the dream she had included what seems to have been a gynaecological examination (later to appear in so many American reports), also that Barney apparently had semen removed; that Barney had a high IQ, suggesting a mind that would not easily tolerate sensory deprivation during that night; and that they were a mixed marriage which would have been a source of stress in puritan New England in the early 1960s.

Another important fact we have to look at at this stage is that Betty and Barney Hill are not — at least prior to their sessions with Dr Simon — a pair of witnesses to the same experience. In many of the analyses of the Betty and Barney Hill sighting, and often when using their encounter as a comparison to other encounters, it is held that they represent a corroborated sighting; an encounter they both shared. In fact at this stage as we can see they have shared almost nothing together: they both saw the light from inside the car and they both saw it apparently reveal itself to be a large object closer to the car. This is reasonable since it seems highly likely that there was some physical stimulus for their experience. However, Betty stayed in the car while Barney ran into the fields to examine the vehicle more closely; Betty's drawing of the craft shows no detail and particularly no occupants whereas Barney's reveals both from his much closer perspective; Betty alone had the nightmare which she independently related to her husband, and Betty alone seems to have been inspired to follow up the experience with learning about the subject of UFOs. They were together that night, but very little of their experience then or subsequently was shared except in the broadest of terms.

We must move on then to February 22nd 1964, when Barney undergoes his first regression hypnosis session following a series of inductions. Barney's memories at this stage are — broadly speaking — recollections of events as we know them now, though one or two points are of interest. At one point Barney recalls 'I believe Betty is trying to make me think this is a flying saucer' and in fact in a later part of the session he appears to be arguing as though Betty was with him, saying, 'Betty! This is not a flying saucer. What are you doing this for? You want to believe in this thing, and I don't'.

Shortly after this, Barney relates a story of being involved in a frightening experience when a jet plane dove screamingly towards him, breaking through the sound barrier and creating a sonic boom near him. This was apparently a frightening experience that has lived with him since and whether the fears generated from this form some part of his overall fear of the encounter is a speculation to be considered.

In a later part of the session, Barney confirms that he has not talked about flying saucers, but in fact corrects himself shortly afterwards merely stressing that he did not believe in them. He does say, however, 'But I have not talked about flying saucers since 1957, when we were talking about Sputnik.'

But this was 1961!

To me this seems highly improbable and far more likely to

be Barney rationalising his recall in order to be believed. The reason for this relates to the background against which the encounter would have taken place: in 1957 the Russians had launched Sputnik, which became the first man-made satellite of the Earth. This was a serious blow to Americans, who regarded it as a loss of national prestige, and one interviewee at the time suggested that it was the result of the American military 'falling down on their jobs'. Although Sputnik was in essence just a small radio transmitter whizzing round the world it probably had as much impact in its time as the first man landing on the moon had years later. However, between the launching of Sputnik and Neil Armstrong's 'giant leap for mankind' there was one other incident which was regarded as even more significant to most Americans. After Yuri Gagarin had flown in space and become the first man to leave the earth's atmosphere, American pride took another damaging blow and when Alan Shepherd became the first American in space he was for a time the greatest national hero. For a considerable period the one subject that all Americans discussed was space and if the launch of Sputnik involved the Hills in a discussion of flying saucers, presumably stemming from life in outer space generally, then surely the Shepherd launching would have done equally so. Two important facts must be considered when looking at this; firstly, Shepherd was launched into space on 5th May 1961, just four months before the Hill encounter, and secondly, and perhaps more importantly, Shepherd came from Derry, New Hampshire: in effect just 'up the road' from the Hills. If the hysteria throughout America, so well described in Tom Wolfe's book 'The Right Stuff', was wild, then it must have been a good deal more so 'in the old home town'. It is virtually inconceivable that the Hills would not have been discussing space and — given Betty's preoccupation with the subject — possibly flying saucers, at this time. Wolfe's book reveals that the politicians were even close to renaming Derry 'Space Town USA'.

So we must assume that the Hills had their encounter and subsequent events during a period of intense interest in space throughout America generally and in their locality in particular, and Barney's apparent lack of interest in the subject must be regarded as a subconscious plea for credibility.

During the session a further possible cause of Barney's fears is revealed; he relates the time when he and his cousin were hunting rabbits and he cornered a rabbit that was unaware he had done so, catching him under his hat. Barney apparently thought much the same was about to happen to him as this memory came to mind in the field, while he was watching the UFO.

This session also involved Barney recalling many impressions which are clearly dream-like in nature and which point to the possibility of some fantasy elements; at one time he says 'I'm just suspended. I'm just floating about'. This is quite typical of dream material, and certainly in later and deeper recollections the aliens physically moved Barney stumbling along the ground, so there appears to be no evidence of any actual levitation. In another section he says he can see 'eyes (that) don't have a body. They're just eyes.' He compares them to the Cheshire Cat in 'Alice in Wonderland' which disappeared and left only its (smile) behind. This is typical of dream material, also.

Barney's extra-terrestrial beliefs come to the fore in this session; he says, 'I wish I had gone with them ... Oh, what an experience to go to some distant planet.'

One last point relating to this session is relevant; it was conducted at a time when Dr Simon's offices were empty of other people because Dr Simon was aware of the possibility of Barney crying out from his emotional recall. Betty was apparently down the hall, but she was able to hear two major outbursts from Barney in the silence of the building. As there was nobody else in the building at this time Betty, in her concern for her husband, had the opportunity to go down to Dr Simon's room and listen more closely at the door. Thus, she could have heard something of Barney's recollections. However, I asked Betty about this when I spoke with her and she was adamant that she remained in the waiting room, and heard only the two cries.

Before analysing further details of the regression sessions we must leave our analysis of this case for a short time, to consider the implications of sensory deprivation, some altered states of consciousness, and in particular some sleep-related states.

All studies in the field of sensory deprivation have shown that the human mind is incapable of supporting a vacuum of thought. The mind needs stimuli and, generally, in everyday life it receives great quantities of various inputs; sounds, sights, tastes, smells, tactile impressions; in addition it receives problems, pleasures, fears and forebodings, lusts and loves. It receives and it is constantly analysing the data, and throughout the day it acts on, or instructs the body to act on, the results of its analysis.

When it is deprived of these sensory inputs it cannot 'shut down' and await the next input as, say, a computer can do. Experiments in sensory deprivation have shown that when the mind is not receiving input, then it prefabricates it. It is capable of self-generating fantasy.

Experiments in the field of this Ganzfield research have been conducted in several countries — at the Psychophysical Research Laboratories in Princeton, USA, for example. Subjects are deprived of sensory input; generally by blocking the eyes and ears, by restricting limb movement and by suspending the body in a bath of water kept at such a temperature as to be virtually undetectable to the skin's sensors. In such conditions subjects have reported the most bizarre of fantasies, and have experienced emotion ranging from ecstasy to horror.

Several years ago I interviewed a soldier in the British Army who related his own story of the army's deliberate 'sensory deprivation' conditioning. Because troops can be isolated for long periods, perhaps in alarming situations behind enemy lines, and possibly in conditions that require stealth, quiet, and will likely involve some form of night-time activity new recruits are put through a simulated version in order that they can learn what their own mind is capable of. My interviewee was left alone in a forest in Germany for a night. He had no mission or tasks given to him; merely to stay in the forest throughout the night. During that night he admitted he heard many strange sounds that caused him alarm, even saw one or two movements in the forest that concerned him. He admitted that his fears built up in the night. He had the advantage of knowing why he was there, and what was likely to happen. Never was he under any impression that his experiences were real in the objective sense, and in the cold light of day he laughed them off very quickly. He told me that he learned from the experience, though; that he became aware of what the mind could do.

The man in the street does not get this kind of conditioning, and may well be unaware of this; yet he is often in similar circumstances. I have spoken to many adult men and women who admit they would be afraid to walk through a 'haunted house' at night — or in one case even in the day! — or who would be concerned about walking through a graveyard at night. They speak not of fearing muggers or rapists, but of various 'spooky' feelings. Many people find it uncomfortable to watch a horror movie on their own late at night.

There are many Altered States of Consciousness. These are times when the mind is not responding in what we would loosely call 'normal' conditions. Such cases are often brought about by drugs or drink; they can also be brought about by illness, physical or mental, or they can occur spontaneously.

The most common altered state is sleep. Sleep itself is not well understood by science at the present time; there are reasonable suggestions as to why we need it but very few plausible reasons given for those cases where people appear never to sleep, nor to conditions in different animals such as hibernation. Most scientists believe that apart from the physical relaxation sleep affords us, which can be achieved as effectively by rest, the main function of sleep is to provide us with a time to dream. Unfortunately, even less is understood about why we dream. The most widely held theory is that we need dreams to sort out and 'dump' the garbage that collects in our minds during the day, releasing them as self-generated fantasies. There is some evidence that the mind can use dreams to sort out a difficult problem: in 1865 the German chemist, Frederich August Kekule von Stradonitz, was working in Vienna, trying to solve the problem of how the Benzene compound of six atoms was shaped. He dreamed of six snakes, all biting each other's tails and in the morning he had the solution to his problem, the atoms were arranged in a ring.

Dream deprivation, where the subject appears not to dream, is known to cause considerable mental stress, exacerbating anxieties and fears, even causing waking hallucinations. Recent experiments with Rapid Eye Movement, the tell-tale sign of dreams, suggests that even an unborn foetus dreams.

However, while the state of sleep is still being analysed by science it is clear that most people know whether they are asleep or not. Some dreams have an alarming feeling of reality which can persist into the waking period, but because of the 'bizarre' nature of most dreams their lack of reality can be identified.

One such experience I had myself was to wake up feeling very depressed at the thought of the recent deaths of my parents, and it was a depression that lasted perhaps forty-five minutes into the day during which time I had made and eaten breakfast. As I was shaving and started to think about their deaths, I recognised that I could come to terms with my depressed mood if I went over the circumstances in my mind. But the problem was I couldn't remember how they had died. Very quickly the house of cards began to fall and I realised that they were alive and perfectly well. The mood had had its effect though; and I telephoned them mostly as a way of finally exorcising the depression. The important point here is that the dream felt very real, and I broke that feeling by being able to 'check out' the facts. What would the case be where I — or anyone else — had a dream that seemed equally real but which was so exotic as to be impossible to 'check out'? Generally, such exotic dreams do not seem to occur simply because the mind creates very unreal situations, believable at the time but not on waking. However, there are two times during sleep when this is not the case, and such sleep periods can occur spontaneously and unexpectedly.

The state between being fully awake and fully asleep is referred to as hypnogogic; similarly the state between being asleep and coming awake is called hypnopompic. The former state can occur, for example, late at night in front of the television, in less than interesting company, or driving a car in a desolate and featureless, boring, landscape, particularly at night. In these cases the state is interrupted before sleep is achieved either because of being 'reawoken' by the end titles of the film, or your spouse waking you. In company good manners can come to the rescue, or in a car swerving or veering might shock you to full wakefulness. However, for that short time you are in a hypnogogic state.

In such a state it is quite normal to see and hear imaginary sights and sounds. In a study of imagery generated by this state, Vogel and his colleagues showed that the mental switching off was firstly a loss of clear thinking, then a loss of awareness of physical state, then the onset of hallucinations.

We must now consider the implications of this analysis in the Betty and Barney Hill case.

Driving is a potential situation of sensory deprivation; a lonely road, the darkness of night, the tiredness of the end of a holiday break. With two people in the car such a likelihood is greatly reduced, and there is very little evidence of it in the recall of either party. However, it is possible that long periods may have passed when there was little communication between Betty and Barney and this may have allowed some 'highway hypnosis' to set in. Betty in particular could have slept for periods since Barney was driving, and he would then have been left alone with his thoughts.

However, at the crucial time of the encounter itself, when Barney had walked across the field to see the object from a closer point, leaving Betty in the car alone, there is a much more likely situation. Betty would have some senses alerted; the car lights were on, Delsey the dog would have provided some comfort, and Betty was actively watching for other traffic. Barney on the other hand had virtually none; he was in the open, in a totally dark field late at night, he would have virtually no visual input, no aural input, little tactile impression, perhaps some smells. All his concentration would be, in this circumstance, on the subject of which he had already formed fears, and about which his mind was comparing it to imagery of capturing rabbits. There is every reason to suspect that in such circumstances a worrier like Barney could flood himself with irrational fear, many people admit they would do so in similar circumstances. He may have run back to Betty in a state of fear almost totally stripped of reason, without any external logic to it. And in those circumstances he would certainly have transmitted such a state to his wife.

I was able to appreciate how this fear can be transmitted in an incident in which I was involved many years ago. I was with three friends in the Lake District, all of us around the same age, and all 'lads together', enjoying the freedom of a camping holiday weekend. We had driven up over night and in the end we were to set up tents at around two in the morning; in the meantime we had stopped at a few lakeside locations to see where we wanted to camp. At around one in the morning we parked the car off the road, facing a lake, and walked towards the lakeside. The car lights were still on. In a scene that still seems incredible to me now, thinking of four adults in close company, a very real fear suddenly went through all of us. For my part, I recall seeing a horrified expression on one of my companions' faces and that was enough for me; along with the other three I raced for the car. We all leapt in and locked the doors. Only then, safe together inside the car did we try to analyse what had happened. Our stories conflicted somewhat, no doubt due to the confusion. But it appears that what happened was that one of my companions had thought he'd seen the car move; from his description it sounded as if we had parked on a rock or branch and the car had slipped off, causing the headlight beams to waver. He had shouted to the driver who had misunderstood what had happened and felt an emergency was underway. Quickly, we all picked up panic messages and ran for safety in the car. Within seconds of understanding all this we were united in laughter at our own reactions, but for a short time we had transmitted pure fear messages. I learned a little about the human mind that night, and the parallels between that incident and Barney's isolation during his encounter occurred to me when I was talking through my tentative conclusions on the case with a psychologist. He did not seem to think the event very unusual, and was certainly in agreement that fear is both irrational and easily transmitted.

Whatever the reality of the events there can be no doubt as to Barney's emotional responses to it; after his first regression session Dr Simon noted 'he showed very marked emotional discharge. Tears rolled down his cheeks, he would clutch his face, his head, and writhe in considerable agony.' Fuller's comments at this stage in his book on this case make a very important point; there had been a marked difference between Barney's recollections of the period of events during which he had been conscious, which Barney had recalled with great clarity and detail, and his remembrance of the encounter itself where his descriptions had become vague and detached.

Barney's second regression session was on 29th February 1964, and in this Barney recalled for the first time in organised detail the encounter on the road later when the humanoids stopped his car near their landed craft and took him and his wife from their car, leading them to the UFO. At one point Barney says, 'I feel like I am dreaming.' Barney was later to consider that the feeling he had was similar to the feeling of hypnosis when Dr Simon regressed him, and this has led to speculation that the humanoids induced a trance-like state in him, presumably to make him more controllable.

The most telling part of this regression was Barney saying, 'And I don't want to be operated on.'

At this stage, there had been no suggestion of an operation being performed. Such a fear can only have come from two sources; either Barney, having actually undergone an operation during the abduction, was recalling that memory under hypnosis; or his natural fears were surfacing. Such fears might stem from either a fear of operations generally, which could well have been the case since he was suffering from a stomach ulcer, or from a fear of recalling what he knew was *the frightening content of Betty's dreams.*

After this session Barney began having 'peculiar' dreams, dreaming for the first time in his life about UFOs. Either the hypnosis was bringing memory to the surface, or it was beginning to create fantasies that were spilling over into memory.

The following week, on March 7th 1964, Betty had her first regression session. She had taken the notes referring to her dreams, but these were not shown to Dr Simon as it was felt better not to influence him with their content. This was an important, and correct, decision. That Betty's eventual recall mirrored the dreams so exactly — whatever the implications of that for ufology — was a tribute to the professionalism of the doctor.

In her first session Betty revealed a good deal about her acceptance of the subject, for instance in one interchange she says, 'And I laughed and asked him if he had watched *Twilight Zone* recently on TV.'

Dr Simon asked if she knew of anything like it on that

science fiction programme. Betty replied she never saw the programme but had heard people talk about it. This gives a few clues to her thinking; she associated the event with science fiction, and she was aware, if indirectly, of what science fiction material was currently in vogue.

In another section she says, 'I was wondering if they were as curious about me as I was about them.' At this stage in the proceedings, as related, there was no 'them' yet in evidence. Betty is recalling her sighting of the distant, flying, object. Any 'them' is in her mind, and clearly it was. It seemed to excite her, too. She continued, 'All I could think of was, I don't know where we're going, but I'm ready for it.'

There is another curious point in this recollection. Betty says, 'and I could see a double row of windows.' during her report of the object in flight. In Betty's sketch made before the sessions she does not draw any such feature, though Barney does. Some material seems to have slipped back from Barney to his wife, or in her recollection she is building on her memory of Barney's sketch. Either way, her memory is inconsistent with her original, conscious, recall. This is unusual, for both of them their hypnotic recall of the material remembered also consciously is generally consistent.

The most important material to arise from this session relates to Betty's conversations with the aliens. We shall see later how inconsistent their own use and understanding of the language seems to be. At this stage they apparently have a very 'human' grasp of idioms and of underlying meaning to words and phrases. They say, 'You'll be on your way back home in no time', also 'the longer you fool around out here, the longer it's going to take. You might as well go on and get it over with, and get back to your car. We haven't got much time, either.' Later, 'Barney will be all right.... as soon as we get through ...'.

Now, many of these phrases have no real meaning at face value, and are in fact poor use of language. They are, of course, perfectly useful and sensible phrases provided that they convey meaning, and they would do so to someone using the same language-style. Phrases like 'in no time' only make sense at a deeper level of understanding, they are illogical if taken literally. Similarly, 'get it over with', 'get through' and others. The argument could be put that if these aliens have been studying Earth closely for thousands of years, as some suspect, then they might well have learnt all levels of meaning regarding our language. Why then do we later hear the aliens, during Betty's next session, asking 'What are vegetables?', and 'What is yellow?'. This suggests a good deal less understanding than the former phrases. Why, then, this inconsistency? A number of possibilities exist, but they rule out the likelihood that Betty was hearing the actual voices of actual aliens. Assuming that the aliens existed anywhere outside Betty's mind, then some sort of telepathic transfer of thought would possibly explain this, since they could transfer the *impressions* of such phrases as 'in no time', which could be translated into the actual words by the human recipient. On the other hand they could transmit clear questions where they lacked understanding. A more simple explanation exists however, and we should look to this before leaping for the exotic explanation of telepathy — particularly since that phenomenon is unproven. Betty could simply be using her own idiomatic language because she is recalling her own fantasies, and makes the aliens speak exactly as she would speak. Why then questions such as 'What is yellow?' We know that she believes in the reality of the events, and we know that she is thinking of an extraterrestrial answer. Is it possible that her subconscious needed to make the aliens *more alien* in order to reinforce her own beliefs? Could she need them to ask questions that betray their lack of understanding and therefore reveal their 'true' origins?

As mentioned earlier there are several examples of witnesses seeming to 'modify' their reports not as a lie, but because they desire both to be believed and not ridiculed. By way of example, consider the witness who sees a solid cube-shaped craft in flight. Since he 'knows' this is not aerodynamic and therefore unlikely, and because he may have some days at least to consider the sighting before speaking to an investigator, his mind might seek to 'round off the edges' of the craft in his report to rationalise what he saw. His report will be truthful, in that by the time he makes the report he will believe it; in fact the more he considers it the more he will reinforce the image. There is evidence to suggest that

Kenneth Arnold did just this with his sighting, he said of his calculated speed of the objects he saw, 'When it kept coming out in excess of 1700 miles per hour I thought "Holy smoke, we're taking the measurement of distance far too high up on both Mount Ranier and Mount Adams" so we took a measurement at the very base, as closely as it could be determined, and which I knew from the map was far below the snow line. The distance was thirty-nine point eight miles, we still had a speed of over 1300 miles per hour.' In other words, unable to believe his first guess he deliberately sought a new guess even though he knew his second points of measurement were too low to be accurate, but he felt the need to 'make sense' of his sighting, partly no doubt because he wanted to be believed. This situation seems to occur very often; in abduction cases it is less easy to prove — given the nature of the material — but it may still be happening.

There are other examples of apparently inconsistent material in the recall; the aliens are apparently amazed when they discover that Barney's teeth are false, and removable, and indeed they try to remove Betty's (natural) teeth; yet they apparently remove Betty's dress very easily by undoing the zipper at the back which as any fumbling teenager will admit takes some practice — their differences in knowledge seem almost stage-managed.

An example of 'cultural tracking' (inconsistent technology), which is discussed in more detail elsewhere, occurs also — Betty was shown a star map which has since been the subject of some controversy. The point here is that the map appears not to have been on a video or television screen as we might expect but on a sort of roller blind in a drawer, not unlike Admiral Nelson might have used at Trafalgar. Betty describes it, 'the map rolled up, and he put it back in the space in the wall and closed it'. The map itself seems illogical; apart from having no scale — which admittedly might not matter — it appears to have had no names or symbols printed on it. In short, it seems to have been useless and could almost be thought of as having one use only — to show it to captured humans. As we shall see in the next chapter, this habit the aliens have of giving tantalising glimpses is one which suggests that we do not yet really understand any of what we think we are perceiving.

We must, then, consider the implications of this analysis of the Betty and Barney Hill case. Although there are several possibilities about the true nature of the evidence we can probably dismiss any suggestion that the Hills deliberately lied — there is no evidence to support this and every reason to deny it; we can regard as unlikely the possibility of dual hallucination, which Doctor Simon also thought improbable.

One possibility is that the event actually happened; that the Hills encountered a spacecraft from another world whose occupants abducted them. Given the contradictory points raised, the known fact of the dreams that Betty had; the dream-like material contained in the recall; the fact that Betty had read a great deal of UFO-related material prior to her having the dreams; the reasons for potential stress in the couple; the social and cultural structure in which the event occurred; and the other points mentioned earlier, I find this alternative unlikely. I should fairly point out, though, that I put this to Betty Hill and she was adamant that the event *had* actually occurred, and indeed that the humanoids were extra-terrestrial. She made a surprising point, though; to my suggestion that abduction reports could be explained as being of psychological origin she agreed that many of the recent reports probably did have this explanation.

For my part, I think the balance of evidence suggests that the experience was basically a non-reality. Certainly the Hills appear to have encountered a UFO during their drive, which could have been natural or terrestrial, but the exotic material of the abduction appears to revolve around hypnotic regression drawing out the substance of vivid nightmares suffered by Betty and related to Barney. This appears to also be Doctor Simon's view, 'The doctor believed this (abduction reality) to be too improbable, and much material was similar to dream material.'

If this is the case then we are faced with a very significant point when considering the whole abduction phenomenon; though we know that Betty certainly experienced the material firstly — possibly only — through dreams, and though we know that Dr Simon, a qualified doctor working with the couple, believed the event to be unreal, the fact is that the material of the abduction report is very similar in a great many details to many reports of subsequent years. If the Hills encounter did not happen, then it is unlikely that the subsequent events occurred either, which would leave us with the very pertinent question of why so many similar reports appear to have been received. We shall now look at this point, but close this analysis of the Hill abduction in Barney's own words:

'*I become quite apprehensive thinking about what might have happened if we had foolishly permitted an unqualified person to hypnotise us, with the emotional impact that did come out, just what damage might have been done.*'

PART THREE

The Abduction Phenomenon

I could a tale unfold whose lightest word
Would harrow up thy soul, freeze thy young blood
Make thy two eyes, like stars, start from their spheres
Thy knotted and combined locks to part
And each particular hair to stand on end
Like quills upon the fretted porpentine

WILLIAM SHAKESPEARE

THE AMERICAN FORMULA

Throughout the decade of the 1980s, the theme of UFO abductions has been so consistent in the United States that many top UFO researchers in that country have made clear that they believe that the methods and motivations of aliens visiting the earth are now understood. Indeed, so certain are they in this belief that current work on UFO abductions takes more the form of confirmation than of research.

It is the predominant belief held on that continent, if not by all researchers then certainly by those who have media's attention, that UFOs are indeed the 'nuts and bolts' space craft of other worlds visiting earth. The humanoids so frequently observed in close connection with these craft are identified as the pilots and crew on the one hand and teams of alien medical researchers on the other.

It must be said that there is an impressive body of evidence which supports that view.

A prominent and leading American researcher, Budd Hopkins, is at the forefront of this work though he is by no means alone. Recently Hopkins became honoured with America's top award to ufologists for his outstanding contribution to current research; the only person ever to have received this award twice. At the beginning of the decade he published his first book, 'Missing Time', which detailed his several years of research, investigating the claims of those who had been abducted. His work seemed to indicate that visiting extra-terrestrials were abducting humans in order to conduct various forms of biological experimentation on them. More recently he has published a second book, 'Intruders — The Incredible Visitations at Copley Woods', which showed how his research had gone further into this theme and in which he was able to demonstrate that the purpose of the experimentation by the extra-terrestrials was some form of genetic breeding experiment with humans. Obviously Hopkins can only speculate on the purpose of this work of theirs, but he suggests that 'this leads to the unwelcome speculative inference that somewhere, somehow, human beings — or possibly hybrids of some sort — are being produced by a technology obviously — yet not inconceivably — superior to ours'. He says that 'I can infer that if human sperm and ova have been taken as the evidence implies, then human beings are possibly being produced in an alien context'. It has further been suggested that one reason for this experimentation is that the alien race has become somehow genetically deficient and that they are seeking a way to improve their breeding stock.

The most detailed report by Hopkins is into the abduction history of 'Kathie Davies', (a pseudonym), who is the principal figure in his recent book. His hypnotic regression sessions over a period of years revealed the following history of multiple abductions in the Davis family:

Firstly, there is some suggestion that she may have undergone an unexplored UFO experience when she was two or three years old; Kathie has recurrent dreams of her mother protecting her from a threat from the sky by hiding her in a closet.

At the age of approximately six she wandered away from her Detroit home and appears to have been abducted by a small, large headed, grey skinned alien who uses a small device to make a sharp cut on her leg. Kathie has a scar to the present day on her leg. Throughout this event it appears that the aliens implanted a false memory of the event occurring in a strange house where the alien was seen to be 'a little boy'.

At the age of sixteen Kathie encounters three young men who act in an odd fashion though there is only a tenuous UFO connection suggested which seems to hinge around the fact that the car they were in glided over a potholed road without being too bumpy and that perhaps its lights were not the pattern expected from a normal vehicle, although Kathie at one points suggests this is because one of its headlights was out. Of the three boys they met it was said, 'that the two men (who never spoke, who were never introduced by name, and whose appearance no one could remember) stood "sort of like guards while the blond guy ran things"'. Hopkins asks Kathie about the fact that she suggests they 'smiled with their eyes'. He says that was 'a phrase I'd heard, in other UFO cases: "their mouths never moved, they smiled with their eyes"'.

Two and a half years later, in December 1977, Kathie is in a car late at night in a rural area. The occupants of the car see an oddly flashing light and the driver stops; Kathie is taken aboard a landed flying saucer where she is subjected to her first gynaecological operation. The sighting of the UFO is consciously remembered, as a series of flashing lights, but the remainder of the session is revealed by hypnotic regression. The suggestion is made that Kathie and one of her companions were abducted separately while the third occupant of the car was 'switched off'; Hopkins refers to this switching off as an ability of the aliens for deactivating people they are not concerned with, in order that they can attend untroubled to those whom they have abducted. Under hypnosis, Kathie manages to 'peek a look' at the alien conducting the operation and she describes it as, 'it's just him ... it's the same face'. She later explains that this is the same small grey-faced figure she had seen before. The operation apparently consisted of a penetration into her uterus which she found distinctly unpleasant with no erotic connotations whatsoever.

A short time later, in March 1978, Kathie is again abducted and undergoes a second gynaecological operation. In this particular case she was abducted from the home of a friend late at night. Hopkins' interpretation of this is as frightening as it is crucial; he believes that in the 1977 abduction some months earlier, Kathie was artificially inseminated and that in the March 1978 abduction the unborn foetus was removed. Hopkins says 'I guessed what had happened, and shortly after I brought Kathie out of the trance she confirmed this. They had taken her baby.'

A year or so later, while pregnant with her son, Robbie, Kathie is abducted from her own apartment and taken into a flying saucer. At least one purpose of this abduction appears to be clear; a needle-like object was inserted into her nostrils and appears to have deposited a small circular object deep into her nose. Hopkins suggests that these could 'function as "locators", in the mode of the small radio transmitters zoologists attach to the ears of hapless, tranquillised elk to trace their wanderings'.

In 1980 Kathie is pregnant with another son, Tommy, and throughout the pregnancy she receives a series of indecipherable phone calls at regular intervals. Hopkins draws no particular conclusions from these but points out that no hypnotic exploration of these events has been made. Hopkins does suggest a somewhat eerie connection to the UFO incident, however; he points out that the voice on the telephone was moaning and guttural, that Tommy apparently had a speech defect at birth and Kathie apparently believes that her son sounds much like the mysterious caller.

On 30th June 1983 the incident occurs which in fact inspires Kathie to contact Budd Hopkins. A UFO lands near her parents' home apparently leaving physical traces — damage to the garden. It appears from Hopkins' narrative that he believes that the UFO was in Kathie Davis' garden, dark and unlit, and that she saw one of its 'balls of light' which was surveying the area, and which resulted in her suffering from a blast of radiation which later nauseated her. Hopkins states, 'when Kathie returned and went outside to look for intruders, she herself became the object of the white lights attention'. During this abduction Kathie also recalls having a probe inserted in her ear in what he believes is an implantation similar to the nasal implant four years earlier.

Three months later Kathie undergoes what Hopkins describes as a 'two step abduction ... unique in the UFO literature'. It seems that Kathie was lured out of her house on the pretext of a visit to the local store, but was somehow steered to a UFO which she only 'sees' as the store. The salesman she is dealing with is actually the small grey skinned alien. The actual motive for this stage of the abduction is unclear but it appears she is being forewarned of something that will happen later on. Sure enough, when she is at home, she is transported out of the house and into a UFO. During this second stage of the abduction she is subjected to some medical examination, part of which cuts her neck, leaving bloodstains on her pillow. When she reawakens she is in her own backyard, dressed only in her nightgown. During this latter stage of the abduction, she later recalls, apparently without the use of hypnosis, that she was shown a small child which she believes is her daughter created by an alien manipulation.

Just over a month later, in November 1983, Kathie has a 'particularly interesting dream' in which she believes she is undergoing some physical inspection by an alien. It seems possible from this that she is having ova removed by the aliens. It appears, however, that on this particular occasion there was a simultaneous abduction of her younger son Tommy. An alien apparently came through the wall and 'switched off' Robbie while he attended to Tommy. Hopkins believes this may have been part of a 'tagging' operation. It is possible that Tommy was abducted from the bedroom and taken aboard a UFO during this incident.

In February 1986 Tommy's abductions apparently continue when Kathie sees the alien figure emerging from the bedroom where Tommy was sleeping. Earlier in the evening, her other son Robbie had been frightened by a dream of a red tarantula in his room and was then sleeping with his mother, leaving Tommy alone. Hopkins speculates that this was deliberately done to isolate Tommy ready for the abduction.

In April 1986 Kathie has another remarkable dream; in this case she is abducted from her home and shown a baby again. She is told that in fact there are nine babies, although she is only shown two. In a bizarre sort of bonding operation she is allowed to name them and touch them.

Later that year, UFO sightings and a serious nosebleed occur to Robbie indicating that perhaps he has now become the object of abductions. These later events have not been explored in detail as of the publication of the book. Since the nosebleed follows an apparent missing time event, Hopkins speculates that the 'usual' pattern is occurring.

The reason that I have chosen the Kathie Davis case for detailed examination equates to the reason for the selection of the Betty and Barney Hill case for similar in-depth study; it is perhaps one of the most thoroughly investigated cases. It has the added advantages of being contemporary, indeed ongoing, and it demonstrates many techniques and approaches to the subject commonly applied by researchers other than Hopkins. It also provides a wealth of detail regarding the intentions of the aliens as seen through the eyes of the percipient, Kathie Davis, and through the eyes of the investigators.

I think it appropriate here to outline some of the conclusions that my own study of this comes to. But let me stress that these are conclusions drawn on an examination of Budd Hopkins' account of the events in his book 'Intruders', and not an examination of the case itself. It is important that the reader should understand this, because I am not attempting to re-examine the Kathie Davis case; what I wish to do is to compare this case with the next two in the book; Vallentuna in Sweden, and Kathryn's case, to show how different approaches to the material can lead to quite different beliefs about the nature of the experience.

I don't believe that the conclusions drawn in 'Intruders' are necessarily correct; indeed the questions raised by the case, particularly when contrasted to matters raised in the following chapters, suggest to me that there is an alternative possibility to an explanation of extra-terrestrial visitation.

I interviewed Jacques Vallee at the 1988 Brussels International UFO Conference and he expressed severe concerns over some aspects of abduction research. He stated that he believed some researchers were 'driving American ufology over a cliff ... (their) ... research is unscientific and unethical. We are losing the ability to reconstruct what is happening to these people (the witnesses)'. In fact Dr Vallee applied this quotation to one named researcher in particular, I have chosen not to name him as it seems to me that if there is fault then it lies with some (not all!) American-style research generally rather than with individuals. Certainly in Hopkins' case I have no doubt that whether or not his conclusions, even his methods, are right, they are undertaken with a sincere desire to reach the truth and to help the witness through matters of stress.

I think there are also pertinent points to be made about the presentation of this subject to an otherwise ill-informed public.

If Hopkins is correct then the motives of the aliens should be of considerable concern to the people of Earth, and to date those people have generally received the UFO subject through severely distorted media. A proper balance of presentation would be appropriate to the public and I do not feel that American ufology in general is presenting matters in a balanced way.

To return then to the specifics of the Kathie Davis case, let us first look at some of the questions raised by apparent inconsistencies in the material outlined above.

Firstly we must look at the time of the events; that is to say not the time of the *occurrences* but the time of the revelations. Matters began with the sighting of 30th June 1983 which inspired Kathie Davis to write to Budd Hopkins. The first incident, where there is considerable verification of Kathie Davis' claims from her own children, occurred in November 1983 onwards. Prior to that there had been some corroboration of UFO sightings and some corroboration of background events, but after this date we find very close corroboration, including her sons seeing the same aliens that she is seeing. For example, Robbie reports, 'Mommy, a man with a big head came in my wall and went in my closet and kept going back and forth and he wouldn't let me move.' I would suggest that there is no way for Hopkins, and possibly for Kathie Davis, to be certain that Kathie Davis' own fears, expressed for the first time in October 1983 in writing and involving the attention of the prominent UFO researcher, could not have been passed on to the very young Robbie. In that event his corroborative stories need be no more than very frightening dreams inspired by the stories she may be telling. We have no way of knowing, but I doubt that she specifically related the details of her fears to her children; nonetheless it seems improbable that they would not pick up a good deal of the material, particularly when Hopkins was visiting the house and conducting his research with their mother. By the time Robbie recalls his events, Hopkins has already commenced his work. It seems that there is some inconsistency in one detail about Robbie's experience; at one point Hopkins asks Kathie Davis if she had inquired of her son for a more detailed description of the man with the big head. She replies 'No, actually I didn't. I was trying to help him forget it'. This seems to be a fully appropriate way of dealing with the child's fears, whatever the stimulus, given his age. However, within a paragraph or two we read in Hopkins' narrative, 'Subsequent conversations lent more detail to this disturbing account. Robbie mentions several days later that the man with the big head "had an invisible mouth"'. It seems that Robbie *was* pursued to some degree for more details.

Hopkins comments on Robbie's statement 'the man wouldn't let me move'. He says that this is, he suspects, a description of physical paralysis. There is no need for this to be the case; abject fear without a physical presence would cause a mental paralysis of its own, and in any case if the whole sequence was a dream then paralysis of movement is quite typical of dream material. I asked one psychologist for a comment on this point and he was quite specific: dream material often includes paralysis because the purpose of dreams is often to express those areas where we feel frustration and cannot control the situation around us. Paralysis is therefore necessary for our dream to work itself out.

None of this refutes Hopkins' conclusions which, after all, could be correct; however, the material as presented seems not to give adequate weight to the other possibilities and presents a somewhat biased view of events, albeit those in which Hopkins truly believes.

The subject of dreams, and Hopkins' view of dreams, also raises an interesting point. Kathie Davis often says to him that she has had some form of dream and he believes this is her way of disguising from herself, as a means of protection, the fact that she knows the dream was a reality. This may well be the case, and makes good sense, but here there is also a serious logical flaw. In every case, Hopkins has been able to analyse the dream, to corroborate his views of the alien presences and to piece together the dreams, examined under hypnosis, into a coherent and logical pattern of alien abductions. In many cases he has been able to find physical evidence as corroboration of these events, bloodstains on nightclothes etc.

In that case, where are the *real* dreams?

Assume that Kathie Davis has genuinely been abducted by aliens, subjected to gynaecological examinations, artificially inseminated and then had her child removed from her.

Assuming that this is all real this is a most terrifying and horrific experience; it should inspire genuine horrific nightmares which are no more than genuine horrific nightmares. But where are they? Hopkins can always find evidence or reason to believe that these dreams and nightmares were *real* and that seems to be an inherhent flaw in the material. There should be dreams where they appear not to be. It suggests that at least some of the dreams are in fact dreams and not realities, *indeed they should be*, but since all of the dreams fit into a coherhent and logical pattern of abduction there seems to be no room for real nightmare material. At least as logical is the possibility that *all* of the material is dream material being reinforced by the regression sessions and the attention of a prominent UFO researcher. Again, this is not offered as an alternative conclusion to replace Hopkins' conclusion, but since it is a reasonable, possible, conclusion to draw from the evidence, the public must consider this balance of alternatives.

Any lack of balance will be inappropriately persuasive to an ill-informed public and will reinforce abductions as a reality where they need not necessarily be so.

The fact is that UFO research throughout the world over the past forty years forces us to accept the *possibility* that we are dealing with a complex psychological modern myth and not a physical reality. Again, this is not put forward as a new final conclusion; it simply asks that we consider this possibility because it *is* a possibility.

With regard to the possible abduction in the winter of 1966 when Kathie and her sister Laura are visiting friends and Kathie becomes lost, we see that her remembrance is of meeting a little boy who takes her into a playroom in a strange house. This at least is a fairly typical young dream, as young children are often inventing imaginary playmates. The fact that it is sited at a particular time is neither here nor there since the imaginative mind *needs* a location and time at which to place the fantasy. What is of interest is that at one point the boy 'metamorphoses into a small, large headed, grey skinned figure standing by her table'. The precise details of this revelation are not described, but it would be interesting to know precisely how, and at what point of the investigation the boy turned into the alien. An objective review of this memory must consider the possibility that the investigation has unwittingly planted the alien into the dream. The consistency of particular alien reports is something we shall return to later.

I am interested in the inclusion of the July 1975 encounter with the young teenage Kathie and the three normal-looking men who she meets. It seems to me that there are a whole host of possibilities, bizarre and normal, which could account for such a memory but they do not have to involve alien visitation. Presumably Kathie's whole life is not designed around and manipulated by aliens from another world; there must be some purely human decisions and activities. The incorporation of this non-UFO, non-alien event into the pattern reflects an interesting aspect of the investigation.

Similar consideration is due to the inclusion of the phone calls in 1980 as they seem to have only the most tenuous connection to the case; Hopkins rightly stresses this and draws few conclusions from it.

The 30th June 1983 sighting contains what seems to be a strange inconsistency with the rest of the material. Lights, presumed to be some form of spying device from the aliens' UFO, are searching areas of Kathie's house and the surrounding ground. Kathie goes out to see them and '*became* the object of the white lights' attention' (emphasis added). It seems to me that Hopkins is describing an *accidental* encounter; the start of things to come, and this is indeed the event which triggers her writing to Hopkins. However, as subsequent investigation seems to indicate, this is in fact just one in an ongoing series of events through Kathie's life, and in all the other instances Hopkins is able to ascribe a deliberate motivation on the part of the aliens, luring her from her home, manipulating her movements and activities and those of her companions. Perhaps the encounter with the white lights was itself a manipulated controlled event but why then the apparent change of style? Are we in fact seeing the first real event from which the others have *developed*?

In the February 1986 event when, it will be recalled, Hopkins believes that the aliens distracted Robbie with the sight of a glowing red tarantula which frightened him sufficiently to make him go into his mother's bed, leaving Tommy alone to become the object of an abduction, there is a strange and inconsistent piece of material. It seems almost unimportant and is not dealt with in any great detail in the book and yet perhaps therein lies an important observation. Let us put it in context. After Kathie has put Robbie to bed in her own room and he is asleep, she is lying on her bed watching late night television when she looks up to see the small grey skinned alien walk past her door. She stresses that she did not see him out of the corner of her eye, she was looking right at him. Her TV is right by the door so there is little doubt that she could see through the door into her hallway where the alien was walking. He walked by 'like I wasn't there' Kathie states. He was apparently coming from the boys' room, where Tommy was alone. Now what are we to make of this event? In another part of the narrative it is apparent from Robbie's recollection that the aliens freely move through the walls of his room and are therefore apparently able to deal with physical bricks and mortar in a manner unacceptable to the physics we understand. It is equally obvious, given the balance of the narrative of the book, that the aliens are perfectly capable of 'switching off' those who they do not wish to be involved with the abduction. Hopkins relates several cases where, even in a car load of people, the aliens can switch off some occupants leaving others open to the abduction treatment; in one case causing the abductee some difficulty because he had to get out of a two door car from the back seat, forcing his way past 'switched off' companions. In this particular instance the aliens have apparently chosen not to switch off the Davis family while the Tommy abduction is under way, rather they have simply frightened off Robbie and apparently left their mother, wide awake and alert, to witness the alien in the hall. Two immediate possibilities arise from this; either they are extremely forgetful which seems ludicrously inappropriate given the rest of the narrative, *or it was their determined intention that Kathie should witness the event.* In fact the event itself seems to lend weight to the latter hypothesis, since we are also left with the question as to why the alien was walking past the door in the first place. The UFO was presumably not somewhere inside the house, and since the alien can, if he wishes to, pass through walls etc., and since there is no reasonable evidence to suggest the alien had a purpose in being somewhere else in the house, then we have to ask ourselves why he was there at all. One flippant comment that was made to me when I was discussing this question was that in the excitement of events the alien decided to go to the bathroom to relieve himself. This was of course a joke but at least it offered a reason, which was more than I could do. In fact, if we accept the narrative as given, there is only one reason why the alien left Tommy's room and walked past Kathie's open door knowing that Kathie was wide awake and that was *because he wanted her to see him.* Whatever motive we ascribe to this it is simply not consistent with the other narratives of the abduction case. It is in fact a *haunting*, not of the sort of ghost that turns up at your bedside claiming to be the spirit of your long lost friend, relative etc; not of the sort of ghost that comes to you to warn you of imminent danger; not even of the sort of ghost that is the troubled spirit of a past dead individual roaming around his former possessions (assuming you accept the existence of any of these kinds of ghosts). Rather it is the sort of ghost who deliberately drapes an eerie sheet over his head and carts along with him a whole load of noisy, squeaky, rattling chains for the sheer purpose of being a frightening nuisance in the middle of the night! To have made such weight of this point forces on me the responsibility of producing some sensible conclusion and I confess that I am at a loss to do so. I do not accept that it is appropriate to simply say 'Well, we can't understand alien logic, can we?' The whole point of Hopkins' narrative is that in fact their logic is very similar to ours and that we are being made the subject of a logical and *well understood* genetic study. If we accept that Hopkins has successfully tied up all the loose ends and made sense of events, then we cannot assume alien logic is that far removed from our own and we must therefore be ready to ascribe our own logic to the events. One possible alternative conclusion to Hopkins' own is therefore that this event is actually dream material. All hauntings of this kind seem to have at least a possible basis in dream material.

Another possible conclusion that I shall be outlining in detail towards the end of the book investigates the possibility that there *is* some alien intervention in our lives but that it is quite different from the events we perceive. More importantly, this probably means that abductions as we understand them are simply not taking place.

Another possible conclusion has to be, as I have already suggested, that we are dealing with a complex psychological phenomenon.

There is also the question of physical evidence on the bodies of the witnesses. It is claimed that this presents substantial corroboration of the claims, but there must be some reservations about this. For one thing, most people have scars on their bodies and many of them cannot recall how they got there; childhood accidents are frequent and if they are not traumatic then they are forgotten, but simply running past a sharp tree branch or bush branch at ground level is sufficient to cause a life-long scar in the leg. My fears again would be that the UFO investigator is treating as significant something he knows already exists, implanting the connection and then claiming the connection is a corroboration. I would stress that this is far from saying that abduction investigators are deliberately prefabricating their claims, I merely think that their efforts to get the 'truth' can sometimes be too enthusiastic. This point is also taken up in the next chapter.

Another interesting factor is the consistency of Hopkins' aliens, and indeed the consistency of abduction reports Hopkins receives. I use Hopkins by way of example only; such similarities exist with many American — and other — researchers.

Practically all of Hopkins' aliens are short, white or grey skinned humanoids with large wrap-around black eyes and reduced other facial features such as nose, mouth, ears. Practically none have hair and indeed the books 'Intruders' and 'Missing Time' are illustrated with many similar pictures intended to demonstrate to us the consistency of reports. The first point of concern is that these consistently reported aliens are, while not actually unique to Hopkins, very much a part of his work. Philip Klass in his much criticised book 'UFO Abductions: A Dangerous Game' puts this point rather sarcastically in his summing up when he says 'If you choose to ignore these warnings and feel compelled to contact an abductionist, I strongly recommend Dr Leo Sprinkle. Under his guidance you are more likely to encounter a gentle and spiritually uplifting type of ufonaut than one who takes flesh samples, ova, or sperm, or removes unborn children from their mothers' wombs'. Klass' style is — I would suggest deliberately — abrasive, but the point he makes cannot be ignored; Hopkins finds one kind of alien, Sprinkle finds another, other alien types are reported by other UFO researchers. There is consistency *within researchers' own work.* It is true that Hopkins' alien is the predominant type, and reported by many investigators other than him; he is similar to the aliens of the Hill encounter though not so remarkably so as to make him identical. For instance, early aliens such as the Hill's had apparently human-type eyes with white surrounding a central dark area. Hopkins' aliens are much more 'alien' having elongated black structures curving around the side of the face. Of course when we consider the claims of contactees — and there is no reason why if we are prepared to accept the extraordinary claims of abductees that we should be prepared to deny the extraordinary claims of contactees — then here we are dealing with a very humanlike graceful people with human features and long flowing hair. Indeed, according to their human contacts, many of them pass amongst us frequently in our everyday life. This must lead to the question of why we have such inconsistency of aliens throughout the literature, yet such consistency within the work of individual researchers.

If we are looking for a logical and down to earth reason then we would have to go to the unacceptably improbably conclusion that one particular type of alien is in fact not targeting particular families or blood lines but in fact eventually seeking to target individual investigators such as Budd Hopkins himself. Similar claims would have to be made for the other groups of aliens. This I find quite unlikely and I have to leave open for the present the question of why, with so many varied aliens apparently to hand, Hopkins only gets the type he is already familiar with.

A second point arising from consistency rather than inconsistency is the fact that Hopkins always finds abductions, and particularly abductions which appear to corroborate his belief that aliens are visiting the planet on a genetic study and experimental campaign. Coming away from the Kathie Davis case, let us look at the first major case which inspired Hopkins' book 'Missing Time'; that of Stephen Kilburn (pseudonym). Kilburn apparently did not have a UFO encounter in his conscious memory when he approached Hopkins. Rather, he had a fear or apprehension of a particular stretch of road. Under hypnotic regression, Hopkins discovered that on that particular stretch of road he had encountered a UFO and had been subjected to a reasonably 'classical' abduction. I cannot refute these claims, perhaps Kilburn did indeed have a UFO abduction at that point and perhaps Hopkins has successfully uncovered it. But a question must be considered; had Stephen Kilburn gone to a researcher of reincarnation, of past life histories, then would he have discovered that at some point in a previous life he had perhaps been murdered on that stretch of road? Had he gone to a researcher of ghosts and hauntings would he have perhaps discovered that he had once encountered a very frightening haunting on that stretch of road? Had he gone to a different UFO researcher would he have discovered that he had met quite different aliens who had perhaps given him a frightening warning for his own life or the life of the human race? In fact, he went to Budd Hopkins and discovered that he had been the subject of a UFO abduction of precisely the type that Hopkins frequently discovers. While this raises questions, there are also mitigating strengths: he did in fact seek out Budd Hopkins knowing what Budd Hopkins' interest was and therefore there is a least some suggestion of involvement with UFOs by the witness before Hopkins dealt with him.

Hopkins' ability to find these aliens and these abductions is impressive. In his presentation to the MUFON 1988 Symposium, entitled 'The Skeleton Key', Hopkins relates the case of 'Sam' who had a childhood phobia of spiders. This phobia apparently arose in the following way. 'One night I awoke and there was a nest of spiders in the corner of the window right near my face. I was terrified and pulled the covers over my head. I couldn't sleep, and in the morning I begged my mother to kill the spiders, and take away their nest. I thought they were black widows, but I found out later that black widows don't nest in sunlit places like the window. Well, the strange thing was that there wasn't any nest in the morning when I woke up, and no spiders. I couldn't understand it. My mother thought I had been dreaming, but I knew I had been awake when I saw them. Ever since then I have hated spiders and been afraid of them.' (Quoted from the MUFON Symposium proceedings by permission of the international director of MUFON, Walt Andrus). Hopkins apparently asked Sam what the spiders' nest looked like. He described that it was a white nest in the corner of the windows. Hopkins asked how many spiders were in the nest and he thought there were two, real black and shiny. Sam apparently held up his hands to show the two black shiny spiders on their white web. Hopkins then states 'He realised as he made the gesture what the truth was; he had seen a white face in the corner of the window, a white alien face with two black, shiny, elliptical eyes'. Hopkins goes on to say 'Years and years of spider-dread, years of hatred of the innocent arachnids all caused by what turned out to be the first stage of a UFO abduction. Sam was more amazed even than I at what "The Skeleton Key" had unlocked'.

I was even more amazed than Sam and Hopkins at what 'The Skeleton Key' had unlocked; spiders we *know* exist, arachnaphobia (fear of spiders) we *know* exists and indeed commonly so. And yet in this particular case, this particular spider phobia of this particular witness turns out to be the same old alien as ever before. Desmond Morris, the world famous zoologist who spend many years studying the development of human beings from their animal ancestry, made pertinent conclusions about arachnaphobia which suggested that it was extremely common and related to the nature of spiders themselves. In his book 'The Naked Ape' he lists the top ten most disliked animals; spiders come second after snakes. Why then does *this* arachnaphobia turn out to be a UFO abduction?

At the same MUFON presentation Hopkins applied his 'Skeleton Key' to the case of Kristina Florence. Hypnosis recalled that when she was five or six years old she had encountered an ant hill and she had dug down into it and discovered in herself a reaction of immediate hatred. Not to the ants, but to the eggs. She thoroughly destroyed the eggs and then searched out other ant hills, repeating this destruction. Hopkins asked if she hated them because they were disgusting looking, she said 'No, I just hated them. I wanted to smash them, but I don't know why. They were kind of whitish and smooth and shiny, and I just couldn't stand to see them there in the yard'. During the hypnosis sessions it appears that Miss Florence had been abducted by the classical humanoid figures and apparently she then guessed 'that the whitish colour and the smooth, almost shiny skin of the UFO occupants was like that of the ant eggs'. Hopkins points out that she was stunned by her discovery, which had come during hypnotic regression.

During Hilary Evans' presentation at the 1988 UFO conference in Brussels, on which Evans was putting forward his considerable doubts as to the methods of American ufologists, I put the deliberately provocative question that if there were no UFO abduction researchers, would there be no UFO abductions? I wanted to do no more than to inspire constructive debate rather than to put forward a personal conclusion and fully expected the immediate reaction, particularly of the American delegates present, to be aggressively defensive. In fact, I was quite wrong-footed. Many of the delegates there, particularly the European delegates but also those from America, first laughed in appreciation of the point and then turned and applauded the question. I appreciated the gesture and was pleased to find that there was an acceptance of criticism from 'within the field'. Incidentally, I felt somewhat unhappy at having stolen a little of Hilary Evans' thunder in what was after all his presentation, and an excellent one at that; I apologised to him when we were together shortly afterwards. I was relieved with his response when he said 'It was a very perceptive question, and a point well made'. I might add that one of the people who applauded the question, and who later commented favourably on it, was Richard Haines, who holds a PhD in experimental psychology and physiology, who has studied UFOs for over twenty years and has been involved in abduction research in America for some considerable time.

Another apparent contradiction in the material seems to be in the subject matter of the alien visitations themselves. The aliens are apparently visiting the earth to seek out genetic material for some purpose, possibly to improve their own physical stock with some of our genes. Certainly that is a reasonable conclusion on the basis of the face-value evidence as presented. But that simply does not fit in with the abduction process. As Dr Jacques Vallee pointed out to me, aliens merely seeking genetic material could land on or near any one of any medical research institutes, including one he had worked at which was the example he was giving, where they would be able to remove blood, semen, ova, even foetus, brain tissue, etc. and the most they would have to do would be to 'switch off' a few late night guards.

Clearly, then, the purpose of the alien intervention is not merely to obtain material; the only possible interpretation of the facts, as presented, is that the aliens are making a study of humanity itself. Hopkins points out that it appears that the aliens are abducting generations of the same family in an apparent attempt to examine bloodlines etc. Assuming that there is any alien intervention at all then this must remain one possibility even though their methods of going about this must be called into some question as we shall do shortly. There is one possibility, however, which does not seem to have been explored in any particular detail, even on the American continent, though I strongly suspect it will be surfacing shortly. Stages of the development of the UFO phenomenon have been accepted piece by piece, presumably as people are more conditioned to accept a bigger bite. At first, UFOs were lights in the sky and discs seen at a distance. It was some time before any kind of humanoid encounter was treated with respect even within the UFO community and the first humanoid encounters were the contactee claims where human-like aliens expressed their concern regarding the way we were conducting our affairs on this planet. Only more recently have the abduction claims been acceptable and I suspect that Hopkins believes he is breaking into new areas of credibility with his claims of genetic manipulation. When the climate is right I would expect that the 'blood line theory' will be taken to further extremes. If the aliens are abducting generations of families and subjecting them to various forms of genetic study and experimentation then are we not likely to hear shortly that there is evidence that current members of these families are in truth hybrid aliens? Perhaps Hopkins hints at this when he makes the comparison between the strange gutteral phone calls to Kathie Davis and the apparent speech defect in her child Tommy.

The point is not whether the evidence leads us to this conclusion or not, or whether it can be *made* to do so, but that it is a logical next step to see this claim coming into the public domain and when it happens I would hope that a forewarned public will be rightly critical of the evidence; not rejecting it, because after all it could be true, but being prepared to examine it alongside alternative possibilities, and in particular the existence of a continuing, developing myth.

With regard to the aliens' method of operation, this brings us back to the 'haunting' to which we earlier compared one of Kathie Davis' sightings. The aliens appear to have a superior control over laws of physics as we currently understand them, and certainly over human beings. They can selectively switch off people when they wish to, and they can block memory when they wish to. But in fact they don't do a very good job of it. They block the memory of an abduction but they leave the beginning and end sections tantalizingly available for an investigator to discover, they 'seal the edges' of the so called missing time period but leave sufficient memory for the abductee or the investigator to pick up the pieces. There seems to be no logical reason for this, they do not have to be physically present in order to effect the mental block as is apparent from the wealth of material available from Hopkins, Jacobs, Sprinkle, et al, so why do they not seek to block out even the beginning and end periods of the missing time. Again, I must stress that it is not appropriate to simply say 'Well, we don't understand alien logic', because the whole point of these analyses is that investigators claim they *do* but if in fact we do understand it then we must accept that we cannot just disregard those parts which are not convenient. The inference must be, as in the case of the rattling-chain style haunting, that the aliens want us to know what they are doing, and want to do it in such a way as to be bewilderingly frightening. Since this seems to be unacceptable by any sensible standards there appears to be some lack of logic in the conclusions drawn, and I think it leads to the whole house of cards beginning to fall. Regarding their treatment of people during the abduction, it appears that they do not properly anaesthetise, but rather perform all of their operations with the abductee in some sort of state which enables them to remember what has happened. This is certainly far behind the technology even of our own time where we are quite capable of anaesthetising a person for an operation and no amount of regression hypnosis will bring out an accurate recollection of events during that operation. To my knowledge, there have been no successful attempts to regress somebody who has undergone major surgery and have them recall with any accuracy the events of the operating room. (This ignores the claims of out-of-body experience which are not perhaps quite appropriate to the matter we are examining.) Again, then, we are forced to the same conclusion; the aliens *want us to remember* these bewildering and frightening experiences.

But do they claim to want us to remember? The answer is a definite *no.* Betty and Barney Hill reported that the aliens had told them that they *would not* remember the events that had happened to them. Many other cases have reported the same instruction, often even more forcibly imposed; the aliens do not wish us to recall what they are doing to us. Yet although we, in our present state of technology, would be perfectly capable of enforcing this command, the aliens apparently are not. In fact, every amateur hypnotist who comes along has only to waive the proverbial gold watch in front of his witness' eyes and all the recollections flood out. Apart from the incompetence of the aliens there is another point to consider here; Dr Benjamin Simon, when he revealed details of alien abduction in Betty and Barney Hill, was certain that he was uncovering trauma-suppressed fears rather than actual events and in fact he was quite clear that he did not believe the events had actually happened. UFO investigators on the other hand reveal much the same information but clearly believe that they are uncovering actual events. Dr Simon was a psychiatrist, UFO investigators generally are not. Can any conclusions on similar evidence arrived at through comparable means but varying so wildly ever be regarded as definitive?

Clearly we have not yet found a final answer and it is proper that we admit this, rather than deceive the public into thinking that our theories are facts.

The missing time itself is another matter worthy of further consideration. If we assume that the aliens are able to abduct people very much as and when they wish, and Hopkins makes the point that they seem to keep their human contacts on 'shorter leashes' than had perhaps previously been suspected, then why are there any missing time periods whatsoever? Why not ensure that abductions take place when the person has no awareness of time, such as during sleep periods. An abduction during the middle of the sleep period, with all of the other occupants of the house switched off from *before* the event starts and remaining so until *well after* the event has finished, and with an effective mental block put on the abductee, would leave absolutely no trace whatsoever of the event for the UFO investigator to uncover. The missing time period seems to be yet another tantalising clue deliberately left for us to pick up. On the other hand it may be argued that the abduction experiments require that people are abducted at particular times and that therefore this is not within the aliens' control; again, though, there is inconsistency in this logic. If that is the case, why are all the missing time periods at times when the remembrance is uncertain? People are abducted during long lonely drives, and they appear to take longer to reach their destination than they had expected to, or they are abducted during long walks in the country and again they are mystified at the time that it takes them to complete these walks. If the needs of the aliens are not in their control then there ought to be occasions when a person has to be abducted from the middle of the factory floor in a busy working day, there ought to be times when a person ought to be abducted on the way to work, arriving two hours late after a journey of, say, ten minutes. This would leave no room for doubt as to the missing time element, deliberate fraud aside.

In fact, as we have seen, the abductions are neither totally revealing nor totally concealed but just tantalisingly dangled.

Another particular inconsistency occurs in the area known as cultural tracking. Cultural tracking suggests that there is a direct connection between the development of alien technology and the development of human technology. This takes many forms. Firstly, let us look at the UFOs themselves. In the 1890s UFOs were reported much the same as the UFOs in the 1940s and 50s: low flying eerie lights in the sky, vague outlines of occupants peering down from lighted windows. However, the claims of the 1890s were of airship-shaped UFOs, just prior to the development of the airship. The claims of circular, disc-shaped space craft only surfaced during the late 40s and 50s in any number when the science fiction culture of film and television was beginning to surface also. During the 1940s the alien craft were held to travel at speeds faster than we could achieve, when we were achieving speeds of, say, 800 miles an hour, they could achieve speeds of, say, 1,500 miles per hour. Now that we have achieved speeds of several thousand miles per hour, and faster still in our Earth-to-Moon spacecraft, so we discover that the aliens can now achieve speeds far faster than they could a few decades ago. One interpretation of this is that they are only marginally more advanced than we are and thus we have been watching their development pretty much in parallel with our own. However, another interpretation could be that we are inserting a certain amount of our own perception into the claim made.

The inference is clear. Since alien technology is held to be so far in advance of our own, given what they can apparently achieve, then advances in their own technology should be almost unnoticed by us in the same way that the difference between a 1960s automobile and a 1980s automobile would be unnoticed by a primitive tribesman who had never encountered technology before. That we perceive these changes, and that we perceive they are keeping pace with our own technology, must give rise to the suspicion that we are at least interpreting what we see through our own technology. This does not mean that UFOs are entirely psychological. In fact it could well mean that they do exist and that we are only able to interpret them within the framework of our own technology because that is a limitation of human beings; this point is indeed explored elsewhere. What it does mean is that *our recollections are unreliable* and again as responsible UFO researchers we should be wary of attempting to draw definite conclusions when we have *evidence of unreliable information.*

What, then, are the conclusions of this section?

Firstly, it demonstrates that there are no hard answers to the UFO phenomenon, and this requires saying because on the American continent particularly claims are being made that the answers are now to hand. It demonstrates that there is inconsistent material within the evidence presented and further it demonstrates that the consistent material within the evidence presented does not necessarily lead itself to the conclusions that seem to be being drawn at the present time.

I hope that it will serve as an aid to both 'abductees' and investigators, in particular as a warning; in the February 1988 MUFON UFO Journal, No 238, in the article 'Abductions — A Comparative Study' by Thomas E. Bullard, the conclusion is made: 'If this study cannot settle once and for all what abductions are, the effort proves one thing about them *beyond the shadow of a doubt* (my emphasis): abduction reports as a body show far more similarities than accident, random hoaxes or purely fantasies can explain. The consistencies in form and content down to numerous minute details demonstrate that abductions make up a coherent phenomenon, whatever its ultimate nature. Any sceptic who dismisses this unity relies on hope rather than evidence to support his case'. The suggestion here presumably is that there is too much consistency of material between different abductees' claims and particularly where the knowledge of one claim would not be available to the knowledge of another. There is one often overlooked major flaw in this logic; there is often a common link between abductees who do not know each other and a conduit through which their experiences can influence each other's recollections and that is the Abductions Investigator. The abductees may not have access to the minute detail but he has, and if in any way he influences by his presence the recollections of one abductee, then he distorts the whole picture.

One conclusion therefore, and one which will no doubt receive criticism of its own, is that some American ufology has failed to understand and consider the alternatives.

Even the claims they are making to justify their own actions seem inappropriate to me and I leave it for the reader to judge. Take for example the following: In the article 'Abductions — A Personal Primer' by Budd Hopkins and David Jacobs, also in the MUFON UFO Journal of February 1988, the authors suggest that one important criterion for selecting an investigator is as follows: 'The investigator and/or hypnotist should be well versed in the patterns of UFO abductions in order to pursue the investigation correctly, helping the subject explore his or her memories smoothly and systematically'. *I cannot more strongly disagree.* If there is an objective truth then that objective truth would be evident to any psychiatrist using the same techniques of hypnotic regression. If the investigator and/or hypnotist has to be versed in the patterns of UFO abductions then it is tantamount to a confession that the subject can only be examined *if the conclusions are already 'known'*. I would strongly urge UFO abductionists to reconsider at least that point.

Take for example yet another statement by American ufologists, in this case by David M Jacobs, PhD, a prominent abduction researcher who presented the paper 'Post-Abduction Syndrome' to the 1988 MUFON Symposium. In this he says 'Many well meaning therapists try to convince the abductee that their problems stem from familiar relationships in childhood, or that their vivid dreams originate in repressed sexuality or in childhood sexual abuse. When the abductee says that his problems might have something to do with seeing a strange object in the sky, a "monster" in his bedroom or an unexplainable missing time event, the psychologist routinely tries to convince him that these are just fantasies and the abductee's problems are based on other psychological causes. "Standard" therapy not grounded in the knowledge of what actually happened to the abductee rarely dissipates their anxieties and the problems continue unabated. *The most harmful situations occur when a psychologist will not admit his or her biases*' (my emphasis).

But what about the biases of the abduction investigator?

They themselves have a belief system into which they must fit their own experiences, including their investigations of abductees. We know that people do suffer problems from family relationships in childhood; they do suffer from repressed sexuality; they do suffer childhood sexual abuse; we know that most children create the occasional 'monster' in their bedroom. If tensions arising cannot be relieved by the therapist, could this not possibly reflect more on the competence of the therapist than on the source of the problem. Do we have to look to aliens and extra-terrestrials to explain things when there are *known* explanations available?

I believe the problem with some American ufology results from the fact that it is being 'investigator-driven', and I think this is having the inevitable effect of standardising reports, therefore seeming to corroborate that which is not in fact corroborated. Less caring investigators than those mentioned here could also possibly cause some harm to the witnesses. Their uncertainties are being replaced by a certainty which is horrifying and traumatic in itself and in which no objective faith can be placed. The fact is that we do not yet know what lays behind the UFO phenomenon and we will not find out by imposing our own opinions on the questions. If we are to discover the answers then we must rely only on the one 'data collection instrument' available to us — the witness. Future UFO investigation must be 'witness-driven'. As Dr Vallee commented in the interview I mentioned earlier 'It should be under their own control or we will hurt these people'.

From the point of view of the objective evidence we *must* let the witness lead the investigation. I suspect then that we will lose the standardisation of reports, we will see considerable inconsistencies and when we have genuinely learned how to deal with these real inconsistencies, then we will begin to understand the true phenomenon.

Hopkins himself does point out 'whenever we consider these large, theoretical questions about the ultimate nature, source and intention of the UFO phenomenon, we must admit that we still have no final answers'.

So, if UFO investigation, and particularly abduction investigation, in the United States is heading down too narrow a road, and if Britain — the only other country with a reasonable number of abductions — is blindly following the American example, then where in the world do we look for an example of how to find the right road?

HISTORY REPEATS ITSELF?

Before we examine examples of alternative abduction study, there is an uncomfortable comparison to be made with the current trends in — principally — America and Britain, a comparison from which investigators, and certainly abductees, should take caution.

Interestingly, while I was researching this area both Hilary Evans and Dr Jacques Vallee mentioned, independent of each other, that they were studying exactly the same point; which suggests that this comparison is giving cause for more general concern.

UFO abductees are not the first people to undergo the reception that they find when reporting their experiences. It is a matter of great concern that there is a close 17th century parallel to their experiences which reflects not so much on the quality of the experience itself, and does not particularly lead to comparisons of reported events, but reflects on the approach of some investigators.

That century saw many of the famous 'witch hunts'. Catholics and protestants, who spent much of their time at loggerheads, were agreed on one main issue; that the devil could possess people and could use their bodies during their life times with their permission, their having sold their soul to him. This could be treated by exorcism but in cases where the devil held out stubbornly the only 'cure' was death, usually burning the so-called witch at the stake.

Let us first look at some of the physical similarities between the witch hunts and UFO investigations. Firstly there was a definitive way in which the witch hunter could determine that the person was a witch and that indeed they had the devil possessing their soul within them; this was by finding the mark of the devil which would be physically apparent on the body of the witch. In other words a scar. This scar was important to the devil as it was his way of imitating baptism and a good investigator could always tell the difference between a 'natural' scar and the 'devil's mark'. Sometimes the scar would take some considerable searching for but if required it could always be found. Of course, most people have scars on their bodies, particularly from the vigours of childhood and often they cannot recall where they got them from, but to the witch hunter this was useful material indeed.

We have, of course, a close parallel in UFO research. Particularly in the United States, current research is such that scars on the body are often used as corroborative evidence of surgical medical examinations by aliens, validating testimony given under hypnosis. In other cases researchers are able to 'predict' where a scar will appear because of hypnotic recall and in still further cases the scar itself is the trigger which enables the UFO researcher to search for, and find, the abduction story. And of course the skilled UFO investigator can always tell the difference between a scar inflicted by aliens as opposed to a scar inflicted by natural causes. We have elsewhere in this book examined the possible motives of any alien research crew and concluded that at least their stated aims are not being logically pursued, i.e. they do not wish people to remember what is happening to them and yet they dangle enough clues to make exposure almost inevitable. In the case of scars at least the devil had a valid motive for leaving his mark on people; he required a symbol of his own form of baptism, but the UFO alien should have no such motive if he doesn't want to be discovered. Presumably technology which grants them the ability to do what they will with human tissue and mind would at least give them the ability to leave no scars from their surgical operation.

What is very clear from reading of witch hunt literature, such as 'Witch Hunt — The great Scottish witch craft trials of 1697' by Isabel Adam, is that the finding of the scar was of great importance *to the investigator* because it conferred on him a special ability over and above that of contemporaries or colleagues because he was a 'witch finder', because he knew the special signs to look for. It also enabled him to select just about anybody he required to be marked down as a witch for whatever purpose he had in mind. In the case of the 17th century witch hunts there are clear indications that some witch finders would 'prove' to a person that she was a witch, convince her that her only salvation was in being burnt to death, and then reveal the fact that he and he alone had special powers which could remove the stigma from her and save her life. Presumably the witch, not uncommonly a young virgin female, was suitably grateful to the witch finder. There is other evidence from the literature that even the search for the devil's mark was incredibly thorough when dealing with such young virgin females. At least UFO investigators, at least to date, are conducting themselves with more propriety but does the question of special powers and conferring special status on the investigator not ring warning bells when looking at some investigators' own motives?

Another intriguing comparison between the witch hunts and UFO investigation is in the matter of 'pin pricking'. If one stuck a pin in the devil's mark it would almost always bring forward a confession of witch craft from the witch. If the mark could be pierced by a needle without bleeding or pain then witch craft was firmly established. We do not have such direct comparisons in the UFO literature, but it is interesting to consider the frequency with which the abductees are reporting that the entities themselves are indeed pin pricking them. There are many reported cases of long needles inserted in the nasal cavities, in the ears, in the case of Betty Hill and Betty Andreasson of long needles inserted through the navel, all of which have been interpreted as forms of medical examination. In some cases they are interpreted as the implantation of tracking devices, or the removal of such. In the 17th century we have exorcism, in the 20th century we have medical examination and technology.

With regard to the motives of the investigators themselves there is also much room for comparison and cause for concern. Despite the stated aims of the witch hunts it is perfectly clear from the literature that at least part of the intent was the acquisition of political power and the elimination of opponents. This is not to say that opponents were all burnt at the stake, but rather that if one had the magical powers of being a witch finder it was probably best to steer clear of a similar person in case he should suddenly 'discover' that you were a witch yourself. UFO investigators do not seek political power, but then the true power of the 20th century is probably the power of the media and there is little question that some UFO investigators seek that.

It must also be remembered that the treatment of witches was not intended to be a torture, although they *were* frequently tortured. Witnesses would be subject to intensive interrogation, they would be made to repeat over and over again the stories they were telling in order to catch them out in lies or verify their statements. Stretched out on some instrument of torture they would scream, sweat, plead, with their interrogators. All of these have direct comparisons in UFO research; the witnesses are indeed asked to recall again and again their stories using not torture but hypnosis; under hypnosis they scream, sweat, plead, etc. with their investigators. And in both cases the investigators are ostensibly performing their task for the witch's (or witnesses') own sake. If they tell their story it will relieve their problems, it will ease their pains, and the investigator can help them. Even when witches were burnt at the stake it was not as a form of punishment or torture but to relieve a tortured soul from the possession of the devil, and thus ease the likelihood of the witch being able to go to heaven. We do not yet have a direct comparison in UFO literature to burning at the stake and to my knowledge no investigator has yet suggested that a witness would be better off dead than the subject of alien intervention. However, from outside the field of research itself we do have a comparison; a recent case told of a grandmother who was so concerned that her grandchildren were going to be sucked aboard a UFO by alien entities visiting the earth that she protected them from this fate by the simple expedience of killing them both. Clearly, UFO investigators and researchers cannot be held responsible for this poor woman's delusions, but if they have in any way contributed to them, and if they have done so recklessly by presenting false frightening images to an unsophisticated public, then equally they cannot absolve themselves from criticism.

Another comparison in the two forms of literature comes

from the stated motives of the investigators; in the case of the witch finders they wanted to know how the devil worked and what could be done to prevent him establishing his kingdom on Earth. Does this not sound very similar to the stated aims of UFO investigators who want to know what the aliens are doing and indeed possibly to try to prevent them getting a foothold in an invasion of the planet?

Even the famous old 'ducking stool' may have a counterpart in the 20th century. The ducking stool was an infallible way of testing to see if a person was a witch. Basically, the subject thought to be a witch was tied to a chair which was then lowered into the local pond or river completely submerging the subject. They would, the story had it, be held under water for longer than a person could hold their breath. If they were dead from drowning when they were brought up then clearly they were not a witch and they could be buried with God's blessing; however if they were a witch then they would survive the ducking when they could then be burnt at the stake to exorcise the devil and allow them on their way to God. In short, if this particular type of investigation was to be conducted you were lost from the outset. Is the modern ducking stool regression hypnosis where, if the 'UFO finder' applies the technique and seeks confirmation of this modern UFO witch craft, then the witness is lost because the 'truth' that is sought will *almost always* come out.

Bear in mind it is not regression hypnosis that is at fault here, any more than stools or ponds are necessarily dangerous; it is the application that matters, and we should consider the opinion of Barney Hill whose words closed the chapter on his own abduction.

VALLENTUNA, SWEDEN

As is so often the case, my involvement in what is turning out to be a most significant UFO case started by accident. Bertil Kuhlemann had telephoned to tell me that he would be in London in the summer of 1988 and would like to meet up for lunch with me. I had long admired his work, and perhaps more importantly his approach to the work, and our association had reached a basis of friendship. Accordingly I decided to make the most of his being in London and organised a bar-b-que for the evening of Friday, 29th July, inviting him together with his family, several colleagues from UFO research and others. During that evening I mentioned to Bertil the work I was doing on the writing of this book, and showed him drafts of some of the then existing chapters; areas where I knew he had an interest.

Bertil is a gentle, quiet man but often has a mischievous twinkle in his eye, and, with deliberate understatement, he said to me, 'You know, we have a case in Sweden that might interest you.' I asked him to outline the details, but he said he could not. He implied that the case was too complex for him to summarise, that the current investigator's work was not very typical of UFO abduction research and that it would be best for me to talk directly to him. 'Did he think I ought to go to Sweden for this?' I asked, and he replied 'I think it would be worth your while.'

I did not think twice; Bertil knew me too well to waste my time and I immediately made arrangements for the trip. Personal and business circumstances delayed this until Thursday 27th October.

Bertil is a former chairman of ICUR — the International

Committee for UFO Research, and I am one of its present administrators. This is not a research organisation, it exists only to facilitate efficient exchange of information across national boundaries, to provide a truly international forum for debate and study and to move towards compatible standards for electronic data storage and retrieval. There is much disagreement in ufology, even rivalry, between researchers and organisations and frankly co-operation is not always very effective. The example set by Bertil could well be a model for a better future.

Firstly, in order that Bertil, the other principal researcher and I could get the maximum work done in the time I was there I was invited to stay with the family in their home north of Stockholm, and conveniently near the abduction location. This meant that we were able to work late into the night, sometimes just talking through our notes to clarify points arising in the day's sessions.

Secondly, before I arrived Bertil had made all the necessary arrangements to ensure that the various people I would want to interview would be available. This included even the local head of the 'home guard' who in Sweden is a very important local official.

Thirdly, Bertil had made the arrangements in such a way that I would be introduced to the case, and indeed to Sweden itself, while living within the family home deliberately to allow me to appreciate the significance of small facts of Swedish life that would seem unimportant if their perspective was not understood. These minor points, which we shall come to in the course of the narrative, add much understanding to the 'atmosphere' surrounding the case.

Fourthly, they understood that I would not be able to absorb all of the material in the short time available. While I was there, Bertil and the other principal investigator made a video tape of our discussions, recorded our field trip to the abduction site, adding as much narrative as possible. They even obtained a special macro-lens with which to then film maps of the locality, adding other important details. I noticed that Bertil was narrating in English and I assumed at the time that this was partly because they planned to give me a copy of the tape, and partly because they might feel it would have a more international use. On the second count I was quite wrong; the whole arrangement was made entirely for my benefit and at the end of the time the tape was simply ejected and handed to me.

'Don't you even want a copy of it for yourselves?' I asked, after all the trouble they had gone to.

'No,' replied Bertil with that mischievous smile, 'after all we have the land itself.'

Lastly, and quite simply, I was received by all those involved with great warmth and openness; I believe that was partly due to their knowledge that my own approach to their case would not be aggressive. As we have seen, there is much valid criticism of the way many researchers are currently approaching their work.

In the months before I left for Sweden I had studied the background to the case. Bertil had provided me with his own notes, with summaries of the other related events of the time, with records of a home-guard assisted 'skywatch' that took place at the time and other maps and notes. Some of these documents were in Swedish; fortunately my secretary is Swedish and was able to provide me with a translation of all material. By the time I arrived in Sweden I was well versed in the background, but the real case was yet to surprise me.

I arrived late on Thursday night, finally arriving at the house around midnight. There was little to be done that night, but even so Bertil and I spent over an hour just planning out the next few days; I had to return to London on the Sunday.

THE WITNESS

'Anders' (pseudonym) is the son of an electrician, whose work he followed in. Following some injuries to his neck he gave up this work, becoming a schools caretaker. He is now a technician at the Royal Institute of Technology.

THE INVESTIGATOR

Arne Groth is sixty-three years of age. He has a university degree in Chemistry equivalent to a doctorate (the education structure at that time differed from the present day). He was a professional chemist with the National Defence Research Institute.

More recently he has been researching into survival in different terrains, for the military.

During the past twenty-five years he became interested in a deeper understanding of the different factors which seem to intermingle, resulting in nature as we know it. The Anders case has formed a part of that work, though opening up areas of which he had not previously known, let alone considered.

THE CASE

In many ways the actual UFO abduction is the least important aspect of the case. It was a reasonably routine event, inasmuch as any such event can be called routine, and will be summarised here. However, it has been the events in the years since that may be of such significance to UFO research.

It was around midnight on Saturday the 23rd March 1974 that Anders left a small school hall near Hagalund, south west of Malmhagen. He had been attending a 30 year anniversary celebration of the local section of the Centre Party (formerly the Farmer's party); a local political body. He had drunk a couple of glasses of wine, and a little schnapps, but was not drunk, and could probably have taken more before being affected. He stepped outside for a breath of fresh air, and decided to walk off, presumably towards his home. He lives four or five kilometres away at Lindholmen. However, it is the opinion of both Anders and the current principal investigator, Arne Groth, that at this point he was under the 'control' of the entities that were shortly to abduct him.

There are two basic routes that Anders could have taken to his home; a main road to Haga, then turning south at the crossroads towards and through Granby, or alternatively a short cut through Gustavslund, joining the main road at

Granby. In fact Anders chose the latter and it was on this road that the abduction took place. This is a very desolate and dark road and might appear — at least looking at a map — to be a strange choice for a man on foot. However, I have walked all over this area and now understand the choice; it was quicker and more direct of course and that was the major deciding factor. But the 'main' road is also equally dark, there are no street lights and the probability of more traffic is just an added danger since there are no pavements or reasonable verges on which to walk. Remember also that Anders is a country-man, and long and lonely walks in the dark are a natural part of his life. Whether the choice was, therefore, Anders' or that of controlling entities is not decided by this fact. The circumstances of the evening were such that Anders was not in a place that he habitually visits, however he has been there before and he confirms that he had used that road on other occasions.

The night is clear and cold, bright starry and with a full moon. A fine layer of snow powders the ground. Anders passes a small cottage, and sees a circle of runic stones to his left, just off the side of the road. Around the bend of the road ahead, and directly ahead of Anders where he is now walking, is a small bare hillock.

Anders detects a light first on the side of the hillock, and it gets stronger. There must be some impression of speed of approach of the light because at this point Anders veers off of the road onto the grass to his right and throws himself to the ground. Anders probably believed at that time that a car was fast approaching from behind in which case there would be a need to step away from the road surface. However, very soon he realised that the light was in fact a full circle all around him and coming from above, and his actions then appear to be those of some panic.

Anders has no further conscious memories of events until he is outside his house in Lindholmen; his wife opens the door in response to his frantic ringing of the doorbell to find him agitated, bleeding from a wound in his forehead and his cheek is burned.

When she sees the injuries to his face she apparently becomes very upset; though this may in part be due to the fact that as a youth Anders was injured by the branch of a tree while he was climbing it and seriously damaged one eye. She was afraid he had damaged his other eye.

Having undergone some sort of strange experience Anders contacted the most logical body in the circumstances: K1 'the Cavalry' who are a part of the National Defence. They advised him to call Hardy Brostrom, the local chief of the Home Guard. This is a form of Home Guard much like that which existed in England during the War, and is a very active unit. I asked why they had not suggested the police, the reason lies in social changes in Sweden in recent years; many local police stations have been closed down or merged, 'areas' have been made larger and people have become more distant from the police. The Home Guard have filled the gap this policy has left.

The public in the area became quickly aware of what had happened, although nobody seems able to pin-point exactly how. At that time there was a £100 reward for a 'good story' by the media, but certainly Anders would not have been so motivated, indeed he is a shy person by nature; nor would Brostrom, given his position. It is probable that an acquaintance of the family leaked the story.

The press moved fast. When I interviewed Hardy Brostrom, through Bertil Kuhlemann as translator, he told me an amusing story. He was going to his office when he was warned by his secretary that newspaper and television reporters had besieged it, and she advised him to avoid it. He also had to avoid his home which was similarly besieged (in his position this address is commonly known and listed prominently in the telephone directory); he ended up having to stay with his mother-in-law for over a week. Soon he received a call from the oil delivery company which delivers the gallonage needed to refill the domestic central heating. They needed him to be there to sign for the delivery, and when he arrived newspapermen were lying in wait with the delivery truck. Brostrom explained to me that this was very unusual and he was alerted by this; deliveries are automatic and invoices are simply sent afterwards in the normal course; clearly the reporter had gone to some trouble to catch him.

The reporter was a young man from a local newspaper and

it was Brostrom, not Anders, that he interviewed. Since Anders real name was used I am withholding the name of the newspaper at both his and Bertil's request.

Shortly after this the Educational Radio Section of Radio Sweden did a programme on the Universe which included some material from the abduction. This has been run repeatedly for several years and schools can hire the tape for their use. Anders, though, was not on the programme.

Hardy Brostrom reminded me that his own involvement was not unusual at this time; there was a major 'flap' on at the time which the Home Guard took seriously, even attending a UFO skywatch in official capacity. We shall look at some of these other cases later.

Following from the publicity, not courted by Anders and not directly involving him, Anders was approached by UFO investigator Sten Lindgren (of Arbetsgruppen for UFO-Identifiering — the workgroup for UFO identification) who believed that hypnotic regression would provide insight into the case. Lindgren set up two sessions, on April 1st and May 20th 1974, with hypnotherapist Dr Ture Arvidsson of Danderyds Sjukhus hospital. The sessions were also attended by Robert Larson, a 'new age' publisher; all those I spoke to were certain that his involvement was of genuine interest and not for publication reasons.

During the hypnotic regressions the story of the abduction was revealed:

At the point when Anders threw himself to the ground he missed! Instead, he was lifted up, unable to free himself from the force that surrounded him.

He appears to have been sucked up into a vehicle, where he was confronted by four semi-transparent entities. They are described as rather tall, about 190 cms, Anders claimed at one point they looked like Indians, he described eyes, mouth, nose, but no hair or ears. This may be because of an impression he had that they were wearing hoods.

There was a hazing glow around the creatures, and they communicated by a series of musical tones.

Anders recalls that at one point he fought violently with the entities because they approached him with an instrument. From the May session, as translated:

Anders: 'I defended myself. They were going to pierce me.'
Arvidsson: 'Were they to pierce you?'
Anders: 'They put an instrument . . .'
Arvidsson: 'How did it look like?'
Anders: 'I'm not allowed to say that, no.'
Arvidsson: 'Have they threatened you in some way?'
Anders: 'No, No.'

Despite his resistance the device was placed against Anders' forehead and it created a fierce burning pain.

It appears that the entities then delivered him to his home; certainly when I interviewed Anders, through Bertil Kuhlemann, he confirmed that this was his impression.

There appears to have been no obvious missing time period, an evidence strongly emphasised particularly in American cases; from start to finish the event appears to have taken around half and hour to forty five minutes. Quite the opposite in fact as to travel on foot the distance covered would probably take at least that time, and probably only then at a very fast pace. It could even be a case of 'added time'; if Anders is right though they could have taken most of that time to 'deal' with him while they were giving him a lift home.

After the first session Larson asked of Arvidsson 'Is it the truth that comes through at occasions like this?'

Arvidsson replied 'Yes, one usually tells the truth during hypnosis.'

It is worth remembering, however, that Dr Simon, who regressed Betty and Barney Hill, believed that under hypnosis the truth revealed would be the truth as perceived by the witness, and not necessarily an objective truth.

The regression sessions were halted after these two as Anders had become very distressed, often reacting violently during recall. Whatever the objective truth of the events, it is clear that Anders believed them to be real. In the end, Arne Groth found a new way into Anders' memory.

For a number of reasons Anders did not believe that he was being well treated by the investigation. There is no particular criticism of the individuals; I got the impression that it was the nature of the investigation that troubled Anders. Sten decided to introduce Bertil to Anders as a sympathetic supporter. Bertil was able to explain to Anders that these abductions were not unknown, and were in fact oft-reported on a world-wide basis. Bertil's professional background impressed Anders; he was then on the staff of one of the scientific technical academic institutions in Sweden.

It was Bertil who recognised a need for a new direction in the investigation and introduced Arne Groth to the case. It was realised that he would be sympathetic to the needs and emotions of the witness; also that he was not particularly interested in UFOs, which eased Anders' mind. Indeed, Arne is sceptical of UFOs generally, due partly to the absurd media coverage they attract. At this point a very significant matter occurred, and is the key to the difference between the approach to this case and to many other cases; Sten and Bertil dropped into the background and the case was not pursued by UFO investigators. From this point on the case was witness-directed, rather than investigator-directed, and the witness was able to start to understand his experience in a way that helped him. In America and England so many witnesses have complained that the investigation often appears to have little concern for their own wellbeing, even for their own opinions. Of more concern is the fear that the investigators hunt down and 'reveal' the stories that they are searching for; in the Vallentuna case the witness led the proceedings. Since Betty and Barney Hill were regressed in order to ease their tensions and not to seek out their story there have been few, if any, cases that have been directed by other than UFO investigators; I believe this to be the real value of this case.

THE VALLENTUNA WAVE

The abduction of Anders was an isolated case of its kind; indeed the magazine 'AFU Newsletter', published in Sweden, described the case in 1986 as 'the only well documented case of an abduction in Sweden'.

It was not, however, an isolated UFO incident, and in fact occurred during a major wave of sightings in the area. One of these, as we shall see, corroborated some of the story, and this is one of the very few cases of abduction where there has been an independent witness to events.

Below is a summary of some of the documented sightings of the time, which gives considerable weight to the belief that *something* was happening and, apart from confirming in part Anders' claims, also explains the involvement of the Home Guard. A map of the area is reproduced in the book, showing the close proximity of these events. Witness names have all been withheld from the transcripts sent to me.

March 23rd 1974:

At the exact time of Anders encounter a woman, who wishes to remain anonymous, observed a light from the crossing at Haga down towards Gustavslund. She was in fact cycling on the 'other' main road that Anders could have — but did not — take. Her description of the light matches the exact time and place that Anders reported and is certainly a corroboration of his description. I have been to both the abduction site and the location of this woman's sighting and it is clear that both witnesses are consistent. Anders believed that the light was a cone around 200 meters wide and lighting up the hillock in front of him; the woman described the cone of light as lighting up the hillock to the left of the clearing from where she stood. This is the same hillock, and the cluster of trees to Anders left, to the right of the clearing from where the woman observed, would certainly have obscured her view of Anders, about which she makes no report.

Sunday morning 24th March. Mr X, and a completely independent Mr Y, reported that they saw a metallic object on the ground, in the field between the crossing at Haga and Granby Gard. It could be seen from the road between Granby and the crossing at Haga looking towards the west. Therefore it must have been situated on the eastern side of this part of the woods near Gustavslund; *more or less exactly where Anders had his encounter.*

24th March at around about 5 p.m. Miss V, from Radio Sweden, was travelling home with her fiancé from Stockholm to Rimbo. Near Soderhall, 10 kilometres east of Karsta, they saw in the forest what they thought was a water tower with lights shining out of the windows. They thought the tower was newly built, but later observed that there was no tower there.

24th March, 7.15 p.m. H B and his mother were travelling south by car from Lindholmen towards Vallentuna. At Nygard they saw four light beams high in the air over Lake Uddbysjön. They were like bus headlights in a row. From the ground at Nygard weak light beams shone up from the ground towards these 'bus headlights'.

24th March, 3.15 p.m. M B, who lives at Vallentuna, and works at Granby Gard, observed together with a friend a white glowing, luminous object travelling from Stenby towards the north, which disappeared behind a big hill north of Granby.

24th March, 7.20 to 7.25 p.m. M B had a second sighting. He was at the henhouse at Granby and sighted, towards the east, a bright luminous object. At the time he had been standing talking to a friend about his earlier sighting. The object moved towards a small valley near Soderby. As we shall see from the next case, this was corroborated by an independent party, Mrs H Andersson.

24th March at 7.25 p.m. Mrs H Andersson had her first sighting, confirming M B's above. She is to become an important person in UFO matters in the area and we shall return to see why in due course.

The first sighting took place when she was driving with her three children north towards Vasaskolan school north of Lindholmen. She saw a lady on the road who had put down her bags and was looking east towards the fields at a lighted object which moved on a northerly course. She thought at first that it was a helicopter, but noticed later that the light was unusually bright. Continuing her drive without stopping, she saw that the object went into the small valley near Söderby, north of the crossing at Granby and just behind the hillock near Anders' encounter. Then it descended near Hästberga, behind the forest. She said 'let's drive there and stop on the road and look down at the field, because it must have landed there.' They drove along the road to a point just south of the crossroads at Haga and looked east where the object should have landed. They got out of the car but heard and saw nothing in the dark. She then drove further to Malmhagen to collect her parents, whom she had earlier tried to contact by telephone which was out of order. On her arrival, her parents laughed when she and the children excitedly told what had happened.

24th March, 7.45 p.m. Mrs H Andersson again, now at her parents' home at Malmhagen. There were interferences on the television, forming 'wave patterns'. They switched the television off and she went out with her children and parents to investigate further. She observed a large bright object which came from the south towards the north through the forest east of Malmhagen. It went over the gravel pit and had an irregular radiant yellow-white glow. The distance from her was approximately 200 metres, the size between ten and thirty metres. The object descended over the ground to a height of 4-5 metres and oscillated somewhat between the vertical and horizontal. Suddenly a light beam rose from the ground three times at five second intervals, up towards the object. The object then travelled slowly, lighting up the whole forest and accelerating at high speed towards the sky. Mrs Andersson then drove farther to her brother's at Skrattbacken, with the children. At her brother's they saw the object again, observing that it moved like a 'figure eight'. I visited the area of the sighting at the 'gravel pit' near Mrs Andersson's mother's home and was able to confirm that the description she gave seemed in keeping with the terrain. There appears to be no speculation on her part, and her recollection is the more reliable for this.

24th March at approximately 7.45 p.m. K J, a retired smith, an active 90 years old, lives just south of Malmhagen.

He took his dog for a walk and observed a very bright glow above his house, twice as bright as the sun. He saw a large globe travel towards Malmhagen to the exact place where Mrs H Andersson and others later observed it. He could also see the glow between the trees in the forest in the direction of the gravel pit. He later experienced a feeling of nausea.

24th March at 7.30–8.00 p.m. Mrs Z saw an orange object over Malmen. She watched it travel between Skrattbacken and Malmhagen.

24th March. At Yvlinge Gard, a couple of kilometres north

east of Markim Church there were reports of interferences on the television that evening.

24th March. Mrs H Andersson was now, as noted above, visiting her brother at Skrattbacken, 1.5 km south east of Markim Church. When she left her brother's house he got into his car with his daughter, with whom she was going to travel back to her home. They observed possibly the same object again at a clearing just east of his house. It moved around on the field and then across the whole forest, travelling south, and then east again. As they moved off it crossed the road after Mrs Andersson's car had passed but before the other car reached the spot. Her brother sounded his horn to the others ahead, but they did not notice, so he accelerated to reach them. Just past the school at Hagalund, they saw through the forest towards Malmhagen, in the direction of the gravel pit, a bright light through the forest. Mrs Andersson stopped at the crossing at Haga and they observed a large object at a distance of 400 metres at a height of 10 metres above ground, probably the same large object which had been seen earlier. It moved off in the direction of Yttergärde Farm.

A smaller orange coloured object was seen at a distance of 300 metres over the field between Orkesta Church and Yttergärde Farm. It was in the shape of a half-globe. Over the crossing at Haga there were another two stationary objects at a higher altitude. It passed two aeroplanes higher up at approximately the same time. Mrs Andersson and the children left the area and soon after, near the power station, the children saw through the rear window five smaller objects in a circle high above the car. They were accompanied by objects on each side of the car to Lake Uddbysjön. The objects moved at varying speeds, and thus were either in front of or behind the car.

There was an aftermath to these sightings: the children got headaches and stomach aches and Mrs Andersson had a pain in her kidneys during the few days following.

Mrs Andersson summed up her feeling on events, 'It was so horrible I wish it had never happened. I got the impression that we were checked out by someone — like a big torch that swept the area.'

24th March in the evening. A J was at home in Granby. The television set blacked out completely at 8.30 in the evening for a short while.

24th March. Television interference was reported at Lundby, 1.5–2 km north of Orkesta Church, with 'wave patterns' overlaying an otherwise clear picture.

24th March. Annalund Farm. The telephone was out of order that evening. This is noted only because Mrs Andersson had visited her parents that evening because she could not reach them by telephone.

These cases, all of which seem to indicate that *something* was happening in the area, are selected from transcripts of over one hundred cases with which the Swedish investigators presented me. The majority of these cases occur within a two year period, 1974 being the peak of the activity. Of the remainder, five occurred before Anders' encounter, seventeen at more or less exactly the same time, five in the following month of April, four in May, four in June and then a new peak wave in August and September where eleven and twenty-five respectively were reported. These are not exhaustive but have been selected for study in this case because of certain factors. Firstly, they often corroborate each other's claims. This is much less common in England and America and has much to do with the nature of Sweden and its social structure. Although a population considerably less than London is spread out in an area several times the size of Britain it is in fact a much more close knit community. The local Home Guard is an active force and Hardy Brostrom has served as a central figure in the flaps. Also, Mrs H Andersson who had several sightings, and in fact was involved in a great number of the August and September wave, has become something of a local 'mother-figure' on the subject. In the USA, and to some degree in Britain, abduction researchers are considering the setting up of 'self-help' groups for abductees, where they can share their common experiences and derive strength from themselves. Although Sweden does not have the same needs in respect of abductions Mrs Andersson has in effect started something similar for UFO witnesses in the area around Vallentuna. It works because it does none of the things that are being done in America and Britain, which have caused so much heartache and failure in those countries. There are no regular meetings, no newsletters, no formal discussions. Apparently you just 'pop' down to the local supermarket where Mrs Andersson works and have a chat; if you like you can get together with her after work. If several people want to get together she helps to co-ordinate that but on a very informal basis. Without setting out to do anything special, she could well be the role model half the world is looking for to ease abductee problems.

Secondly, there is considerable mention of what might collectively be called 'earth mysteries'. In the industrial west, Sweden is most often thought of as a highly efficient, business like country, the 'U.S.A.' of Europe. In fact it has a long history of folk-lore not unlike that in Britain, peopled by gnomes and elves and the like, and the people of the country are not only well aware of their legends but are probably closer to them than most in Britain. Certainly it was regarded as significant by many people I spoke to that the light beams which in some cases were reported searching around fields, lakes and forests, were often seen coming *up* from the ground to the UFO above, and generally gave the impression of some sort of 'one-ness' with the Earth. This, in fact, is the dominant impression of UFOs I received; most people felt there was a real event happening, and the number of corroborated sightings seems to suggest this is true, but few had much time for the extra-terrestrial hypothesis.

Anders most overriding impression was that the entities that abducted him were from Earth, that they were not human but had been thousands of years ago.

A third matter of importance was the involvement of the Home Guard; an official and active unit regarded as an unofficial part of the military. Given the governmental disinterest in the subject of UFOs in most other countries, their involvement seems to be a surprising factor. Between 31st May and 2nd June 1974 a 'skywatch' was organised, led by the Home Guard chief, Hardy Brostrom. Three prominent members of the Swedish UFO identification group Project URD — Bertil Kuhlemann, Arne Groth and Sten Lindgren — co-ordinated events. All three have worked on the Anders case. In the end, the three observation points and the central command were manned by fifty Home Guard personnel and fifteen ufologists. Sightings were generally of the lights-in-the-sky variety; often corroborated by other observation points. The significance is again that this is suggestive of *something* being in the air at the time, and observed by people trained to some degree in aerial activity. Bertil pointed out that unofficial investigations at the time indicated that perhaps only ten percent of all sightings were being reported; if the rule holds true that of all sightings ninety percent are explainable by simple means, then it still leaves an impressive amount of 'exotic' sightings, mostly made by people familiar with the area, some by trained observers, usually corroborated.

Bertil believed that the area was in fact a focus for activity.

I interviewed Bertil on several aspects of the case, having realised that some local knowledge was necessary. Firstly I questioned the interest of the Home Guard. Bertil pointed out that Sweden is a very military country with problems not shared by America or Britain. Saab produce advanced airfighters, and two companies produce tanks and other military hardware. Although neutral, they are aware that if Russia decided to attack Europe it might well move through Scandinavia; it would have to deal with Norway and Denmark both of whom are in NATO, but it could not afford to ignore Sweden though neutral and Finland with whom it has a non-aggression pact. Bertil believed that if Sweden had to fight it would do so vigorously, as did the Finns in the Second World War. The military are very aware of this possible overland border invasion threat.

I questioned Bertil further on the social structure that allowed the Home Guard to be so effective within the community. I pointed out that generally speaking officials are regarded as oppressive in Britain. In Sweden, he explained, the general, working class people are imprinted with *Medelsvensson*, a product of Social Democratic politics, which emphasises that officials truly are representatives of the people, not oppressors. Also, that they are caring for the ordinary people, who expect their problems to be dealt with. The Home Guard would therefore be expected to 'deal with' the problems that arise, including UFO flaps. Bertil pointed out that UFOs are not particularly newsworthy, generally speaking, and viewed by the country people as perhaps something to do with the devil. Sweden is a mainly Protestant country, the result of a 17th century struggle, with often strong religious feeling.

I asked Bertil for his views of Anders, and of the case. He believed Anders to be a genuine truthful person, certainly not lying about his experiences as he felt them. In fact his wife encourages him not to talk about UFOs, partly due to her own religious background.

Of the case itself Bertil believed that abductions should be viewed separately because of the different attitudes and methods required for investigation. The many other phenomena associated with abductions rightly place them within the UFO field, but with special overtones.

'The significance of the case is that it has been handled as it was. It has opened a path through which we can investigate energies of a subtle nature, that cannot be investigated with normal scientific instruments.

'We are using the human mind and body system as a measuring instrument, a derivation of this case. And we are reviewing the results of the investigations. We find a successful widening vista of different types of qualities, characteristics, structures and dynamics. That leads to an opening for a new understanding of nature. That is the real significance of this case.'

While I was in Sweden I was fortunate enough to also interview at length a 'repeater' witness of several night lights and daylight discs. Her sightings were not particularly out of the ordinary, and contain no exotic material. However, again it was the effect that the sightings had on her which was so important. And significantly, her opinions were very similar to those of Anders.

She was around 12 years old at the peak of her sightings, which lasted over two years. This was during the 1974 flap period; she is now about 26. Her original suggestion was that, given the 'commonplace' nature of her sightings, I should use her real name. In the end we agreed that I would not for a number of reasons; firstly she was not yet married and any notoriety that might attach to her could be unwelcome by her future family, secondly the material would be exposed in England and America through this book, where the media is not as honest as in Sweden. In fact when I described some of the antics of British tabloid newspapers to her she was quite unprepared to believe them until Bertil confirmed what he knew of them. If her sightings were not important enough to attract that kind of attention, then equally they were not important enough to need her real identity revealed. I have gone into this relatively insignificant detail only to emphasise another difference between Sweden and America/Britain; namely the media appreciation of the subject.

Her background must be put into perspective; her father was somewhat involved in the study of UFOs at the time and presumably actively so at the time of the 'flap'. Her attitudes, however, are hardly those of conventional UFOlogy.

Marianne, as we shall call her, had a total of eighteen observations in the period. The closest observation, and probably the most important, was on the 27th April 1974, just a month after the Anders encounter. Marianne was sitting at her desk drawing; she found she had drawn a flying saucer, and indeed that it was a better image than any she had ever created before. The picture she drew is reproduced in this book. At this point she felt compelled to go to the window and there she saw a silvery disc moving across the fields behind the house where she lived then, and still lives, with her family. It was just above treetop height and moving slowly, and appeared to be about one and a half centimetres at arms length. As the disc started to descend so Marianne went downstairs to see it through the living room windows. She wondered whether or not to go out, and felt she should not. Consequently, possibly because of the trees, she did not see a landing, nor did she see the disc again. Her belief was that this sighting was destined for *her*, that it and other sightings were designed to give her a more spiritual dimension to life.

A second sighting was corroborated by her father; they were walking home together in the evening when she saw a large, white light moving in the same direction. When she looked at the light it suddenly climbed very high, and made extremely strange movements above them. There was no sound. Marianne believes it reacted to her; though on this occasion she said she felt fear throughout the sighting, despite being with her father.

A third encounter was very similar, a white light that appeared to move quickly away when she looked at it. On this occasion she had no feeling of fear, or indeed any emotion.

I asked Marianne what she felt the objects were, not because I thought she would necessarily have the answers, but because her opinion would reveal something of the significance of the sightings to her. She felt that perhaps they were a force designed to search out those who were yet to become 'aware' of the Earth as a resource, and help them to do so in a beneficial way. Certainly this is the result for Marianne, for whatever reason; she is passionately concerned for the ecology, and feels a unity with the planet. She has had no sightings since, and believes this is because she is now 'awake'. She does not feel that she was intended to direct her attention to a study of UFOs and indeed has not done so; in fact she always believed that UFOs were natural, never strange.

THE AFTERMATH OF THE ANDERS CASE

Anders believed that his experience had given him a feeling of one-ness, of unity, with the Earth itself, and indeed it is his belief that the entities came from the Earth. Arne appears to have recognised this need in him quickly. He appears to be 'sensitive' himself and certainly impressed me in some of the fieldwork I watched him in. Anders responded well to this approach believing, correctly, that Arne was going to try to help him to discover the truth, which was important to him. They discussed the scar on Anders' forehead. When Anders placed his own left hand over the scar he felt a pricking, stinging feeling deep in his head, about two-thirds of the way back. Sometimes he would feel more of a 'sucking' feeling. Arne had been reading of 'fields' of energy around people and suggested to Anders that he slowly bring his hand towards the scar. At six inches from his head, Anders started to feel this sensation. Since Arne was at that time following up the mid nineteenth century work of Baron von Reichenbach on crystals and magnetism in life energy forces he applied this to Anders. First he used a magnet and the influence was felt at a greater distance, around eight to twelve inches. Then they used rock crystal; the sensation was clear from six to seven feet. Different distances from Anders' head gave different feelings, alternating between stinging and sucking. For later experiments they used a grooved wooden slide to give some accuracy of measurement to these differences. Control experiments were conducted on others at the same time; no such effects were felt. Further, as a second control the same experiments were conducted on Anders by others, one Lennart Lidfors, the other a physicist who has asked to remain anonymous. Anders felt the effects whoever did the experiment.

I asked if they had considered that this 'force' was inherent in Anders, and that the UFO incident was a way of rationalising heightened powers, of giving him a reason for his gifts. Anders and the investigators were sure that these gifts *were* inherent, but that they had been heightened by an external influence (though not an extra-terrestrial one). Since we had an independent witness to aspects of the abduction, this seems likely to be true at some level. Arne also pointed out that he had made a close study of Anders biorhythms and for reasons we shall also see later, believes that the force *must* have been external.

I suggested that there were doubts about the technique of hypnotic regression; that at its worst it might implant and create the abduction experience, and even in this case the abduction was only uncovered by these sessions. Arne had no particular comment on this, though he was certain that hypnotic regression was unnecessary and that easier, natural recollection would come with patience. It seems to me that this is a further example of good sense not often applied by those who hasten to 'get to the truth'.

About one year after the event Anders had a dream. Part of that dream was the message 'You have had my sword within you for a year, but you don't know for what to use it.' In the dream he also received the message 'Search in Yttrium'. Anders reported this to Arne, believing Yttrium to be a place where they would find answers to the enigma. Arne at this time had no knowledge of the name, but later found out that yttrium is a metal; and one hard to come by as it is laboratory processed. Arne obtained some and used it in his experiments replacing the rock crystal; Anders said that the effects were very powerful, that in fact it felt like a flow of electric power. Only *after* this did Arne tell him that the metal was yttrium.

Arne had isolated 'lines' in Anders' body similar to acupuncture lines but influenced by the rock crystal, and then the yttrium. Using these Arne was able to develop 'natural' regressions which he believed better and more likely to reach the truth than hypnotic techniques. Their strength is in the fact that the recall is all under the witness' direction, and that since the witness was leading the investigator into the areas he wanted to study, the recall was of matters considered *relevant to the witness, not the investigator.*

The witness, and Arne, believe that the influence was external, though not extra-terrestrial, and that those who controlled it directed his attention to these lines of enquiry in order that they should enjoy a better association with the Earth; this echoes very strongly the opinions of Marianne in her sightings. It also offers a wider perspective in our understanding of the phenomenon. Later in the book we shall look at alternative 'origins' for these 'aliens'; this case opens up the possibility of a consciousness of Earth itself, the Gaia concept that the Earth is itself a living organism. However, since such a concept is — at best — very speculative this line will not be pursued here. But since the object of this book is to suggest alternative perspectives with which to consider the UFO and abduction phenomenons neither should it be totally disregarded.

Later experiments have been complex; they draw away from the subject matter of this book and so are not discussed in any detail here; however it must be made clear that they are far from irrelevant to the abduction phenomenon — indeed they may begin to show the way to understand its true nature and its true significance if we can understand the implications of them.

Such experiments have included:

— Anders' discovery that he could move a compass needle with his hands placed nearby, but obviously not touching. A scientific study of this was undertaken; fine iron filings being spread over a sheet of paper, placed under a large petri dish and the whole assembly laid on Anders' stomach as he lay prone. He was stripped, so that there was no question of metallic objects interfering with the experiment. A pattern of force was evident in the filings, of which I have seen photographs, which later experiments suggested were the result of emanations from the spleen. The best location for the filings in this test was discovered by passing a compass over parts of Anders' body.

— Arne has for some years demonstrated considerable ability in 'dowsing'; not only for water but for lines of energy in the Earth. I felt that this was an area where I would have to take him on trust as it was not easy to prove, and offered to do so, but *he suggested* that he could prove at least something of his abilities. I have to say that I was sceptical of this, as I felt that it was all too possible for the dowser to influence the dowsing rod. Arne handed me the rod — which in fact he later gave me as a gift — and placed me where he said I was over a powerful energy line. I felt nothing, and said so. Anders placed his hand over the rod, approximately nine inches above it, and lowered it never closer than six inches above the rod. I felt a surge of energy and the rod pressed downwards *against my efforts to prevent it.* Bertil Kuhlemann was watching this and I heard him laughing; he said afterwards he saw real shock on my face.

At least able to understand a fraction of this ability, I was better able to appreciate that of the next hour, when Arne dowsed the entire area of the abduction site, repeating for me what he had done years before. A diagram of the energy and water lines at the abduction site is included in the book; it shows that the event took place at the convergence of several such lines, near the site of an ancient runic stone circle. In fact, the actual abduction point is where major lines meet.

— When Anders was on the west coast of Sweden, after the abduction, he reported seeing the vibrant, *living*, aura of the sea. In more recent years he believes that that aura has diminished, from vibrant blue/violet to lifeless brown which he believes may be a product of pollution. Certainly in the last few years fishermen have had difficulty making their living from the sea which yields less fish-stock. This is a matter for belief since it cannot be proven, but it reflects a concern for the environment that several people tell me is stronger in Anders since the abduction.

— Arne and Anders together have been mapping 'grids' in the Earth which, they believe, reflect the 'chakra ' of different energy fields where humans interact with the Earth. In particular they have experimented with the spleen chakra, a grid of 185.83 cms. One such experiment consisted of both Arne and Anders standing over selected points on the grid, but in their separate homes 20 kilometres apart. One would then touch either gold, yttrium or a magnet with rock crystal, the other would know which it was that was being touched. This was confirmed by telephone link, and witnessed by others. Of course, it would be easy to fake such experiments but nothing in my conversations with those involved suggest any desire for deceit on their part.

Interestingly, there may be some significance here to a point referred to by Budd Hopkins, which also appears in the Betty and Barney Hill case. Hopkins believes that the witnesses are repeatedly abducted, and kept 'on shorter leashes' than previously considered. Betty Hill was told by the aliens 'Don't worry, if we decide to come back, we will be able to find you all right. We always find those we want to.' Energy lines particular to each individual that can be 'tapped into' would be far easier to deal with than implanting ball bearings in the skull.

— Arne and Anders experimented together to study Anders' biorhythms; and the analysis revealed that the abduction took place at the exact moment when the three rhythms peaked at a triple maximum, which occurs only every 46 years and for some therefore only once in a lifetime. Furthermore the event happened at the spring equino and under a new moon, which is the strongest position for Anders' biorhythms. It is this coincidence which supports Arne in his view that the event, whatever it was, was external and not just the product of Anders' mind. Interestingly, there may be some answers here for 'standard' ufology; the fact that some witnesses seem to be repeaters — having series of UFO and other paranormal events throughout their lifetime — has been documented, but without any reason ever being suggested for this other than aliens checking up on their 'marked' targets; here may lie an answer to why some people repeat these experiences. In the case of biorhythms, there are

Kenneth Arnold: the man who started the 'modern era of UFOs' – but what did he start? *(Photo: Mary Evans Picture Library).*

Betty and Barney Hill with their dog, Delsey. The importance of their encounter cannot be overstated, but it has rarely been properly understood.

George Adamski with illustration of 'his' alien. *(Photo: Mary Evans Picture Library).*

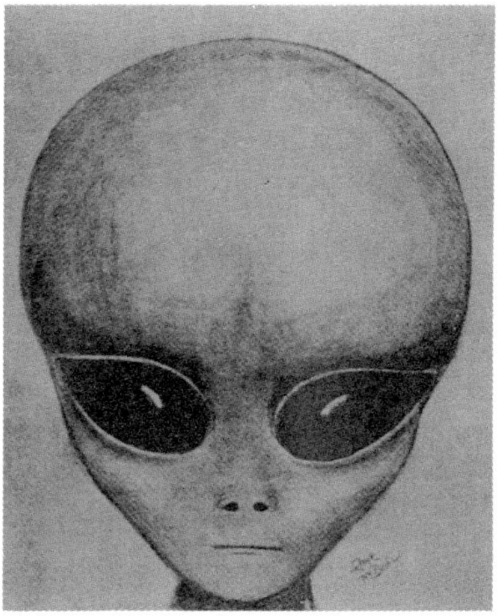

Abductees report a very different type of alien, as this artist's impression shows. *(Photo reproduced by kind permission of MUFON and its international Director, Walt Andrus).*

Stephen Gamble, Robert S. Digby, Walt Andrus and John Spencer (author), the executive officers of the International Committee for UFO Research which exists to harmonize work across national boundaries *(Photo: John Spencer).*

Delegates at the Brussels International Congress of 1988. Among those pictured are; Ken Phillips (UK), Robert S. Digby (UK), August Meessen (Belgium), Richard Haines (USA), Michel Fiquet (France), Denys Breysse (France), Vladimir Rubtsov (USSR), Eduardo Russo (Italy), Pierre Lagrange (France), Hilary Evans (UK), Jacques Vallee (USA), Jacques Scornaux (Belgium), Claude Mauge (France), John Spencer (the author, UK), Stephen Gamble (UK), Bertrant Meheust (France), Walt Andros (USA). *(Photo: reproduced by kind permission of SOBEPS – The Société Belge d'Étude des Phénomènes Spatiaux).*

Drawing made by 'Marianne' (then aged 12) on 27.4.74. She looked up from this and saw a disc outside her window. *(Reproduced by kind permission of 'Marianne').*

Photo taken from location where independent witness saw the light that abducted 'Anders'. *(Photo: John Spencer)*.

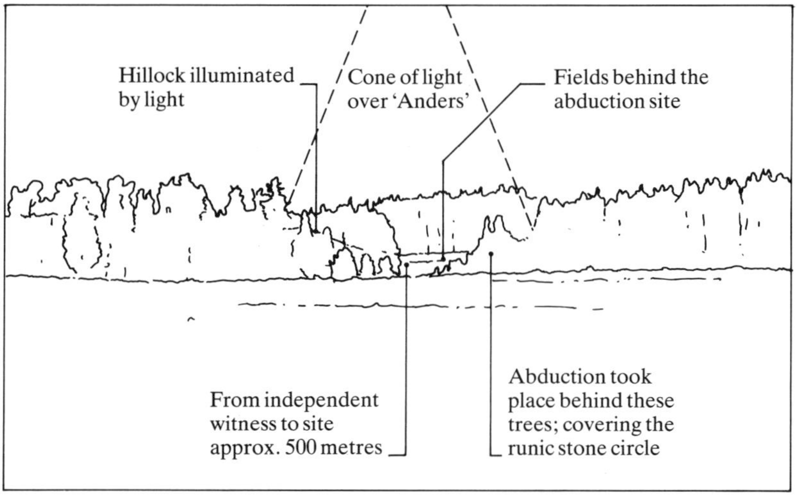

Diagram of above photo showing key features.

Photo shows the desolation of the 'Anders' abduction site: in the foreground is the area of grass onto which Anders threw himself – and missed! *(Photo: John Spencer)*.

Left to right, Arne Groth, John Spencer (author) and Bertil Kuhlemann discussing the 'Anders' abduction and consider some of the experiments used in the case. *(Photo: John Spencer)*.

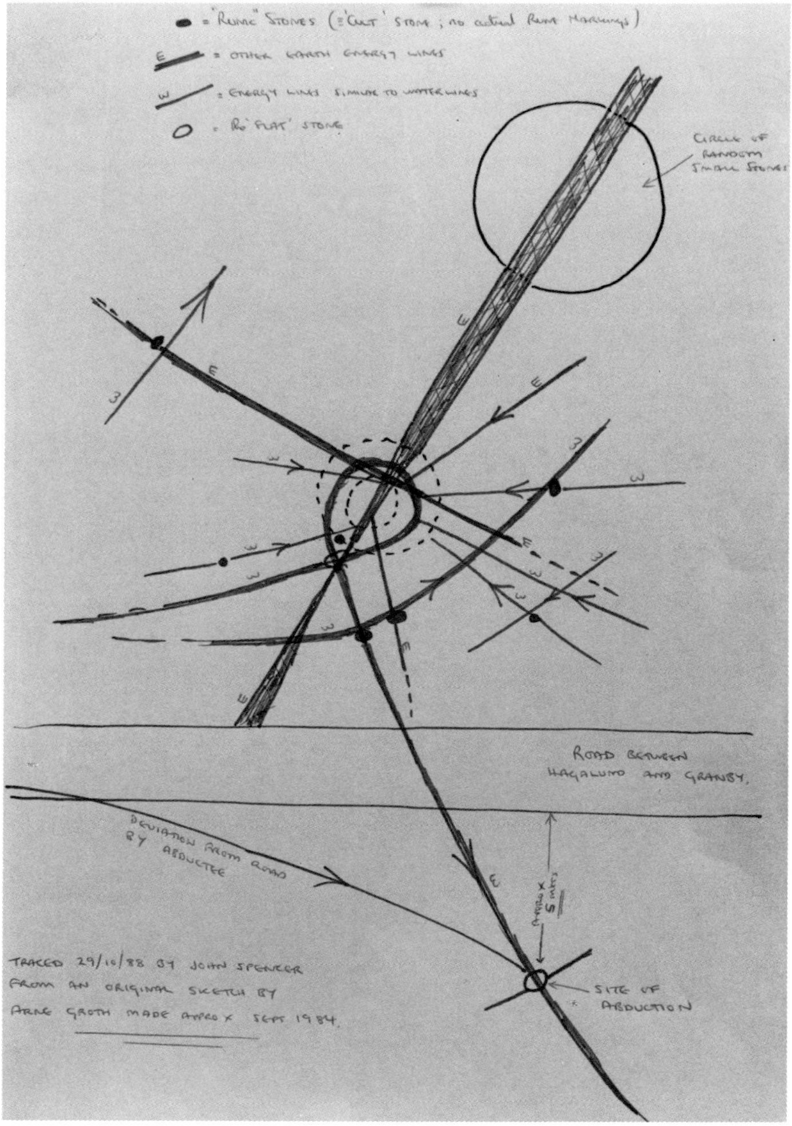

Sketch of Arne's 'dowsing' of the area of the 'Anders' abduction showing water and energy lines converging at the site. The runic stones are shown.

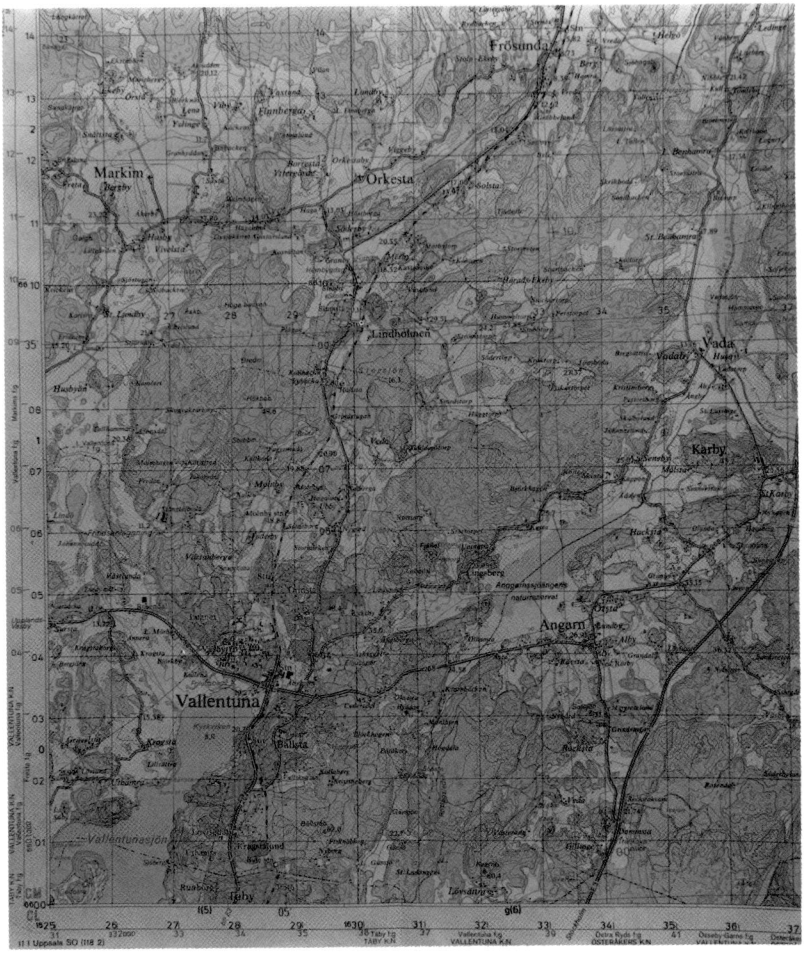

The area around the 'Anders' abduction showing the close proximity of corroborative sightings (refer to text). *(General map material from Lantmäteriverket, permission number 88.0233).*

many maximums each year (the triple maximum being a special case) and they may co-incide with events. Arne is following up this work, which is in its early stages yet.

This case is one of the most interesting I have been involved with, and the wealth of material *not* included here adds to that interest. None of the remainder specifically relates to abductions, but it all adds to the belief that the abduction phenomenon may not be what we think, and may represent forces more subtle than we have previously supposed.

Of particular significance is that this case has not been investigator-led, but witness-led; with Anders exploring those areas that he feels he wants to explore, often with only a tentative feeling that it is connected to the event. As such, it is a case rare, if not unique, in abduction history in that *it has not been investigated with UFOs in mind.*

The case is clearly similar enough to those of Betty and Barney Hill, Kathie Davis and many others, to be regarded as a UFO abduction; a structured UFO is believed to have been involved, and it seems to have been witnessed by others; an abduction of the witness from the ground onto the UFO is part of the experience, and entities have been reported; yet because of the nature of the investigation, the case raises issues not uncovered in other examples and asks questions not previously considered about the nature of the experience.

We do not yet know what the answers will be, but the lessons are clear; researchers must be prepared to discard their own prejudices, and be ready to accept the abduction phenomenon as part of a range of events rather than as some isolated plot from poor science fiction if they seek the truth, whatever it turns out to be.

KATHRYN — 'ON THE EDGE OF EARTH'

My visit to Sweden resulted in an introduction to yet another very interesting case and one in which the witness was able to make interesting comparisons between Sweden and the United States.

Bertil Kuhlemann gave me the address of a woman who had had an abduction experience nearly twenty years earlier in Sweden. She had briefly been the subject of an investigation there but had lived in the United States for the last seven years.

As before, Bertil gave me no information about this woman's experience — he very properly refuses to lead me by the nose but rather lets me roam as I will — he said he was sure I would be interested. He gave me her name, address and telephone number in the United States and suggested I contact her, having earlier discussed my involvement with her.

When I returned from Sweden I was determined to contact this woman, but knew that the next two weeks would be extremely busy for me as there were a good many business matters I had to attend to before preparing to go to Brussels for the International UFO Congress being held there. However, on my first day back at my desk on returning from Sweden I found I had received a letter from her in my absence. It turned out that she had considerable, and in my opinion justifiable, reservations about UFO researchers, particularly in America and presumably in England which tends to follow the American lead. She told me in a subsequent interview that she had never been able to complete reading any of the American books on UFO research as they disturbed her in a number of ways and it was clear to me that she had approached me only because Bertil had assured her that I was not the type of UFO researcher who would 'pin her to the table for the purpose of extracting information'.

'I never would have written to you about this if you hadn't been acquainted with Bertil,' she wrote.

Her initial letter to me ran to five pages and was wonderfully incoherent; nothing could have expressed her emotional response to the experience more clearly than the disjointed recollections and outpourings I read. Her words expressed her awe, her excitement and her multitude of questions.

I had glanced at the letter very briefly and filed it amongst many 'action papers' that I intended to deal with when I was in Brussels; I knew I would have some spare hours away from the pressures of my professional work during the Congress. As is not at all unusual with me, I ended up reading Kathryn's letter in the bath one morning and it says much for her narrative that I read and re-read the letter several times, in such an absorbed fashion that I got nothing else done that morning and was scarcely ready to join my colleagues for breakfast some two hours later. This 'missing time' experience is, however, very easily explained; it was a pleasure to absorb and re-absorb the excited emotions she had expressed.

As a 'case' Kathryn's experience bridges several phenomena. There was an abduction experience by a craft which Kathryn is certain was a 'nuts- and-bolts' reality; there was undoubtedly a religious experience in the broadest sense, which the strongly religious would call a revelation; there was a flood of imagery which can have no physical basis; there have been premonitions and much more. There are also many phenomena which Kathryn has indicated to me have happened which she has not discussed with me.

If the reader finds my approach to cases, and particularly my willingness to leave questions open-ended and let cases drift for a considerable time, irritating, then while I regret this I make no apologises for it. I simply do not believe the intensive investigation — almost interrogation — approaches of many investigators to be appropriate. I believe it brings out distorted memories; I am certain that it extracts memories affected by, or in the worst cases, implanted by the investigator himself and I believe such an approach harms the witness. I never lead a witness, at worst I might encourage a witness to share their experience with me but usually I am content to listen to the relevant and non-relevant alike and if I am told 'there is something I don't want to discuss yet' then I simply pass on. Many UFO investigators will criticise me for that and point out that it is very defective investigation. Good. If I were investigating a murder case then it would be extremely defective investigation and quite inappropriate, and the problem is that many investigators treat a witness as if they were the witness or suspect in a murder case, whereas in fact we are dealing with people who have had experiences they don't understand and the approach must be different. If it takes me ten years to collect together a witness's feelings about an experience where another investigator could do it in six months, particularly using intensive regression hypnosis techniques, then I stand by my belief that the story revealed to me will be as near to truth as defective human memory can allow and free of my own prejudices, biases, and the influences of my own experiences and beliefs. If I have not led the witness then even if his or her memory after ten years is defective, the distortions will still be the result of the experience and other influences *on the witness themselves* and therefore will still reveal a truth which comments on and expands on the experience that the witness underwent. I am certainly not alone in this approach; for example Jacques Vallee commented 'It is not always necessary to use hypnotism . . . it (the investigation) should be under their own control or we will hurt these people'. Arne Groth, who is conducting much of the investigation into Anders' case in Vallentuna, commented 'Hypnotism is unreliable. There are easier, gentler ways to let people remember things for themselves'. Kathryn is trying to write a book of her own and perhaps puts it in the best context; she has found herself unable to write the book with the correct emotional intensity because — she believes — the materialistic influences of the United States are too strong to allow her to feel the way she did when she was in Sweden. She comments, 'I have to feel the same way again before I can write about it'.

To return to Kathryn's experience. I shall quote Kathryn

extensively — this is her story.

'My experience was so positive, so uplifting, it completely changed me and my whole way of being. In fact, I have always felt that I was born that day, whatever day it was! I have always written everything down since childhood, but I didn't write it down then.'

Kathryn told me that she could never understand at the practical level why she had never written in her own diaries about what was such an extraordinary experience. She understood, I think, that the written word was totally inadequate at the time because it simply could not express the emotions within her. Even so many years after the event, with so much time to reflect on it, it is clear to me that there is an enormous gulf between the words Kathryn writes and the feelings she experienced. 'I figure it happened around April 6, 1969, it was before the moon landing. The meadows were green (one of the earliest springs in Sweden).'

'It happened in the middle of the day when the sky was blue. I have vivid memories of everything that occurred until I made one statement, and all memory was wiped out to 1985 when I underwent hypnosis. The last thing I said was (with indescribable emotions of love and compassion for the earth and everything living on it), "If Hitler were here now, I would put my arms around him and tell him that I loved him. He didn't know what he was doing. He was not alive yet. He was just a shell".'

After this, Kathryn and her two companions of the time have no further memory until they found themselves sitting on a sofa in the house of one of her companions at eleven o'clock in the evening, when the sky was dark. According to Kathryn, none of them can remember what happened for the rest of the day and evening. This companion's house is only approximately an hour away from the meadow where they had been walking.

Kathryn points out that one of her companions, Harvey (pseudonym) did not experience what Kathryn and her other companion, Martin (pseudonym) experienced. According to Kathryn, Martin and herself had 'the same visual, emotional, physical, mental and spiritual experience'. However, according to Kathryn, Martin shortly after the experience became 'very political' and refuses to discuss the events.

I should point that Kathryn (Howard) is the witness's real name. I have almost never used the witness's real name in the past even when offered the right to do so. However, in this case Kathryn has expressly asked me to use her real name as she believes that it is an important part of the experience that there is complete and open honesty in everything she does and she feels that the use of a pseudonym is somehow not fitting. I have therefore complied with this but will continue to use pseudonyms for her companions as they clearly have different feelings about the experience.

Kathryn recalls 'It all started with the three of us sitting there is the meadow talking about Vietnam and Biafra. At the time, I was (and I always have been) extremely upset by the violence and lack of caring from the masses. I just couldn't understand it. I started to cry about it. Just then, directly above us in the sky, appeared an object. Martin and I looked up and saw it at the same time. "What is that," I asked. He didn't answer. It was oval shaped, it seemed to have what looked like legs coming out of the bottom of it. It's impossible to describe really. And just like that, soundless the entire time, it disappeared. Shocked, I said, "Did you see that? What was it? It couldn't be an aeroplane. An aeroplane can't go straight out, away from the earth — it has to go round the earth." And he agreed. At that moment, the colour blue disappeared and the word "sky" no longer existed to Martin or me. We turned our heads in front of us and saw the moon (exactly the way it looked later when the Apollo footage came back to us via TV and photographs). We could see the natural size of it, the craters, the colour, and it seemed to be revolving in space (that to us appeared to be a colourless, almost-fluidic grey eternity). On the left side space of the moon there was total darkness. If you look at the moon pictures and imagine the space around it, there was a distance of the grey and then darkness (which was curved too). We didn't seem to look behind us at any time, only straight ahead. I said, aghast, "My God, what is that? Do you see it too?" (Martin nodded.) "It must be the moon," I said. Meanwhile, Harvey thinks we are playing a joke on him and laughs. "Don't you see that, Harvey?" I asked, incredulously (of course). He didn't. I brought my knees up to my chest and wrapped my arms around them and as I watched, said, "I must talk. I will forget if I don't talk. Look at the sky. There is no sky. We are sitting in the universe. This is the universe." As I said that, the earth seemed to be expanding in front of my eyes. It was enormous and round. I stood up and started to walk. "My God, Martin, walk on the Earth. (He didn't). What a feeling this is. I am walking upside down, sideways, and every which way. The only thing that keeps me here is gravity. Gravity." (And I seem to understand what gravity was instantly). "If I walk on the edge of the earth (pointing to the moon) I could fall off and land on the moon!" And then I laughed because I realised how stupid I was. Of course, I could fall off right here, I thought to myself. "I feel like a puppet on strings". I lifted my arms up high above me. The earth continued to expand. It felt as if I were looking at the earth from way above it, and at the same time standing on it with the same consciousness that I have right now, as a human body and all that. I was talking and looking at Martin (who was crying as I was), just as I would normally, and at the same time seeing all these things. Then a sound came that seemed to permeate the entire universe — a very loud and slow beating sound (just like a heart through a stethoscope, except much slower). "Oh, what is that? It is pulsating. It's the rhythm of the universe," I said.'

Budd Hopkins believes that extraterrestrial aliens 'switch off' those that they do not wish to abduct, leaving them free to deal with those who they have targeted. I have never believed the UFO phenomenon to be so prosaic, so mundane. Forty years of varied, contradictory, and illogical experiences reported by reliable people from all over the world has always led me to believe that what we are we dealing with is more likely to be a common stimulus of a type we simply do not understand, be it extraterrestrial, terrestrial, or psychological, but which is interpreted by each individual according to his or her own character and make-up. Can this experience merely be Harvey being 'switched off' while Kathryn and Martin are abducted?

Surely if any case cries out to demonstrate the complexity of the UFO phenomenon it is this one.

Kathryn continues, 'And then the feeling of love and compassion that came within us was as enormous as the visual experience itself. I was weeping for the human race at the same time that I felt the greatest joy I have ever known. I felt one with everything. I read later that was called cosmic consciousness.' This echoes the statements of so many witnesses, including both Anders and Marianne in Sweden, that the experience is about the Earth and Man's relationship with it.

'And then, not outside, but within our minds, we seemed to be seeing the evolution of the human race from the beginning of time to the end. This happened so quickly (the way people say they see their lives on a film reel when they are close to death). It seemed like seconds. I can't remember what I saw then, but I know that we started to feel more compassionate and I said, "Why can't we do anything? If everyone could feel and see as we do now, there wouldn't be any more wars, starvation or anything negative on the earth. It doesn't have to be that way." And as I said that, a strange thing occurred. It didn't seem to matter what happened. "That's just part of the evolution", I said.'

Kathryn admits that there is probably much she has forgotten and she is continuing to, gently, explore her memory. For the present time she believes that it was about this time she made the earlier remark about Hitler and then everything went black.

During a visit to Sweden three years ago Kathryn underwent hypnotic regression. I have already expressed my concern with the use of this technique, and many psychiatrists and psychologists have made clear that they believe recall under hypnosis is, at best, often unreliable. However, it seems significant to me that throughout her period of time in the United States Kathryn did not feel able to approach researchers or hypnotists to investigate her story but rather waited until she was able to return to Sweden. The hypnotherapist who conducted the sole hypnotic regression session in Sweden was one that both she and Bertil Kuhlemann trusted and believed to have no 'UFO axe' to grind. Kathryn's conscious recall was of beauty, compassion and compassionate sadness. It is perhaps significant that her recollections under hypnosis also contain fears and apprehensions. Some would hold that this is because the hypnosis has revealed buried trauma, others that the process of hypnosis is, in these cases, inappropriate and even damaging to recall. Kathryn does intend to undergo other hypnotic regression sessions and particularly if she can return to Sweden at some time, certainly she and I will share the unveiling of this experience in the future in any way she feels appropriate. She has been careful in selecting the people to do the hypnosis and I feel sure she will continue to be so.

For the moment, this one session is a fact and the following is some of the information which the session revealed.

'"The legs" that were sticking out underneath the object were cylindrical and after going through incredible darkness and then blinding light, I found myself inside of the object (the cylinders had been pulled into it with me in one) and looking between my feet through a lens (where I first saw the treetops and the earth). When asked if I were standing, lying, sitting, I answered, "I am free floating but my wrists and ankles are being held by something". They seem to be like loose straps that held me there. It was barrel-shaped inside but I felt comfortable. In fact, there wasn't any fear until I couldn't see the earth any more, and then I freak out on the tape (four times — every time he brings me back to that moment) because I am so afraid that I will never return to the earth. "Oh! (I screamed) Please take me back. I am not ready to leave yet." Just before that, I was enthralled by the beauty of the earth. The colour was so blue, it was the brightest thing in that space. Nothing compared to its light. It was all black space everywhere else — just the earth in all its glory. Then it started to disappear. In the circular see-through lens that I was looking through, it "in its natural size" suddenly only appeared in part (just like it does in photos by the astronauts). I come back to that on the tape and each time my hysteria is the same. I cry and scream. And then, while under hypnosis, I remember some dreams that I have had. I hear a voice say to me, "If you touch the Earth, you must go back." When he (the hypnotist) tries to get me to tell him who I am talking about, my voice completely changes and I answer very sternly, I cannot tell you that. Don't ask me that." There is another part where I find myself in a strange place and I actually see something that looks like an enormous cigar taking off in the distance and I cry out not to leave me there. It seems to be on another planet somehow, but, I never tell where it is.'

'Clairvoyants and the like have talked about seeing a "crystal mass", "head-dress", "helmet", or something like that on my head. I saw this when I was under hypnosis. I talk about it several times, describing something I see over my head when my eyes look up.'

In a later discussion with Kathryn she told me that the entities she had seen were transparent which is certainly not the 'normal' description of UFO aliens and I have yet to explore with her more details of this if she has any to offer. However, again it is worth noting the similarity with her own experience and Anders' experience where he reported that the aliens were translucent.

It seems to me that there is enough similarity between this case and what might be called 'classic' American UFO cases to show that there is a possible common stimulus, a commonly-shared experience. The abduction through darkness and into light is very commonly reported, 'instructions' from the abductors not to remember certain information is commonly reported, and yet there seems to be a world of difference between the meaning that the experience has for Kathryn and the meaning that is interpreted by others in other cases. It seems to me again to be the difference between investigations which are 'investigator-led' and those cases which are 'witness-led'.

Although the experience occurred during just one day, its meaning and its significance have continued for Kathryn to the present day. She has found that she has been able to discuss experiences with people in a way she would have felt unable to do before and that this has unlocked other knowledge within her. She has had experiences of what it means to have lived another life, and much more. There have been prophetic dreams which Kathryn comments she hopes will not occur in her life time. I asked her what sort of dreams she had had and she described one to me where she was standing on the earth as an enormous giant able to see the whole horizon around her, and in the sky the stars disappeared. One light got bigger and approached the earth which was oozing fire-like lava and spitting out flames similar to solar flares. She was crying and felt a love for the earth. She knew that there was no way to stop the earth from burning and that it was the end of civilisation. The light was coming right at her and she felt incredible joy because she and possibly the race would be saved. She feels that the premonition may be of a future or a past time. She does not feel that this was a physical experience, and indeed it could not logically be so, but she believes that although it was a dream it had deliberate significance and that it is part of a continuing experience.

Her experience clearly shows a separation of physical and astral bodies even at the time of the abduction itself; there is a time when what appears to be her 'astral' body is looking down at her own physical presence still in the meadow. Other recall has related what she believes to be recollections of her own previous lives, all of which she believes to be connected to one ongoing experience.

I made the comment earlier that one of the apparent faults, for me, of regression hypnosis, is that it is too consistent within the ufological field. To reiterate that point again; if reincarnation is true then logically we must all have had past lives; if, say, ghosts truly exist then many people would have seen them. When an investigator of past lives is searching for past lives he discovers either past lives or nothing, when an investigator of ghosts is searching for a memory of such an encounter, he either finds them or nothing and similarly when an UFO investigator is searching for a UFO event he either finds them or nothing. It seems to me to be an inherent fault in the research that UFO investigators do not occasionally uncover a past life or ghost experience, that past life investigators do not uncover a UFO experience, etc., etc. Kathryn's case seems to indicate that when the investigation is 'witness-led', the borders between these phenomena break down, and that many experiences are uncovered. This suggests to me that a much more impartial approach on the part of the investigator dealing with a case is needed and lends me to believe that the recall is, if not more accurate, then more true to the experience *as perceived by the witness.*

Kathryn commented to me that ever since she was young she has felt that her life had special meaning; this experience appears to have triggered the unlocking of that meaning to her and she writes, 'Ever since that day, I have felt strongly that there is a message I have to get out, that I know how to get people to open their eyes in a way that they have never done before, that everyone wants to express their hidden desires and secrets with me, and on and on I could write about these things.'

What the future of this case will reveal we cannot tell but it seems to me that if Kathryn pursues her own 'investigation' in the way she has done so far, then a reliable truth will be drawn from her memories and, more importantly, the experience will be one which helps and uplifts her and perhaps allows her to help others.

As UFO researchers, we must realise that through the past forty years times have changed and that we must change with them. In the early years it seemed to be apparent that UFOs were probably only some sort of physical object in the skies which had to be understood. To do this we merely had to capture one, or unambiguously photograph it, and we would have the solution to the whole problem. I have a tape of a recording made between a reporter and Kenneth Arnold the day after his sighting in 1947, which was generously given to me by Pierre Lagrange. In that, the reporter announced 'I understand United Press is checking . . . and we hope to have some concrete answer before nightfall'. He was out by quite a margin!

We know that a proper understanding, not perhaps of what the UFO phenomenon was, but of what the UFO phenomenon has developed into, involves a journey not through the skies or the files of the Air Force but through the mind of Man himself. You cannot dissect a mind as you can dissect a file or a photograph and investigators must be ready to apply quite different techniques to investigation. Techniques which will assist the witness in finding answers, benefit the witness and help us to understand more than the UFO phenomenon, possibly a whole aspect of human perception. We may even be past the day when we can talk of a UFO phenomenon; the events of June 1947 may only have served to trigger a long-term development of human understanding.

And the first new important rule for researchers is that we must listen — listen with open ears and minds — to the witnesses.

PART FOUR

Regression Hypnosis

I have been here before
But when or how I cannot tell
I know the grass beyond the door
The sweet keen smell
The sighing sound, the lights around the shore
You have been mine before —
How long ago I may not know
But just when at that swallow's soar
Your neck turned so
Some veil did fall — I knew it all of yore.

DANTE GABRIEL ROSSETTI

"THE MAGICAL AND ROYAL ROAD TO TRUTH"

The key technique used in unlocking hidden abduction memories, as we have seen throughout our narrative, is the technique known as regression hypnosis. In the vast majority of cases it is this technique which has been used to reveal the abduction itself when only a UFO sighting was apparent, sometimes the details of the abduction when only a broad outline is remembered and more recently whole UFO and abduction experiences when no such memory was ever apparent before the technique was applied. It must also be borne in mind that there are many cases where full details of UFO encounter and abduction events have been recalled without the use of any form of hypnosis, and we shall come to this point later.

There are two vitally important points to understand from the outset; the technique is a combination of two applications, hypnosis and regression, and *neither of these is properly understood either by science or by the people applying them.* Many psychologists and psychiatrists, and particularly those involved in the UFO research field, will disagree with this point but since even within these groups of people there is some disagreement about what lies behind regression hypnosis, I think it is a fair statement of the art at the present time.

Hypnosis

There are a number of myths about hypnosis which are known to be incorrect and which stem basically from the most public use of the technique in what might be termed music hall and cabaret entertainment. Hypnosis was once known as mesmerism after Mesmer who studied this in the 18th century and who proposed the theory that it was an influence exerted by the hypnotist over the subject. Stage acts of 'performing hypnotists' are full of examples of the hypnotist putting the subject, usually supposedly randomly picked from the audience, 'under his influence' and then instructing him to do bizarre uncharacteristic acts for the amusement of the audience. On being brought out of this supposed altered state of consciousness the subject then expresses amazement when he is told of the things he has done and the implication is clearly set out that the hypnotist has exerted a form of magical power over him. Some years ago at a nightclub just north of London I watched such an act with some companions. One of these friends volunteered to be one of six subjects that would be placed under hypnosis by the performer and they were led off backstage to be prepared for the event. In this particular case the hypnotist was less than subtle; he simply suggested that if they played along with his instructions they would be able to appear in his television show that was being broadcast in the north of England if they so wished. One of the other subjects admitted that he had been planted specifically in the audience and had been the leading subject in each of the shows at that nightclub. This was of course rather blatant and possibly reflected more on the lack of ability of the performer. I suspect that other performers are far more subtle, indeed that some of them employ some true hypnotic techniques. However, as this example suggests and as is now known, there is no external influence over the subject. It is now recognised that hypnotism is some form of psychological effect which is a result of the state of mind of the subject, though considerably aided by a practised hypnotist. The title of this chapter is taken from Dr Benjamin Simon's introduction to the book 'The Interrupted Journey' — the story of the Betty and Barney Hill abduction. He points out that 'there is little produced under or by hypnosis that is not possible without.'

Opinion in the medical profession is somewhat divided on hypnotism, with some experts believing that there is no such state and that it is a term covering a range of levels of relaxation, others contending that there may be some degree of altered state of consciousness but that it is quite in the control of the subject.

Certainly there is evidence that the hypnotist can instruct a person to remember events recalled under hypnosis or to forget them according to his wishes, though the degree to which the subject could fight off that instruction is in debate. Part of the success of hypnosis appears to be in the trusting relationship between the hypnotist and the subject and there is little doubt that no one could hypnotise a person who was locked in rigid fear of the hypnotist unless the hypnotist was able to first overcome that and obtain a degree of trust.

Experiments have shown that a person under hypnosis is still perfectly capable of constructing totally prefabricated lies and so there is no question of hypnosis being a definitive pathway to truth; on the other hand it is recognized that where there is a trusting relationship between the two, then it is likely that hypnosis will reveal the truth *as perceived by the subject*, assuming both subject and hypnotist are in fact seeking the truth. Again, this is not to say that hypnosis will reveal an objective truth where the subject believes otherwise, it will merely reveal the subject's own true perceptions. As Dr Simon says, 'it must be understood that hypnosis is a pathway to the truth as it is felt and understood by the patient. The truth is what he believes to be the truth, and this may or may not be consonant with the ultimate nonpersonal truth.'

Another point to consider is that this degree of trust between the hypnotist and the subject does tend to lead to a situation where the subject will try to give answers which please the hypnotist, or at least which do not offend. This was very clear in the case of Betty and Barney Hill with their psychiatrist Dr Benjamin Simon and was in fact recognised by Simon at the time.

It is also clear that hypnosis does place the subject into a state of heightened suggestibility and that a hypnotist can implant a totally untrue memory if he should so wish. In the case of an unscrupulous hypnotist it would be possible to prefabricate a memory, implant it and have the subject recall it with earnest belief; we shall come to an example of this shortly; but in the UFO research field I believe it unlikely that any of the investigators would do this. However, I believe it quite possible that, subconsciously, investigators present at hypnotic regression sessions may well implant some false memories by virtue of the leading questions they ask. Indeed this is quite evident from the narrative given in many articles and books, even when written by the investigators themselves. Given that the state of hypnosis leaves the subject wishing to 'please the hypnosist', then a corruption of even the perceived truth is possible, let alone details of an objective truth witnessed.

There could be an example of this in the case of Alan Godfrey, a police officer who had an encounter in 1980. During a hypnotic regression session in which he describes his abduction he believes that one of the aliens is called Joseph. I was very interested in this as it is unusual for abductees' aliens to have names and I wondered if there could be a filtering of information to him through the hypnosis session. When the case was presented to a public lecture of the British UFO Research Association I asked the leader of the investigators' team, solicitor Harry Harris of Manchester, for the names of those who had been performing the actual hypnosis. He confirmed that it was Dr Robert Blair and Dr Joseph Jaffee. Harris, however, was adamant that the safeguards he had built into the session would have prevented Dr Jaffee's name influencing Godfrey's memories. As I was not at these sessions and have only seen video tapes of them I am unable to comment on this but feel it remains at least an impressive coincidence.

In the BBC television programme 'The Mind Machine' psychiatrist Martin Orne points out that the mind is not a recorder but a synthesizer 'It is the way in which we recreate the past and we have the illusion that this now is the past, it is always distorted to some degree'. Orne goes on to point out that 'under some circumstances such as hypnosis the ease of distortion is greatly *increased* (emphasis added)'.

Orne then went on to perform an experiment with a subject, Melissa, demonstrating that hypnosis can not only alter the unconscious mind but can also interfere with the conscious memory.

Orne first asked Melissa when she had gone to bed and when she had reawoken on a given night, and her responses and their conversation was recorded. Melissa confirmed that she went to sleep at around four o'clock in the morning and that she slept until around eight o'clock in the morning; she confirmed that she did not wake at any time in between. Orne then put Melissa under hypnosis, and asked her to relive her night and asked her whether she could hear two loud bangs outside her window after approximately an hour of sleep. Melissa nodded that she could. Orne suggested that the noises were like the backfire of a car, or gunshot sounds. To check the accuracy of his implanted memory he asks her if there are two or three noises and she confirms there are two, he again asks 'Are you sure there is not one' and she confirms two. At this point a very interesting event occurs; Orne asks her what time it is and she says 'It is about five o'clock I think', which is in line with the suggestion of an hour passing. Orne asks her to look at her watch or her clock to know exactly what time it is and she confirms five o'clock; Orne asks her if this is exactly the time and there is the suggestion of criticism in his voice, that such an exact time is improbable. Without prompting she falsely creates a new time and confirms that the watch or clock says that it is 5.01. At one point Orne asks her whether the noises were close together or far apart, a point he had not instructed her on, but rather than simply say she does not know she instantly responds with an answer; that they were close together. Orne then brings her out of the hypnotic state.

Orne then asks her the same questions he asked her prior to the hypnotic session. He asks her what time she went to bed at night; again she confirms she went to bed around four o'clock in the morning. She also confirms again that she woke up around eight but she then states she also remembers waking up around 5 o'clock because she was awoken by two noises like the backfiring of a car. Another very interesting point occurs here; she rationalises her memory by saying that she assumed it was the backfiring of a car and not gunshot sounds because there is a parking lot under her open window. None of this had been suggested by Orne and clearly her mind is seeking to rationalise the memory. In fact she further rationalises from her conscious memory because when Orne asks her to confirm that it was indeed that night and not some other night she recalls being angry about being woken up because she had been up late working on a paper and she needed her sleep. All of this is now conscious memory being created by Melissa, not by Orne, in order to rationalise the suggestion implanted by the hypnotist.

Orne played back the tape recording he has made of his original questions to her when she confirms she had not woken up, and she was visibly startled and in some state of disbelief that her voice was saying what she 'knew' to be untrue. In fact she defended her memory strongly against his own negative questions.

Orne makes a very revealing statement which is of great significance to UFO research. He says '*Hypnosis has a great deal to do with the mind, it is a window to the mind, it shows that we are able to translate beliefs into memories and convictions and you confuse what you fantasise in hypnosis and having seen them in actual recollections. And when you do that you have great convictions in what you say, you have strong beliefs that they are accurate, and you are very convincing to an observer because you think you know the truth and you describe it as such. You are what can be called an "honest liar"*'.

Regression

The second part of regression hypnosis is the regression technique. Broadly speaking, this is where the subject under hypnosis is instructed to reach back in time and to recall events that had happened previously. This technique is employed extensively in UFO abduction research since almost invariably such work is a search for the details of a historic event.

The technique is held to have merit as it has been suggested that there is some increased accuracy in recall of detail in experiments where, for example, a person has been regressed to their childhood and has been able to recall details of early friends since forgotten. However, even in this we must recall the point made by Dr Simon that the truth so revealed will be the truth as perceived by the subject and not necessarily the objective truth. We should also be wary of Martin Orne's experimental proof of false memory. In fact, experiments in the early 1970s on just this point showed that the subject was able to recall classmates with incredible detail and describe them with great precision and it was some surprise to the investigators to discover that these memories were in many ways incorrect.

A further point to be wary of is that the more times a subject repeats his memory the more likely it is that it will become firmly fixed as a truth in his mind. This reinforcement of possibly false memories is certainly of concern for UFO abduction research where researchers will frequently go over and over the same point in an effort either to verify facts or to discover more.

The strength of regression is held to be that when the person is hypnotized and regressed to a particular point that he is actually there at that time, describing events as if he is seeing them 'in live action'. Many UFO investigators have indicated to me that they believe this to be the case and even those who do not believe so appear to place such reliance on the recall that they demonstrate such a belief.

This is clearly not the case, as some uses of this technique have shown.

Let us step away from UFO abduction research for the moment and consider the use of the technique in reincarnation research, i.e. the search for past lives. In the most spectacular of those investigations, Morey Bernstein's 'search for Bridey Murphy', the subject, Ruth Simmons, (a pseudonym once used for Mrs Virginia Burns Tighe) was regressed to a time prior to her birth and recalled a previous existence as a 19th century peasant girl, Bridey Murphy. During the sessions Ruth Simmons spoke in an Irish brogue using Irish phrases of which we were told she was not normally aware and referred to details that were supposedly not within her framework of knowledge. The purpose of this narrative is not to re-examine that case and we shall therefore assume for the purpose of argument that all of these are true and that Ruth Simmons was once Bridey Murphy as the regression suggests. (I emphasise that we are accepting this for the point of argument only.)

During one of the regression sessions Bridey Murphy in her Irish brogue refers to sweets as 'candy'. Since Ruth Simmons was a mid 20th century American young woman this phrase would be a common one for the 1950s but clearly not so in the context used for Bridey Murphy. It would seem therefore that even if Ruth Simmons' recall of Bridey Murphy is true that her memories are being overlaid by the memories of her subsequent existence as Ruth Simmons. In short, even if Ruth Simmons' recall is correct, then it is being distorted by events that have happened subsequent to her former death.

Since UFO research is generally speaking contemporary and events are held to occur within a reasonably short time frame, i.e. most sessions are within a year or so of the event and rarely more than say, 10 years, then anachronisms are not likely to be discovered. However, we can speculate that there is some fear that between the time when the person believes they may have had a UFO encounter, which may be no more than a light in the sky, and the time when they are put into regression session, their sighting may inspire them to read detailed UFO material which would include all of the necessary imagery of abductions. In fact, given the high public profile of recent books on the subject such as Whitley Strieber's 'Communion', it will forever more be impossible to be certain to sort source from signal. If we compound this problem with the hazards of unwitting introduction of material by the investigator himself, then we can see that regression is not likely to be a reliable tool for recalling accurate memory. We can also see why reports will tend to standardise themselves and corroborate each other.

But what of recalls that we do not require regression hypnosis?

The question of why we have accounts that do not come through regression hypnosis is only partly a consideration for this chapter and is also taken up in the other relevant chapters. However, as a general rule it would be fair to say that recall without regression hypnosis produces somewhat more varied stories than those that are produced through regression hypnosis. For example, Jose Antonio da Silva, a member of the Brazilian armed forces, was abducted in May 1969 and taken aboard a landed flying saucer. However, his aliens were bearded dwarfs, the spacecraft and the room he was in were reported as being stone-walled and he was apparently offered bribes to spy for the aliens (which he refused). He reported the naked bodies of dead humans and a host of other details which do not frequently occur in other reports.

In the case of Antonio Villas-Boas his abduction contained a virtual rape scene not entirely devoid of erotic material and certainly with more sensual qualities to it than are reported by, say, Hopkins' abductees who regard even sexual encounters with some distaste. Villas-Boas was apparently somewhat disturbed by his mate barking like a dog during the experience but he nonetheless described the experience in part at least as 'agreeable'.

Travis Walton reported a case much more similar to the standard American alien type although this type was well known by this time in America following the Hills' and other accounts and in any case there have been considerable doubts raised as to the motives for this abduction claim. Even accepting that it was true there is the possibility of contamination of recall from highly publicly exposed material; for example the story of the Betty and Barney Hill sighting had been filmed and was televised in America only just prior to the Walton claim.

The point therefore is not that hypnotic regression produces UFO abduction reports; rather that it may be a way in which some reports are created, and is almost certainly the way in which many reports are 'standardised'.

The fact that individual investigators receive similar reports, but that these reports are not similar to the reports received by other investigators, suggests this strongly.

Within the material we know that there must be a percentage of hoaxes and frauds, we know that there must also be unreliable but truly believed fantasies which perhaps do not require regression hypnosis to draw them out.

The phenomenon of UFO abductions is not therefore dependent upon regression hypnosis. The seemingly apparent corroboration of the phenomenon, and the implied answers that recent work has given, are likely to be a product of regression sessions which are more probably distorting the truth than revealing it. This is not to say that there is not a truth, merely that hypnotic regression will not help us to find it with any certainty.

CONTROL EXPERIMENTS

Imagine a UFO witness laying, relaxed, on a couch undergoing regression hypnosis. He or she reveals what might be called the classic American scenario of small grey foetus-like aliens with large wrap-around eyes forcibly controlling them onto a landed UFO, conducting a systematic form of medical examination, possibly gynaecological examination, and subsequently releasing the subject back to his or her car to continue on their way.

What would be the significance for ufology if it could be demonstrated, *without question*, that this was a prefabrication in the mind of the subject?

In fact, this is not a hypothetical question. In 1977 Alvin Lawson and colleagues conducted what became known as imaginary abductee experiments. The initial reason for the experiment was to enable them to compare the stories created by imaginary abductees with those revealed by real abductees. They reasoned that some insight would be given into the differences between human imagination and the 'real' activities of the alien visitors.

However, Lawson and his colleagues were forced to drastically rethink the basis of their working hypothesis. What transpired was that there was virtually no difference between the deliberate and unquestionable prefabrication of imaginary abductees and the stories of 'real' abductees.

In outline, the experiments were conducted thus:

Advertising was used to collect an intake of volunteers for what was described as an 'interesting experience in hypnosis and imagination'. Some of the questions in the initial interview were designed to allow Lawson and his colleagues to eliminate from the test sample UFO enthusiasts and those with probable detailed knowledge of the subject.

Having then got together the selected group of target subjects, each were placed in hypnotic trance by one of Alvin Lawson's colleagues, Dr William C McCall. The bare bones of the abduction was introduced to the subject, who would be told to imagine that they had seen a UFO, that it had turned out to be a flying saucer, that they had been abducted aboard the flying saucer, that they had been given a medical examination by the occupants of the flying saucer and then released back into their earth environment.

Each subject was then taken through the abduction and asked to describe in detail what had happened to them. They gave remarkably clear descriptions of the inside of the flying saucer, of the alien abductors, of the nature and tenor of the medical examination that was conducted on them and so on. In fact, Lawson's first report on the experiments stated 'What startled us at first was the subject's ease and eagerness of narrative invention'.

In fact, as Jenny Randles writes in a summary of her experiments, 'Dr Lawson ... found that there is relatively little difference between UFO contacts deliberately imagined under hypnosis and those which are supposedly genuine. In other words, it is feasible that even the most plausible abduction story has a psychological basis deep in the sub-conscious'.

Lawson's experiments have been heavily criticised within the UFO community, and yet for me they remain one of the most significant pieces of work undertaken. If I have any criticism of Lawson and his colleagues, then it is only that they did not continue the work as, in my view, the results demanded of them.

One criticism levelled at the experiments is that there are no 'UFO-virgins'; in other words virtually all intelligent, literate adults have had some exposure to UFO material — even if the source is only the wildly distorted tabloid press reports. The concern was that material so absorbed could feed into the recollections. Since the experiments were conducted in the mid 1970s in California, where exposure to what might be regarded as 'new-age' material was widespread, then this appears to be a valid criticism. However, it overlooks the obvious counter argument; if imaginary abductees have been exposed to such material then so have 'real' abductees. There is no reason why a person selected by alien experimenters for a real abduction should not have the same background material in their reading and knowledge.

Another criticism levelled at Lawson's work was that he structured the events of the abduction. As Thomas E Bullard points out in his comparative study of abductions (in the MUFON Journal of February 1988, No 238), abductions seem to fall into eight structured components: capture, examination, conference, tour, other-wordly journey, theophany, return, and aftermath. Bullard points out that not all of these events are always disclosed in an abduction story but that whatever events are disclosed tend to follow the same order of unfolding. In some cases this is inevitable, for example the subject must be captured before he can be examined but in some cases it seems to be part of the 'technique'. In prefabricating the skeleton of the abduction to his subjects, Lawson gave them the order and it is therefore not surprising that they recalled the same order when relating their detailed story. This *is* a valid point but it *is not* a criticism of Lawson's work. The experiments were not conducted with a view to testing this particular point, though it would be interesting to see if later experiments could be done with this end in view. The experiments were conducted to discover what fine detail the imagination could put on the bare bones of a structured abduction and to this extent they were highly successful. The interiors of the craft that were described by the imaginary abductees, indeed the descriptions of the external shape of the vehicles, matched in many fine details with those of 'real' abductees. Similarly, the descriptions of the humanoid entities matched with great precision, as did the descriptions of the medical examinations that were being undertaken.

These similarities must lead us to the conclusion that there is the *possibility* that abductions are psychological in origin. As Jenny Randles, in her book 'Abduction' suggests, 'Imagine you were trying to decide if the same car was involved in two separate road accidents. Witness accounts such as, "It was big and blue and had four wheels" would not be much use, that is standard for many cars. But if the two versions mentioned a tiny, ornamental pink frog hanging from a string in the rear window, we might sit up and listen.'

This is precisely what Lawson's experiments have shown. Real abductees reported the 'pink frog', and the imaginary abductees saw it too.

Another criticism of Lawson's work was that there was some structuring of the event simply because the subjects were instructed that they had had a UFO encounter and the point was made that this would channel the person's mind to 'think UFOs'. Again, though this is a valid point it is not a criticism; there is good reason to believe that the experiences of abductees are similar in substance to divine revelation and other religious experiences and indeed to a host of other paranormal activities. Those people who approach UFO investigators and say, in effect, 'I have had a UFO experience' are themselves channelling their own interpretation of events into 'thinking UFOs'. The experience of Fatima in Portugal showed that of the many witnesses to the events, some saw visions of the Virgin Mary, some saw balls of light, and others saw UFOs. Is this 'self-channelling' not as valid as Lawsons's channelling of his subjects' thinking?

The strongest criticism of Lawson's work is that there was one major difference between the recall of imaginary abductees and those of 'real' abductees; the massive gap between the emotional responses of the two types of subject. In the case of the 'real' abductees they would recall their experiences in great personal emotional pain, often sweating, crying, screaming, often having to be forcibly held down by the investigators; they would subsequently suffer nightmares and often they would appear to have suffered some character change. In the case of the imaginary abductees none of these characteristics were present; basically they recalled their events in flat level description rather as if watching a television programme or film. Does this then in fact give us the way to determine 'real' abductees from imaginary abductees? And is this a criticism so important that Lawson's work is invalid because of it?

Not in the slightest; in fact if anything it adds to the probability of a psychological basis, or part psychological basis, of the experience. The imaginary abductees had nothing to fear because they *knew* that the experience was a fake whereas the 'real' abductees believed it to be genuine. This in no way confirms that their experience *was* genuine, only that they genuinely believed it to be. I doubt that anyone closely involved with abduction witnesses would question their sincerity and the depth of their beliefs. Even amongst those people it is important to note that many do not automatically assume that their recall is accurate and that their experience is extraterrestrial; many in fact express doubts about that hypothesis and some even reflect on a possible psychological experience.

But worse still if the 'real' abductees are scared witless and forced to face trauma if in fact the experience is being implanted, albeit subconsciously, by the investigator himself as considered elsewhere in this book. For many witnesses, particularly those less sophisticated, the close attention of a prominent author and perhaps television personality, is sufficient 'proof' of the validity of their experience and if they therefore believe the stories he apparently reveals from their own subconscious then they have genuine reason for fear.

Rather than falling at this hurdle in the search for a psychological basis for abductions, Lawson's experiments leap very gracefully over it.

I suspect that in fact the basis of the criticism of Lawson's work comes not from these experiments but from the conclusions he drew from them which were, even if valid, an imaginative leap, and difficult to substantiate at least on the basis of the experiments alone. Lawson speculated that the reason for the similarities between events was that 'real' and imaginary abductees all shared one thing in common; their birth. He speculated that the UFO experience was a reliving of the birth experience: that the UFO entities described by many as foetus-like were indeed recreating the foetus-like body of the abductee himself, that the UFO was in some way descriptive of the womb and that the medical examination was in fact a reliving of the moment of birth itself. Work on this suggested an interesting, even amusing, circumstance. The vast majority of people leaving the UFO were, as in the case of Betty and Barney Hill, steered out of the UFO and back to their vehicle by supporting alien entities. Some of the abductees were forcibly pulled out of the UFO apparently in a state of not wanting to leave and these were, it was believed, people who had undergone forceps birth. To cap it all, there was one story of an abductee who was not guided down the corridors of the UFO, held to be comparable to the birth canal, but was in fact brutally ejected from the UFO and he turned out to be of caesarian birth!

Criticism of the suggestions were manyfold; why should the UFO resemble the womb when the womb is dark and warm and UFOs are often described as extremely bright and somewhat cold, why should the UFO entities be foetus-like when they are presumably the doctors and the abductee is presumably the foetus, etc., etc.

The idea is an interesting one though scientifically invalid at the present time simply because it has not been effectively researched. It is based on pure speculation and not on evidence from the experience itself and in any case presupposes much about the birth experience which we would have to understand before we could apply it to a comparison of UFO encounters.

It is this, however, which I suspect incurred the wrath of the UFO community, and particularly that large segment of it which seeks only extra-terrestrial explanations. They discredited Lawson's work in the 'in house' literature, but the two aspects should have been separated in the minds of serious researchers. The birth trauma theory was at best highly speculative, the imaginary abductee part of the work was well conducted, valid experimentation and produced results which cannot be ignored if serious research into the subject of UFOs is to be conducted. As I said earlier, my one criticism of the work is that it has not been continued and I would urge a continuation of these experiments, not necessarily by investigators or researchers within the UFO community but by psychologists and psychiatrists whose work would then be of much value to us and presumably to them.

I had some interesting insight into the thinking processes that go into such experimentation when I was one of 20 test subjects in a small ad-hoc experiment based on Lawson's work. The experiment had no scientific validity and indeed did not use hypnosis which may well be one of the important keys to the 'believability' of 'real' abductees. But it forced me to consider where I would obtain stimulus for UFO story fabrication. Half of the subjects, including myself, were known to have a good working knowledge of the UFO phenomenon and the other half were an attempt to find as near to 'UFO virgins' as possible. We were asked to imagine that we were driving late at night and saw a UFO and that we should describe what we saw, we should describe how we were taken on board the UFO by the occupants, what the inside of the UFO would look like, what the occupants would look like, etc., etc. I should stress that this was simply a questionnaire we had to complete, there was no hypnosis or intensive interrogation. So I had to fabricate a UFO encounter. I had never created a deliberately false picture of an encounter at that time, and to put myself in the position of an abductee I had to decide where I would construct my surroundings from. I gave free rein to my imagination, describing each of the circumstances as I thought most typical. And in most cases the descriptions I gave were typical of the UFO literature, i.e. I described the dwarf-like aliens with the wrap-around eyes, etc. But then I had actually seen these creatures with my own eyes prior to that! Not in reality of course, but in books and literature on the subject. Where I could have fallen short was in the description of the inside of the UFO itself because although these have often been described by witnesses they have rarely been drawn and never photographed and there was no visual image for me to pick up for my recollection.

However, I found I had no trouble creating the image, I visualised the ramp leading to the saucer, the circular corridors within the saucer, the doors opening to a medical examination chamber within the saucer, etc. And as I was describing them I had a clear visual *memory* of the image I was describing. Even as I was describing it I was searching in my mind to find out where the memory was coming from and it was with some surprise that I realised I was, in this instance, recalling in black and white rather than in colour and then I knew specifically where I had taken my flying saucer from; it was the inside of Gort and Klaatu's saucer in the film 'The Day the Earth Stood Still'.

In other words, where I had no memory from the UFO literature, I had no difficulty in finding one from pure fiction. There is little question that the cultural influence of fiction, and particularly science fiction, is overwhelming in the reports of UFO witnesses. The point is made elsewhere, but to summarise; it is not an immediate cause and effect situation where you can press button A and produce image B but rather a state of social conditioning. The fact that a particular type of UFO or a particular type of humanoid is depicted on film does not, and should not, lead to a sudden rash of reports of that kind of UFO or that kind of alien but what does happen, and can be demonstrated to have happened, is that those particular shapes of UFOs, those particular characteristics of the aliens, perhaps their manner or approach rather than their physical description, becomes incorporated into the cultural image of 'what an alien really is' and from that the reports begin to be coloured from this description.

Without consciously doing so I had myself done exactly what it is suspected some abduction witnesses *may* do; I had simply called up the best memory I had.

Hilary Evans in his 'case for scepticism' in the book 'Phenomenon' makes the point that, 'While the experiments do not prove that the "true" abductees are making up their stories, they do suggest that anyone who unconsciously wishes to do so is able to find within himself the necessary resources.'

Lawson's paper was entitled 'What can we learn from hypnosis of imaginary abductees?' The answer is we can learn a lot and we must be grateful to Lawson for opening what I hope will be a future avenue of research.

PART FIVE

The objections

The marble index of a mind forever
Voyaging through strange seas of thought
alone

WILLIAM WORDSWORTH

A SUMMARY OF DOUBTS

As we have seen so far, we are faced with a surge of belief in the Extra-Terrestrial Hypothesis (ETH); to pave the way for alternative thinking we must first summarise the reservations we have considered already to this working model:

— the response to the Arnold sighting shows that the ETH became a front runner theory immediately, despite little or no evidence at that time. This suggests that the theory *did not initially develop from the evidence.*

— it can be demonstrated that the media promoted the ETH immediately following the Arnold sighting. Subsequent years indicate that it became a bandwagon driven mainly by the media.

— the popularity of the stories related may well have laid down the foundation of a modern mythology; and as it provided answers to those seeking 'something' — an alternative religion, a reality to science fiction, a vicarious broadening of horizons, etc — it may well have created followers who came to truly believe in it.

— the stories of the contactees were the first significant proof of extra-terrestrials. It is an alarming co-incidence that a theory based on no evidence should so soon be proven to be correct, particularly given the nature of the evidence the contactees provided.

— the stories of the contactees were conflicting with each other, and conflict also with the later stories of the abductees. This is made all the more improbable by recent claims that abduction memories have been traced back to before the contactee era, suggesting that both were happening simultaneously.

— the stories of the contactees and abductees mirrored the expectations created by science fiction. Some isolated cases even appear to be direct copy-cat reports of such fiction, though obviously this is rare.
— one of the most thoroughly researched cases of abduction — the Hill's encounter — was held unlikely to be real by the one non-UFO expert involved in the case (Dr Simon).
— we know *for certain* that the stereotype abduction arose from Betty Hill's dreams. It is speculated that these dreams were memories; but that is impossible to verify.
— the claims of subsequent abductees, while significantly similar also contain directly contradictory differences in the attitudes and knowledge of the 'aliens', the appearance of the aliens, and the activities of the aliens.
— the aliens have developed over the years, becoming suspiciously more 'alien' in the same manner that Hollywood box-offices require that a sequel betters the original. Betty Hill reported very similar aliens to the version discovered so frequently by later American researchers, yet she was sure they had human eyes and other 'normal' features; the same apparent alien in later years has developed very alien eyes and features.
— virtually all aliens are suspiciously humanoid, yet there seems no reason why this should be, other than it might well be the expectation of human arrogance. On Earth we see an enormous variety of life forms, many of which may well have levels of intelligence akin to our own in their own way; certainly their social structures are advanced. If we are indeed the dominant race on Earth then it is probably because of an accident of evolution which could presumably have caused any of our competitors to have become dominant. Across the universe the variety should be even larger given different planetary and stellar conditions. It has been pointed out that far from being a 'typical' solar system we could be quite rare; many stars are binary whereas we have a single star; also we have a 'double planet' environment with the Moon very large in comparison to the Earth — a factor not found in any of the other planets in our solar system. Could this not lead to the possibility that other life forms would in fact be very different from our own, rather than very similar? Jerome Pearson spec-

ulates on this in his article 'Lonely life of a double planet' in the MUFON journal of November 1988, number 247.

— occasionally there are reports of robot-like creatures and even these are humanoid. This seems very unlikely except in the creations of science fiction; in fact real robots rarely look anything like human — they are designed in specific ways for specific tasks, usually this means anything but human form since it is usually designed to get over the limitations of that design (for example, car assembly robots in car plants). If the robot-like appearance is a factor of their movements and unemotional attitudes, then does this not reflect the creations of science fiction?

— the aliens seem sometimes very vulnerable on Earth, often wearing spacesuits, etc just as we have to when we go to the Moon. Yet we expect that when we are of a technological ability to travel to the stars — if ever — that we will also develop the ability to create cyborg (artificially enhanced) humans especially adapted to the new lifestyle. Already, we are advancing in our genetic engineering. Surely we might expect superior races — *who seem to be acting as we would* — to have solved these problems.

— if American researchers are correct in that the aliens' purpose is genetic engineering with human subjects, perhaps for the very point raised above, then they are going about it in a curious way, with frightening and frequent abductions. They could 'raid' the laboratories of several hospitals and research institutes in one night and collect all the material they need without difficulty.

— the aliens do not act in the way they themselves claim; they appear not to want us to know of their activity yet they leave a plethora of clues scattered about to point us in the right direction; for example they forbid photographs (at Gulf Breeze — as we shall see later) and then make special arrangements with the principal witness to ensure he is warned of their arrival in time to get his camera ready.

— there is a great deal of illogical inconsistency in abduction material; in the Betty and Barney Hill case, for example, the aliens appear to have inconsistent knowledge of the language, of everyday artifacts, etc. Of more concern is that this type of inconsistency is *typical* of dream-material.

— despite their obvious technological abilities, their desire for secrecy and their ability to 'switch off' any witnesses they do not want involved they are apparently bad enough pilots to crash in considerable numbers their flying saucers and then fail to ever recover the bodies of their lost comrades or the saucers themselves, which presumably they could easily do by 'switching off' the personnel at Wright Patterson for a couple of hours.

— they are not only bad pilots, they are unethical and inadequate doctors; they demonstrate their need for secrecy and their ability to 'switch off' witnesses yet they switch them off after giving a short tantalising glimpse, and switch them on again in time to catch a glimpse of them leaving. They leave scars where even we would be unlikely to do so in our operations since they apparently still use scalpels and have not discovered laser-surgery, they fail to apply proper anaesthetic during their operations which would in any case aid their desire for secrecy.

— subjects undergoing 'medical examinations' are often strapped down, are stripped naked, and have their will suppressed. While this may all be necessary to conduct such examinations it is also heavily symbolic of Man's modern condition; of lack of control over his environment, of being powerless against outside force. The symbolic interpretations of these activities seem to have been ignored by researchers who ascribe prosaic meaning only to the events.

— particular investigators seem to find the stories they expect. Despite the fact that throughout the world all sorts of paranormal activity is being researched, everyone finds their own field of study answered; it is too pat, and suggests that the answers are being implanted by the investigation, or that the actual source is not what we understand.

— when witnesses are not investigator-led their similar stories seem to produce quite different meanings.

— we know from Lawson's experiments that anyone wishing to fabricate an abduction story has the resources within them to do so, based on our present day, science fiction, culture.

— hypnotic regression is used in many cases, and has certainly provided *investigators* with a stereotype to apply across the board; yet experts in this field claim that the technique is unreliable, and quite able to implant false memories.

From these objections we have a duty (while not rejecting the ETH) to rethink the strength with which we apply it; and this must lead us to consider other possible answers to the phenomenon, and also perhaps to rethink the very basis on which we believe we understand it.

We must re-set our perspectives.

SCIENCE, SCIENTISTS AND UFOS

Having considered many objections to the ETH, some of them of a purely scientific nature, we might take this opportune moment to look at the love-hate relationship between UFO enthusiasts and some scientists, particularly astronomers. There is considerable friction between these groups, apparently centred on the respective belief systems of each. In May 1988, I — along with a number of others associated with the UFO phenomenon — was a guest speaker at the Jodrell Bank Radio Telescope Centre in Cheshire. I arrived early having had to drive up from London that morning and met one of my colleagues before the Centre had opened, at around eight-thirty. He warned me that before we got underway we were to be summoned before the Director of that famous installation, Professor Sir Francis Graham-Smith.

The tone of my colleague's warning was clear, he assumed that we were to be 'put in our place'. In fact this was not really so, and Professor Graham-Smith proved to be a pleasant, intelligent and considerate man. Being arguably Britain's Number One Astronomer, he was above petty squabbles but alas his colleagues were not. His meeting with us was to warn us that we were going to get some considerable flak from other scientists at the Centre who had made a number of complaints that for the Centre to associate itself with UFOs was a debasement of science generally, and Jodrell Bank specifically. During the course of the day he and I spent some time discussing UFOs and it was clear that while he was above the pettiness of his colleagues he nonetheless shared their opinions.

One of his contentions was that it was significant that no

astronomers had ever reported UFOs. In fact I have never found the point he was trying to make particularly significant, because it pre-supposes an answer to the UFO phenomenon that I doubt is likely. However I listed a few to him: Halley, Croste, DeRostan, Messier mentioned elsewhere, also Astronomer Gruythuisen in 1824, Astronomer Wartmann in 1831, Astronomer Maunder in 1850, Astronomer Carrington in 1859, Radcliff Observatory in 1868, Astronomer Flammarion in 1883 and observations at Zacatecas Observatory the same year, Astronomer Coulon in 1893. And others. He pointed out that these were long ago, that technology had moved on. Rather mischievously I asked what he thought his successors in the year 2200 would be saying about him. He took it in good cheer as I knew he would, but he remained adamant; in the past they hadn't known what was known now.

So I pointed out that there were many modern astronomers who had been involved in UFO work, and in particular Professor J Allen Hynek, a United States astronomer who was internationally recognised as the most important 'ufologist' up to his recent death. Having been engaged by the United States government to 'debunk' UFOs he had become convinced that there was a significant phenomenon to study, and devoted the remainder of his life to this cause. This did not impress Professor Graham-Smith, who made no comment.

However, in the event his warnings to us were very well founded. My colleagues and I met with considerable public popularity at the Centre, too much for the residents. A lecture on the UFO phenomenon was given in the Planetarium on site by author/investigators Jenny Randles and Peter Hough, one standard show having been cancelled. It was a full house, but we found that outside a hoard of people were complaining that they had been unable to get in. The clamouring got louder, and the staff were pretty well forced by public demand to stage a repeat. They could not cancel other planned shows of the Planetarium so they stopped one of the fixed slide show programmes and a repeat lecture was staged there. Still the demand was not sated and in the event the lecture ran twice more. This proved too much for the astronomers; they stopped seeing stars and saw red instead. The public was then treated to the spectacle of a young astronomer loudly berating everyone connected with the UFO groups represented. We were a disgrace to science, we were unscientific, we had no right to be in the Centre, and so on. Hot-headed colleagues of ours joined in the spirit of the 'debate' and loudly listed every failing of astronomers that came to mind, starting with once believing that the Sun went round the Earth and ending with claims that the Apollo moon landings were the result of engineering achievements, not the efforts of astronomers. (Jodrell Bank was proudly displaying an exhibition of the Moon Landings, presumably as evidence of the successes of astronomers.) The astronomers proudly denied that engineers were the driving force, but in a discussion about the difficulties of the Giotto probe to Halley's comet the astronomers blamed the engineers entirely!

I was able to take a back seat on this and enjoy the show; for me the UFO phenomenon is not — at least significantly — an astronomical one and whether or not astronomers had seen UFOs did not mean a lot to me. But their reaction *did* because I am particularly interested in the reaction of people to the phenomenon, and of their perception of it. I was forced to think back to a television debate on UFOs where a protagonist of extra-terrestrial UFO theory — Tim Good — had shared a panel with, and been in discussion with, astronomer Heather Couper, a noted television personality. I recalled that a member of the audience had offered what he believed to be evidence of some UFO experience (some stressed metal coins that he held out to the camera); Ms Couper dismissed it out of hand, denying the man's claims of some tests that had suggested an exotic explanation. I cannot say that the evidence impressed me much, but I was a little shocked by Ms Couper's immediate rejection of it, without apparently any scientific questioning or debate. It seemed, to me, that her usually scientific approach had gone out of the window in the face of this heretic UFO subject. I recalled also that Jenny Randles, a co-director of BUFORA, had reported a television debate with astronomer Patrick Moore where he had shown similar signs of intolerance for the UFO subject, apparently not applying his fine scientific mind when discussing this emotive subject.

The amusing point for me was that it seemed that few ufologists were actually asking for the opinions of astronomers on this highly popular and topical subject and astronomers seemed only able to 'get in on the act' by shouting loudly that there was nothing to shout about.

It is unfair to be too hard on astronomers; they are not in fact reacting to the UFO phenomenon, they are reacting to one popular possible explanation of it — that UFOs are extraterrestrial spaceships — which they find unacceptable basically because of the great distances involved across space. I think such an attitude probably shows a lack of imagination and we shall be looking into the various theories in a later section; however, if they are reacting to this one possible explanation then it must be admitted that we in the field of UFO study suffer from the same problem. Many — and more likely — theories exist to explain what is certainly a genuine phenomenon but as one who is frequently on radio and in the newspapers on this subject, I have found 'ETH' is the only theory that the public seems to want to hear about. And the media, as we have already shown, have not been slow to promote this highly marketable idea.

But if astronomers at the end of the day are going to play no more than a small part in the search for answers, what then of other sciences?

It is likely that many scientific persuasions will be involved and it must be said that already many notable people from many fields have worked on the subject: Stanton T. Friedman in the United States is a nuclear physicist who has worked on nuclear submarines for the US government, world famous psychologist Carl G. Jung published his book on UFOs in 1959, Boston psychiatrist Dr Benjamin Simon spent years on the hypnotic regression of Betty and Barney Hill, the 'first' abductees; lesser famous though none less worthy names have assisted UFO research groups the world over, such as BUFORA, in analysis of physical traces, in examining the so-called 'cornfield circles', various medical people have been involved in hypnosis and regression sessions, people from aerospace technology, radar technology, hosts of other physical sciences have been involved. Many of these people have specifically asked to remain anonymous because of the 'stigma' that the subject can attract through the media; few of these people have any great respect for the 'ETH' theories, but all have recognised that there is a phenomenon worthy of their considerable time and effort.

The UFO research organisations have been accused of not being a scientific discipline, of not approaching the subject scientifically enough. It may be that this criticism is unfair given the involvement of those mentioned above, but even if fair does that make it a bad thing? If UFOs are a physical reality — perhaps other-world spaceships visiting the Earth — then it is probable that only true physical sciences need be involved and that experimentation can be done in strict scientific conditions. But if, as seems likely, there is at least some perceptive, cultural background to the subject then is science the appropriate response? Can science *prove* to us that the Mona Lisa is a masterpiece whereas, say, my own awful attempts with a paint-brush are not; can science *prove* that, say, Sir Ralph Richardson is a better actor than another given thespian; can science *prove* that love exists, even when we all recognise that it does.

In fact, as science understands more so it seems to need to lean towards what was once the unscientific. The chair I am now sitting on to type this article I always thought was made of wood; now I know it is in fact just a mass of whirling electrons. It might be hard to persuade, say, Admiral Lord Nelson, that his ship was also just a mass of electrons; will our descendants sympathise in the future with our difficulty to understand that — for example — telepathy is 'just' the transfer of an electrical impulse (as they might then have discovered). And what will the future say about scientists and their views on UFOs?

In the end, we live in a world that must consider aspects of both what we loosely refer to as the arts and sciences; not one or other of these categories. And while it is right and proper that we encourage experts to study the material we have to hand, let us not rule out the enthusiastic amateur. There is, and has been, a very significant place in research for him; Percy Shaw was no expert on 'cats eyes' when he invented them (obviously, as they previously did not exist) yet his invention is credited with saving many thousands of lives.

Thomas Edison, perhaps the most famous inventor of all, was an amateur in 'phonographs' and electric lights — because there were no experts — yet his insight has benefited the world ever since. The discovery of penicillin was an accident, not the result of scientific research, and so on, and so on. Experts in any field are learned, and have greater knowledge than those outside the field; but they are not necessarily wise people, even clever people, nor are they in any sense infallible. In the medical profession one has only to look at the recent furore surrounding experts in child abuse in British cases of this nature to see fallibility.

This is not to suggest that science and scientists do not have a role to play; if a scientific technique — such as hypnosis — is to be used then it should be used by those expertly trained in its use, but we should not necessarily expect scientists to be able to solve the UFO phenomenon; they have no monopoly on intelligent thought.

When considering science and experts, remember that such experts in a journey of approximately three to four days put a man on the Moon.

In a journey of similar duration experts put the Titanic on the floor of the Atlantic Ocean.

IN THE FOOTSTEPS OF KLAATU

Having examined the role of science in the development of ufology, we might take the opportunity to examine its alter-ego; science fiction.

It must be remembered at the outset of this chapter that the influence of science fiction on UFO claims is not direct. We do not expect, or get, 'real' claims based on films or books recently released. Rather, we expect, and get, a general level of background to claims that can be seen to have been inspired by the overall reinforcement of science fiction themes. With that in mind we can examine the effects that this genre has had on the subject of UFOs.

Science fiction is not new. It is difficult to pin-point a time when science fiction started but some landmarks are obvious. Before the turn of the century Jules Verne had created the Nautilus, an electric submarine which enabled its inventor, Captain Nemo, and his companions to make one of the first voyages to a new world. In this case the new world was under the sea, in 'Twenty Thousand Leagues Under the Sea'.

Before 1900, H G Wells had written 'The Time Machine' (in 1895), depicting a voyage into the future, 'The War of the Worlds' (in 1897) depicting a Martian invasion of Earth, and 'The Invisible Man' in the same year. At the turn of the century he was writing 'The First Men in the Moon'.

It is clear that by this time science fiction literature was already established as a genre, but it would have been the fiction of intellectuals. It took the breakthroughs of the cinema and television to bring science fiction to the majority of people.

The first science fiction films were of course silent, and can reasonably, but arguably, be held to start with Georges Melies 'A Trip to the Moon' in 1902. The first visit to the Earth by an alien would appear to be in Percy Stow's 1908 film 'When the Man in the Moon Seeks a Wife'. 1925 saw perhaps the first really significant science fiction epic, Fritz Lang's 'Metropolis'.

The next decade saw the first real thrust of science fiction; in 1936 Korda's 'Things to Come' was made from H G Wells' publication 'The Shape of Things to Come' with Wells himself writing the screenplay. Like 'Metropolis' before it, this film had as its theme a warning that Man was not conducting his affairs well, and that he would suffer in the long run for the consequences of his actions. The thirties also saw the development of the so-called horror genre, Boris Karloff as Frankenstein's Monster in three films in particular, but the distinction between science fiction and horror blurred quickly — into which would go 1933's 'King Kong', for example?

The thirties may have been most significant for the arrival of the film serial, and it is through these that the most famous 'pure' science fiction found fame. Flash Gordon, in 1936, dealt with evil extra-terrestrials in the form of Emperor Ming the Merciless and his minions from Mongo who were trying to destroy the Earth. Two other serials followed; 'Flash Gordon's Trip to Mars' in 1938 and 'Flash Gordon Conquers the Universe' in 1939. Buster Crabbe, the star of these serials went on, in 1939, to become Buck Rogers. Both these serials left lasting impressions; in fact both have been remade in recent times as films and serials.

Horror rather than sci-fi dominated the forties but again some of the serials were on the theme of evil extra-terrestrials; 1945's 'The Purple Monster Strikes' depicted a Martian who could make himself invisible and take over human bodies.

Up to this time the modern era of UFOs had not been born, coming to the public's attention as it did in 1947 with Kenneth Arnold's sighting. It is important to note what the content of science fiction was in the years before. As we have seen, the early years tended to reflect on Man's handling of his own affairs, extra-terrestrials were not a part of the major scene though curiously one stereotype may have been starting life in the 1929 film 'Mysterious Island'; the inhabitants of an undersea world were short, with rounded bald heads and odd, prominent eyes.

In the serials of the time the extra-terrestrials such as Ming were just 'the bad guys'; their other-world origin really had no significance. These serials were in effect just an updated version of the 'cowboys and Indians' films involving some good guys, some bad guys, and a lot of shooting. With regard to the hardware, Flash Gordon, for example, flew in what amounted to an advanced airplane, shaped something like a squat bullet with fins; the flying saucer had not yet come to the fore.

Science fiction probably never rode higher than in the fifties and it must be remembered that this was after Arnold had created his 'flying saucers' with the help of some media distortion. Suddenly, we had an image of what an extra-terrestrial should travel in; and from then on he did. It kicked off in 1951 with 'The Thing from Another World'; the story of an extra-terrestrial spaceship that crashes into the polar ice and ejects a humanoid alien that later runs amok. All that can be seen of the vessel is a fin sticking up through the ice so the discovering party mark out the shape of the object that they can sec through the ice; they form a perfect circle and one of the team exclaims 'We've found a flying saucer.'

The same year saw the release of 'The Day the Earth Stood Still' the story of Klaatu, a very human-like extra-terrestrial and his robot Gort. They arrive to warn humanity that it must control its use of atomic weapons or forces out in space will destroy us. Having entered the atomic age in Hiroshima in 1945 this was perhaps the most dominant fear of the time — later to arise in the sixties as the Cold War — and it was the theme to which most of the 'real' visiting extra-terrestrials would return to time and time again in the 'contactee' era of Adamski and others. Adamski's book was released shortly afterwards.

1951 is an important year for UFO development in the movies; that year also saw 'The Man from Planet X' who very closely resembled aliens later to be 'photographed' in crash retrievals. He wore a large plexiglass space helmet with various tubes leading from it and some internal lighting, wore a machine on his chest, and he was — true to form — the possessor of a large bald head and almost invisible slit-like mouth. 1951 also produced a serial 'The Flying Disc Man from Mars'.

'War of the Worlds' in 1953 was of course the classic flying saucer invasion from Mars; it is no coincidence that H G Wells' Martians arrived in flying saucers rather than the 'bullet' projectiles he had originally envisaged in 1897; George Pal who made the movie said, 'With all the talk about flying saucers, War of the Worlds had become especially timely. And that was one of the reasons we updated the story.' 1953 also saw 'Invaders from Mars'; a flying saucer had landed and created a secret base from which to abduct humans whose form they could take over. We were leaving Emperor Ming behind, no longer were extra-terrestrials merely alien humans, now they were a race apart, with sinister motives.

1955 saw the release of 'This Island Earth' where an alien fifth column was living amongst us disguised as humans, while getting our best scientists to work out the solution to their planet's problems for them. In America the story became popular that an alien was really working in the Pentagon alongside human confederates.

In the following year the cinema went wild on the subject, no doubt following on from the interest created by the first few 'contactee' books. They took flying saucers as their theme, but not the stories of the contactees. While the contactees were claiming that the aliens were basically friendly, well meaning and beautiful types the films were re-inforcing the idea that aliens were in fact aggressors, with evil intentions against Man and the planet. There was, in that year, 'Earth versus the Flying Saucers', 'Invasion of the Body Snatchers', 'Plan 9 from Outer Space', in addition to a whole host of other 'flying saucer' films of a slightly different type such as the classic 'Forbidden Planet', actually a sci-fi remake of Shakespeare's 'The Tempest'.

1957 continued with 'Invasion of the Saucermen', 'Enemy from Space', 'Not of this Earth'; 1958 saw 'I Married a Monster From Outer Space' and 'It! The Terror From Beyond Space'.

1959 had 'Teenagers From Outer Space' who used classical flying saucers for travel.

The flying saucers they travelled in were clearly copied from the claims of contactees, but the films did not follow their claims; they made aliens an enemy of mankind, not its saviours. Very shortly, the contactees would give way to the abductees, who met aliens that were much more like enemies than friends.

By the time the fifties ended, the cultural reinforcement was firmly in place; aliens from space were hostile, they had a desire to conquer the Earth and to enslave humans. In addition they generally acted like robots, totally devoid of emotion; witness the manner of the aliens-in-human-form in the films 'It Came From Outer Space' and 'Invasion of the Body Snatchers' particularly. In abductions the victims often make the same claims; that their abductors have no emotions, or they offer platitudes without real feeling to make the human subject more controllable. Abductees began to report robot-like aliens, sometimes alongside other creatures.

Against the background of these films, and television series such as 'The Twilight Zone', Betty and Barney Hill made their then-novel claim that they had encountered aliens who were not benign, were unemotional and seemed to have ulterior motives in their actions. Betty and her doctor even have an interesting conversation on this subject:

BETTY 'and I laughed and asked him if he had watched Twilight Zone recently on TV.'
DOCTOR 'Why did you mention Twilight Zone?'
BETTY 'Because the idea was fantastic.'

To some extent, as other sections of this book will show, the science fiction influence on the subject of UFOs may well have done its worst by this time. Having influenced a general perception of extra-terrestrials, and of course *reinforced the assumption that they exist at all*, other forces came into play. In effect the subject which had rolled into the fifties took a turn here, and having taken it, was able to roll on again under its own steam. However, throughout the three decades since, UFOs and science fiction have continued to influence each other, sometimes obviously, and more often subliminally.

Another important aspect must be noted also; science fiction itself took a change of direction as Man reached out into space. In 1957 Sputnik put Man's influence into orbit, by 1961 Man himself was there. By the end of the decade he would leave footprints on the Moon.

The cinema itself was undergoing change; in the fifties the cinema was a social meeting place and almost always crowded. It was usual to go to the cinema regularly, on a given night each week, and see then what was on. Today, the tendency is to see where a particular film is on and go to it, a quite different arrangement. Today, the cinemas are often virtually empty, sufficiently so that an advertising agency has been engaged to boost cinema attendances, while people now stay at home and watch television and videos. So future influences, after the fifties, were likely to come not from the cinema but from the TV and, more recently, video.

In the early sixties, television series in addition to 'Twilight Zone' were coming to the fore. 'The Outer Limits' was very successful with a similar format, and in fact one interesting episode showed actor David McCallum as a man thousands of years ahead on the evolutionary scale. His one particular characteristic was an enlarged bald head.

Several films have actually been on the subject of UFOs; 'UFO' in 1956, 'The UFO Incident' in 1976 (The story of Betty and Barney Hill's abduction), 'Hangar 18' in 1980, the story of a crash-retrieval, and of course 'Close Encounters of the Third Kind' in 1977. These draw from the UFO experience, but of course they also feed back into it, reinforcing the aspects they cover. When the popular American soap opera, 'The Colbys', ended with the UFO abduction of its star, I wondered what the effect would be given that the audience of that programme was one that would not have generally been exposed to the material before. In fact the star was reintroduced to a sister soap opera, 'Dynasty', where her abduction was recalled. Within weeks BUFORA received a call from a woman claiming a genuine abduction which followed, almost exactly, the detail of the programme that had been broadcast the night before.

That case was initially investigated by BUFORA's Jenny

Randles who immediately noticed the connection. Such direct copy-cat claims are very rare, but it must have been an awkward moment; in her recent book 'Abduction' she had stated 'What seems to happen is that science fiction sometimes uses UFO interest after the fact but does not stimulate it.'

In fact it is quite clear from any objective study of the material that science fiction has played a large part in not just stimulating but creating much of the UFO material. It is, however, a subliminal effect. It would be naive to assume that cause and effect would be immediate; the fact that a film comes out in one year should not mean that there is a rush of reports the next year, which in fact rarely happens; what happens is that science fiction in its many forms, but principally films, introduces or reinforces a concept which begins to surface in the claims of witnesses during later periods. A study of the material makes this very clear, following the development of science fiction as we have done, and the development of the UFO claims over the past forty years shows the parallel changes.

One would also not sensibly expect — and nor do we get — a direct correlation between the details of the films or the claims of abductees. It must be remembered that abductions are *real* to the percipients, whatever they are in reality, and the recipient has the task of making sense out of confusing data, and of relaying it to a republic that is sceptical. The self-conditioning process that is undertaken is discussed elsewhere, but suffice to say here that what will happen is that the witness will filter out those obvious details that seem to come from science fiction films, books, etc, or will modify them to a reasonable and acceptable degree in order to be believed, and perhaps to believe it himself. For example the obvious and dramatic interiors of flying saucers are unlikely to be reported shortly after a film comes out; however, there will be a tendency to see those features arise over a long period as they become part of the accepted culture. The most obvious example is glaring for all to see; the interior of Klaatu's spaceship in 'The Day the Earth Stood Still', released in 1951 before anyone had claimed contact with, let alone abduction by, aliens is exactly what later witnesses would claim the interiors of spaceships to be; including the platform couch for medical examinations. That particular detail took a decade to emerge as a claimed fact, however.

Too close a similarity to science fiction would be unlikely, it would be as ridiculous as expecting abduction claims of seeing aliens like Mr Spock just because 'Star Trek' had been televised. In fact Brad Steiger reports that he has received claims of aliens with pointed ears, but generally we don't get such correlation; Spock is, however, a popular character and we would expect him to begin to influence reports. In fact, perhaps he does, almost all aliens are, as we noted earlier, cold and emotionless towards their human victims, just like the fictional Vulcan. Of course he also follows a tradition in fiction in this characteristic, but it is interesting to note that Betty and Barney Hill, in 1961, while describing 'their' aliens as unemotional also described them as reasonably chatty. Later aliens seem to have been much less communicative. Star Trek came out in the late sixties.

One theme that holds reasonably constant through both science fiction and abduction claims is that of humanoid aliens. There have certainly been attempts to produce grotesque, non-humanoid forms such as the 'true form' of the creature in 'It Came From Outer Space', but these were obviously produced from a desire to frighten rather than to be credible. The way that the creature in that film is kept away from long or detailed exposures to the audience until the end is exactly as any suspense horror should do, as the shark was treated in 'Jaws', as the monsters of many pure horror films of the time were treated. Serious attempts to produce a realistic alien invariably ended up being humanoid. There are probably two very down to Earth reasons for that; you can dress up a man in an outfit leaving him basically man-shaped at far less cost than building some complex special effects creation for all shots of a long movie, secondly we think in terms of the human form when we set up fictional situations and non-humans end up appearing limited and weaker than humans because we seem unable to consider a world built for other than humans. As an example look at the most famous of Dr Who's adversaries, the Daleks. They were created specifically because the BBC did not want more 'bug-eyed monsters'. Yet they suffered immediately from limitations; for example the city on their own planet consisted of floors connected by lifts, whereas machine-bound creatures of that shape would have presumably been happier with floors connected by long, slow sloping ramps. Jon Pertwee, who played the Doctor for many years, said he was not greatly impressed with the Daleks because you only had to run up stairs to escape from them. (In fact a recent Dalek episode of the programme, now starring Sylvester McCoy as the Doctor, deliberately set out to challenge this and had a Dalek gliding over a flight of stairs!)

As a curious example of possible interaction of science fiction and UFO claims we can look at a children's puppet show of the early sixties. In a 1962 episode of Fireball XL5, called 'Robert to the Rescue' several factors we are all well aware of from UFO literature were present; the aliens were short creatures with large, bald heads, they could suppress the will of Earthlings and impose amnesiac blocks on them. They could even 'switch off' those they did not want to be involved with their work. Since the material of the Hill encounter had not yet been uncovered and released to the public we can assume that the creators of the puppet show did not draw from that for their imagery. Nor is it possible that the Hills could have drawn off of the programme. More likely, both sources were drawing from earlier, fictional, images of aliens and alien activity, but that such similar claims can arise from 'fact' and fiction suggests a closer interaction than is often suspected.

But more importantly, it does seem impossible to conceive of an alien life form that we could accept as intelligent if it is not humanoid. That is true of sci-fi and abduction claims, generally. Look at the recent films 'Star Wars', where the bar-room scene featured a wide selection of alien life forms, all humanoid, and 'Star Trek 4', where the final court-room scene is similarly decked out. It may be that the only intelligent life forms that do exist are humanoid but it is my suspicion that this is an anthropological assumption on our part. In fact, the humanoid form is rare even on Earth, and it appears that intelligence may exist in some considerable degree in very non-humanoid forms such as dolphins. If that is true on one planet then surely it ought to be true throughout the Universe. It seems almost certain that the dominance of humanoid forms in UFOs is a factor of the same human thinking that produces science fiction.

The Future holds a problem for any realistic investigation of abductions, given the effects of the reinforcement of imagery from films and other literature. In 1987 Whitley Streiber, an American novelist, published his account of his own perceived abduction in the book 'Communion'. That book was an international bestseller and is to result in a film being made from the reported events, much as Betty and Barney Hill's sighting inspired the film 'The UFO Incident'. It is likely to be a successful film and therefore from now on there will be no UFO abduction virgins, over the next few years the stereotype is likely to be reinforced strongly, the stories will first probably rationalise around the 'Communion' theme, then there will be a deliberate drawing away from the detail of that book/film. But such a strong influence, in so direct a way, must forever change the way that we look into cases of abductions in the future. There may be direct copy claims, just as were inspired by the 'Dynasty' programmes, but these will be easily seen for what they are, the subliminal effects will be less easy to spot.

UFOLOGY IN THE USSR

In November 1988 I was one of six British delegates at the International UFO Conference in Brussels, Belgium. Indeed I was honoured to chair one session of the proceedings. The meeting was notable for several matters, in particular that it attracted the first ever Soviet officially invited to give a lecture on the subject of ufology.

Dr Vladimir V Rubtsov is a sociologist; a senior research fellow in the Ukranian Extra-Mural Polytechnic Institute. He holds a PhD in philosophy; his thesis was on the Methodological Aspects of the Problems of Extra-terrestrial Civilization. Indeed 'The Problem of Extra-terrestrial Civilizations' is the title of his recently released book.

I was pleased to obtain an exclusive interview with him and for an hour we discussed Soviet ufology, and its western counterpart, probably the first such interview given. There were few surprises, but some cultural overtones were interesting when we are considering the reality of abductions.

In the USSR the UFO phenomenon is 'new'; however this new cultural aspect is overlaid on the 'old' culture, the folk lore and ancient myths. I explained that it has taken the West forty years to shake off the dominance of the extra-terrestrial myth before we could consider such a parallel. He knew of this, but mischievously reminded me that America was going right back to that subject, as indicated by several of the papers at the Conference. As in the West then, he concluded that UFOs may not be what they seem, but they must be *something.*

I asked about the source data for UFO investigations; in the West it tends to be by local groups picking up reports in newspapers or through press cutting agencies. Of course, individual investigators receive direct calls in addition to this. In BUFORA's case such collected data is then redistributed through the internal network to its field investigators. In the USSR, according to Rubtsov, newspapers do not produce many UFO reports, which is probably a reflection of the newspaper's role in that country. UFO reports are generally made on a personal, or recommended level and therefore there are a good deal less in the Soviet Union than in the countries of the West. 'Such a system is not very effective,' said Rubtsov.

The most major change in Soviet ufology is one we all recognised; that twenty years ago UFOs did not officially exist. One Soviet researcher we knew of, Zeigler, had formed an organisation that had been closed down in two months. The new organisations however are apparently going strong.

With regard to the abduction phenomenon, Rubtsov confirmed that there were such reports in the USSR, though he had not investigated them. He had investigated some CE3 cases. Generally he believes that witnesses are sincere, trying to describe what they are perceiving. In other words, the Soviet view of ufology and abductions is similar to its western counterpart.

However, humanoids appear to be somewhat different in description, and reflect to some degree the 'old' folk tales that are a part of Russian legend. They have the dwarf types, and human sized types, but they have a significant amount of giants, much more rarely found in the West. I felt this confirmed the belief that visiting aliens might not be a part of the phenomenon; it was unlikely that they have a special breed just to visit that continent. Again, to me this reinforced my own belief that we were failing to understand what really lies behind the reports we receive.

There is much less contamination of the subject by the media in the USSR than is found in western countries. There is little science fiction in films as we find in the West, nothing like Star Trek for example. Rubtsov mentioned the film 'Solaris' billed as the Russian 2001; in fact it achieved that title only because of the proximity of release date. In fact it is a film more about the nature of humanity and human thinking, which is typical of most Russian literature, according to Rubtsov.

Russian literature is full of science fiction, much more like that of the West. However, Rubtsov believed that there is no contamination, and cited the fact that many witnesses describe their UFOs and experiences as 'not what they expected from science-fiction'. I pointed out that if witnesses said that then it indicated that they were at least thinking in those terms, and that that was a form of contamination. Rubtsov considered this a valid point.

The conclusion seems clear; a different culture, dependent more on its folk tales than visual images of science fiction, sees the UFO phenomenon in a different light. It was what I had been concluding for some time; there is *something*, but it is not so purely external as to be outside national boundaries and beliefs.

GULF BREEZE — RECORDED EVIDENCE?

In our study of the development of the UFO phenomenon, and particularly our study of the public's perception of it, we have looked very little at photographic cases. The principal reason for this is that few photographic cases have very much merit or much in terms of objective evidence to offer. Isolated photographs are invariably of fairly distant objects and from the point of view of this book's subject matter — UFO abductions — they very rarely feature. There have been one or two spectacular close encounters supported by photographs, the first of which was probably George Adamski's meetings in the 1950s, where he was able to supply photographs of the scout ship flying saucer he had encountered; photographs which have been called in to question ever since. There is of course the celebrated case of Eduard Meier who claimed a repeated series of contacts supported by well in excess of a hundred good photographs of the visiting space crafts. This is explored in Gary Kinder's book 'Light Years', although this event puts Meier more in the place of contactee than abductee.

However, in the United States a most extraordinary photographic case has come to light recently which also includes many abduction features and which may well reveal itself to be a classical American abduction in due course. It is particularly worth looking at this case because there are a number of 'firsts' associated with it:

— it is the first case where an extensive series of apparently distinct photographs supports close encounters and possibly an abduction

— it is a multiple photograph case which is being studied as it happens
— it is a multiple witness case including possibly independent photographers of the same event
— it is the first case of multiple-vehicle photographs of its kind (earlier cases which occurred around the Warminster flap in England in the 1960s have either been belatedly confessed frauds or called into some considerable question by photographic analysis)
— there has been considerable photographic analysis of the Gulf Breeze photographs by American researcher Dr Bruce Maccabee
— modern photographic techniques have been applied for the first time in such a case.

It must be stressed that this report on Gulf Breeze is preliminary since the case is still ongoing and since there is a good deal of information being withheld by the researchers of the case pending as much verification as possible before they release it. I have had sufficient access to this information for me to accept the complexity of the case but I have been asked to respect the privacy of both the investigators and the witnesses involved and I shall do so. What I am summarising is information already made public through the MUFON UFO Journal and I am doing so with the expressed permission of the international director of MUFON, Walt Andrus. Some additional material comes from Walt Andrus's presentation of the case to the 1988 Brussels UFO Conference.

Of the witnesses, Walt Andrus personally interviewed Mr Ed and found him to be 'a conscientious and responsible businessman'.

On November 16th 1987, the witness known as 'Mr Ed' presented five colour Polaroid photographs to the editor of the Florida Sentinel newspaper. The witness had requested anonymity though it appears that this has broken down to some degree in the ensuing months and that his identity is fairly well known, particularly in his locality. However, throughout this chapter we will continue to use his pseudonym. The publication of the story on November 19th inspired the MUFON investigation through its state director for

Florida, Donald M Ware. The investigating team was led by MUFON investigator Charles D Flanagan and Gary A Watson.

It appears that at sundown on November 11th 1987 Mr Ed observed a UFO in the sky which prompted him to take his Polaroid camera and shoot four photographs of the event, apparently within three to four minutes of each other. At this point he ran out of film and there was some delay before he took the fifth photograph. At the time of taking the fifth photograph Mr Ed reveals that when he went into the street to take another picture he suddenly found himself frozen in a blue beam of light; his eyes would not move, he could not breathe properly and felt that he was dying. He was apparently physically lifted off the road by the beam and held by a very strong force. He heard a voice in his head telling him that he would not be harmed. He then received a very bizarre impression; he described it as if he was flipping through the pages of a book showing him pictures of dogs. Suddenly the object and the beam were no longer in sight and Mr Ed fell to the ground from about three feet. According to Mr Ed, his wife helped him pick the Polaroid pictures from the drive and she commented that he was 'reeking with a smell of cinnamon and ammonia'. There is some independent witness corroboration of the encounter. Charles I Somerby and his wife Doris apparently spotted a UFO in the sky at the time of Mr Ed's photographs. Mr Somerby is a former editor of the Sentinel and his wife is the present editor's mother. Their description of the UFO is similar enough to Mr Ed's photographs to suggest that they were looking at the same object.

On the same day a Mrs Zammit apparently saw the blue beam, and reported it on the 20th to the newspaper, in response to the article.

Nine days later, on November 20th in the late afternoon, Mr Ed heard a humming noise which he described as being the same sound as when he was levitated from the road on the earlier encounter. Shortly after this, from his front porch he heard a voice which he could not understand but which he thought might be an African dialect. Then the UFO returned and a computer-like voice instructed Mr Ed to 'step forward'. He took a sixth photograph but heard a command in a voice sounding like Spanish 'Photographs are prohibited'. He ignored this and indeed apparently voiced a comment such as 'The hell they are'. (Walt Andrus tells me that this has been cleaned up for publication and he will not reveal exactly what Mr Ed is believed to have said, due, I think, to Walt's own gentle character. He did point out Mr Ed uses colourful metaphors at the best of times.) Ignoring the warning, he took three more photographs and then received a similar impression to that he had received nine days earlier with the pictures of dogs except this time he seemed to observe a catalogue of atrocious and disgusting nude women. Shortly after this the object disappeared. Mr Ed is unsure how but he believes it began to glow and then took off in a vertical direction. It is interesting to speculate whether this series of images was a response to the words Mr Ed had used when swearing at the object!

Twelve days later, on December 2nd, the humming sound awoke Ed followed by the sound of a baby crying, although there are no babies in this household. Mr Ed apparently overheard a bizarre conversation in Spanish; he decided to investigate with a .38 calibre pistol and his camera. In his backyard he took his tenth photograph of the object hovering approximately 150 to 200 feet beyond his back fence. Approximately half an hour after this Mr Ed believed the object had returned because his dog was barking in an unusual fashion and he got out of bed again and went over to the double french doors leading to his porch. When he opened the curtains he was 'eyeball to eyeball' with an alien creature. Not surprisingly he screamed and fell backwards, waking his wife, who appears to have witnessed at least part of this event. The creature is described as being approximately four feet tall with a shield over its head, chest and lower body. It was apparently holding an illuminated rod in its right hand. After the creature had turned, Mr Ed was able to appreciate that the shields were only across the front of its body and that its actual form was distinctly humanoid. In his own drawing of the creature it is interesting to note that, through the clear visor on the head, the creature's eyes are the large black wraparound eyes frequently observed in American UFO sightings, which had prior to Mr Ed's encounter been made famous on the front cover of Whitley Strieber's book 'Communion'.

The creature apparently ran away and Mr Ed — incredibly — chased it. He was apparently prevented from catching it by a blue beam which 'nailed' his leg to the porch. Regrettably he was unable to photograph the creature but he was able to retrieve his camera and photograph the object again, showing the blue beam shining into the field beyond his house. He speculates that the creature was picked up through the beam in a way not apparently dissimilar to a 'Star Trek' transporter beam.

We have considered elsewhere the influence of science fiction on UFO reports; to my knowledge this is the first time we have a report of something so similar to this particular, fictional, invention although 'influences' that draw objects and people up into overhead UFOs have often been reported in the past.

Three days later Mr Ed observed the object hovering over the field behind his house and photographed it.

Twelve days following that, December 17th, Mr Ed was awakened by a sound like a waterfall. He saw the object again and was able to take his thirteenth photograph. Mr Ed went into the field above which the object had been hovering and recovered a small plastic container filled with a light-green liquid which was actively bubbling and was still doing so during an interview with MUFON investigators twenty one days later. Apparently the sample taken from this liquid stopped bubbling when it had no access to air. The sample was taken by Robert D Boyd for analysis. No conclusions have yet been drawn on this.

Shortly afterwards the object reappeared and Mr Ed took his fourteenth photograph, which he believed showed the object landed or very close to the ground. There is certainly some reflection from its underlights on the ground. Mr Ed in a burst of optimism not to be fulfilled claimed 'The son of a bitch is down. It will be there in the morning and everybody will see it. We've got the whole thing full of aliens'. After about three minutes the object took off flying directly towards Mr Ed who was able to take his fifteenth, sixteenth and seventeenth photographs as it left. A survey of the field found a circle of dead grass which might have indicated a potential landing trace. Investigation of this area will be ongoing but there is no specific reason for the damaged grass known to date.

On December 22nd, five days later, Mr Ed heard the humming sound in his head again and went outside to look for the object but observed nothing. However, there is some suggestion that the object was in the vicinity because a second photographer, using the pseudonym 'Believer Bill', sent photographs to the Gulf Breeze Sentinel of objects similar to those Mr Ed had been photographing.

On December 23rd, the next day, Mr Ed went out of his back door and saw three UFOs hovering over an apartment complex nearby. He took his eighteenth photograph showing all three objects and, as he says, 'As soon as I lowered the camera, the top one brightened and went up faster than I could raise my head to follow it'. A second or so later the other two also flew up and the comment was made that Mr Ed had 'got the impression that they *had waited until he took the picture*'.

Nothing apparently upset the Christmas festivities but on December 27th a family friend who had discussed the events with Mr Ed came to the house in the hopes that he would be present when the object reappeared. When he arrived, Mr Ed's wife said, 'It's here.' The friend walked through to the other side of the house, where he simultaneously observed the object and Mr Ed by his swimming pool. The object, however, disappeared and no photographs were taken. Both Mr Ed and his friend believe that the object reacted to Mr Ed greeting his friend and they have speculated on the object being 'aware' of Mr Ed's thoughts.

On December 28th Mr Ed was sitting on his back porch and observed a glow over a nearby field. It was approaching the house but there was no humming noise present. Mr Ed was out of Polaroid film and so used his Sony Video 8 video camera to take two minutes of video film. However, the object on the video film does not appear to be the same object as has been photographed by the Polaroid.

On the 6th January Mr Ed heard a hum for approximately one minute but observed nothing. I have noted this only because the hum appears to be significant to the case.

On January 12th Mr Ed heard the hum again and called investigator Ware's home with the news, hoping that the investigator could be on the scene during the sighting. Unfortunately, Ware was absent and the phone call was received by his son. Having remembered that he was going to check the power meter installations on one of his buildings which was being prepared for electrical inspection, Mr Ed left his home in his pick-up truck. As he was driving away, he encountered the object hovering close to the road; it instantly blasted him with a white beam, paralysing his fore-arms and hands. He apparently managed to ease the truck off of the road, to a position where he could watch the object. Very quickly, the object closed to approximately 180 feet of the truck, and after some discomfort Mr Ed was able to take his nineteenth photograph of the object through the truck windshield. The object apparently brightened up, took off and came towards him and Mr Ed, apparently still semi-paralysed, attempted to crawl under the pick-up truck for protection from the light beam. However, before he could get completely under cover the beam struck his legs, making it difficult for him to move. From underneath the truck he tried to take another picture but it showed only the tyre when it was developed. Mr Ed watched the object rotate and the blue beam deposited five aliens on the road all wearing shields and carrying a glowing rod, similar to the creature encountered on his porch. (Confirming the 'Star Trek' transporter beam analogy?) The thought came to his mind 'if they can't get me with the white beams, they are sending aliens after me'. Now very frightened, Mr Ed crawled out from under the truck and got inside it and was able to drive off and escape any further encounter.

On January 13th Mr Ed was apparently confronted by two men in civilian suits at his front door demanding he hand over the photographs of the UFOs on the grounds that 'it is against the law to withhold them'. Apparently the men left empty handed and have not been identified.

Four days after the previous incident, on January 16th, Mr Ed was awoken by a soft hum and he took his camera to his front drive where he saw a UFO again although this particular object was different in appearance to the very similar one that had been photographed nineteen times already, as this twentieth photograph shows.

MUFON investigators set about a walkie-talkie radio stake-out whenever they could to be in on the event when the object returned. Mr Ed, it was agreed, would call in on his walkie-talkie whenever he heard the humming sound in his head which, whatever its reason, *seemed to be a forewarning of an encounter.*

Five days later, on January 21st, Mr Ed heard the hum and saw the object briefly but neither he nor investigator Bob Reid could photograph the object. The object had left before Bob Reid had been able to observe it. This has again led to speculation that the object 'knew' someone else might see it and removed itself in time.

Three days later, on January 24th, Mr Ed heard the humming sound and called on his walkie-talkie. Unfortunately there was no response and so he drove to the Sentinel newspaper offices and was accompanied by Duane Cook, the editor of the paper, and his friend Dari. Duane Cook is the son of Mrs Somerby, who had witnessed a similar event the previous November. They had video equipment with them in Mr Ed's truck, and Dari followed in her own car. Mr Ed apparently described the humming feeling to Mr Cook as very strong and 'pulling his face off'. It seemed that the aliens were desperate to get him out of the truck and were trying to communicate with him. Mr Ed appears to have been distressed at this time, eager to confront whatever it was and 'get it over with'.

Mr Ed apparently got out of the truck, writhing in pain. There was an unfortunate missed opportunity here because the object did appear and Mr Ed was able to take his twenty-first photograph of the object over the top of his truck. However, Duane Cook was videotaping Mr Ed at this moment and was not able to see the UFO which departed immediately after Mr Ed had taken the picture. Mr Cook's attempts to video the object failed, and all he filmed was the flash of the polaroid going off. There is therefore little corroborative evidence here, though Duane Cook was a witness to the photograph apparently being taken.

On January 26th 1988 at approximately 8 p.m., Mr Ed's

wife observed the UFO and called for Mr Ed to join her. He did this although he came from the shower and in a photograph taken is seen with his towel wrapped around him. He is in fact clenching his fists and waving at the object in desperation for it to 'get out of my life'. The other photograph taken at this time shows the dog next to their swimming pool apparently not reacting to the object.

On February 7th 1988 a blue beam appeared near Mr Ed's wife who was feeding their dog in the backyard. She called for Ed to come out who didn't hear her and therefore their daughter had to call again. Ed ran to the kitchen door with his camera but his exit from the house was blocked by another blue beam apparently trying to prevent him moving. Ed photographed the blue beam from his kitchen window though this photograph has never been released since it clearly shows his wife and he does not wish her to be identified. However, the principal investigators of the case were shown the photograph.

During February 1988 Mr Ed underwent a lie detector test, the outcome of which was that the examiner decided Mr Ed 'truly believes that the photographs and personal sightings he has described are true and factual to the best of his ability'.

Since the case was clearly a photographic case, emphasis was placed on photographic evidence and some tests set up. MUFON supplied Mr Ed with a special 3-D Nimslo camera which has four lenses and was sealed by the MUFON investigators. Mr Ed took ten photographs of the object with this which MUFON believe helped to verify his claim.

At the suggestion of Dr Bruce Maccabee, the chairman of the fund for UFO research and a photo analysis consultant of MUFON, a series of stereo photographs were taken. Polaroid cameras were attached to a fixed wooden slat two feet apart and between them a long broom handle with a nail in the end was extended so that each time the photographs were taken there would be two pictures slightly offset, both giving some points of reference from the broom and the nail. It is understood that Dr Maccabee has spent hundreds of hours in his study of this case and its photographs.

Several stereo photographs have been taken, and seem to indicate the presence of a physical object of some kind. The first of these stereo photographs was taken on the 17th March, 1988; from this Dr Maccabee believes the object photographed in this case was at least 130 feet from the camera, giving a suggestion of considerable size. The second stereo photograph was taken on the 20th March and the series continued for some months, until May when Mr Ed seemed to lose the ability to 'know' when a sighting was due. We shall look at this in due course. The two polaroid cameras have their limitations when photographing a moving object, however, as they have to be 'fired' separately which could cause some inaccuracy in judging size and distance if the exact speed and direction of the object is not known.

On 28th April an independent witness, Truman Holcomb, reported seeing an object similar to that reported by Mr Ed, hovering over Highway 98, only half a mile from Mr Ed's lonely road encounter of January the 12th. The blue beam was in evidence, and dogs in the vicinity seemed to be upset. Mr Holcomb also offered some corroboration of that earlier sighting; he said he had suffered TV interference on the 12th of January.

At this point we must record that there is considerable controversy about Mr Ed's experiences within the United States, where 'for' and 'against' views are polarizing UFO groups. Although they have not said so specifically (rightly, as the case is uncompleted) it is apparent that MUFON and international director Walt Andrus strongly favour the view that the case is a genuine one and that the photographs are not faked. On the other hand, Dr Willy Smith has circularised his views on the case, and believes he can demonstrate that the photographs are faked. Smith believes that only two interpretations of the case are possible: that 'we have a genuine UFO occurrence, substantiated by a large number of photographs, or ... it is a very elaborate hoax perpetrated for financial gain or motivated by intellectual arrogance.'

Smith believes that the case 'will stand or fall on the merits of the photos themselves.'

Using only the first five photographs, Smith believes that analysis of them leads to the belief that cloud movement and direction do not match the claims made for the pictures, that the length of time taken to make the photographs is incorrect.

On the basis of his considerable scientific analysis he concludes that 'it is evident that (Mr Ed) has lied' and that 'the credibility of the witness and the belief in the genuineness of the photos have evaporated, and only a great deal of wishful thinking may preserve the illusion that the Gulf Breeze sightings reflect real events.'

Smith later expresses further doubts of the photographs taken on January 26th, in which he believes that Mr Ed's body language expressed in the photographs is inconsistent with his claims of anger and frustration.

On May 1st 1988 what is possibly the most significant event took place. At 1 a.m., Mr Ed heard the familiar hum in his head as he sat in his pick-up truck and he immediately used his cameras to take simultaneous photographs of the UFO. While trying to take a second set of photographs he was hit by a white beam and remembers falling, but not hitting the ground. He seems to have come round at approximately half past two, leaving speculation that there may have been over an hour of missing time. What is being discussed is the possibility that Mr Ed has been abducted. He states that he suspects he may have also been abducted three times earlier in his life. He recalls an incident when he was sixteen when he saw a strange bald man with big eyes beside his bed. It is speculated that it was perhaps then that the implant was inserted into Mr Ed's head.

The suggestion is that the 1st May abduction was to withdraw his capability to hear the hum, presumably by removing the implant. Walt Andrus suggested to me that this could be because 'they' felt there was some danger of exposure as MUFON 'got closer' to the truth.

Since May 1st 1988, Mr Ed has not had any further experiences nor seen any other UFOs although they are continuing to be reported by other witnesses in the area. At the time of writing there have been hypnotic regression sessions but details from these are being kept confidential and it is understood that Mr Ed and his wife will be publishing a book on their experience, provisionally entitled 'UFOs: Proof Positive'.

Budd Hopkins, who visited Gulf Breeze in February 1988 is quoted in the 'Sentinel' as endorsing the sightings as authentic.

The MUFON summary to date on this case is as follows:

'Many of Ed's UFO experiences and photographic sessions seemed to have been 'programmed' by some intelligence source for an express purpose known only to 'them'. Why was a successful businessman selected to be exposed to these traumatic experiences, which disrupted the lives of his entire family? One can only speculate! As UFO investigators and researchers, we are continuing to probe for the answers, since it seems highly probable that an implant was placed in Ed's head on or before November 11, 1987.'

The antagonism between organisations and individuals caused by this case is apparent from reading of related material by all parties, and from discussions I have had with, particularly, Dr Willy Smith and Walt Andrus. This is a pity but seems to be a fact of UFO research and leads to some speculation that individual belief systems, rather than science, are being challenged. Other cases have caused the same furor in the past, though photographic evidence seems to be a favoured 'boxing ring'. And, it has to be admitted, I have seen more such disagreement in UK ufology than anywhere else in the world, so America — for once — is not leading this particular field!

Of the case itself, I do not propose a further analysis — nor to enter the boxing ring! — and if it turns out to be a hoax then, despite the elaborate mechanisms necessary to have set it up, it will have been simplistic in terms of data 'revealed'. On the other hand if it turns out to be genuine then it seems to me that it further challenges the assumption of a prosaic, extra-terrestrial, visitation. As with the other cases we have looked at in this book, and the wealth of other data on the subject, it seems to me that the objections raised by this case suggest that whatever lies behind this mystery it is not what we think, and it will require a different perspective before it is understood. Any answer to this case, where an extra-terrestrial visitation is believed to be *understood* must answer the following questions:

— why does the first instruction to the principal witness, 'Photographs are prohibited', lead to one of the most photographed cases in the literature, including video, stereo and 3–D photography?

— why does a visitation that implies a desire for secrecy, for example disappearing when certain other witnesses appear, start by implanting a device in the witness's head to give him sufficient warning of a sighting to allow him to call more witnesses, to get his camera ready, and to generally prepare for the event? At the same time it seems to do nothing *with* Mr Ed except wait around to be photographed like a Hollywood starlet seeking publicity?

— at the time when Duane Cook just missed seeing the object but Mr Ed managed to photograph it, the inference seems to be that it was waiting for the right moment to quickly appear, then disappear again. Why, then, does Mr Ed seem to have been selected for what — as we have considered before in the Kathie Davis case — seems to be more in the nature of a *haunting*?

THE NEXT FRAUD

In considering the history of UFO reports and UFO–related entities, we have to accept that there have been many frauds perpetrated on the public and the 'UFO community' alike. Some of these are proven frauds, some of them are belatedly self-confessed frauds but the largest percentage are suspected frauds.

We can learn much from these and it is a worthwhile exercise for us to consider the ideal environment for a fraud. Thus we can not only be forewarned of one developing but also possibly stay the hand of would-be perpetrators. There again, frauds give us some insight into the way 'outsiders' perceive the subject.

The first criteria for anyone seeking to commit fraud must be motive and the question of motive in UFO reporting is a complex one. Even considering someone who has experienced, or believes they have experienced, a genuine UFO encounter, the reasons why they bring that encounter to the public's attention are complex, and sometimes difficult to understand. Quite often they become shunned by family and friends; their jobs or careers may suffer and their standing in the immediate community can fall in the estimation of their peers. It would certainly be simplistic to suggest that a case which exhibited these characteristics was necessarily true merely for those reasons, but clearly the absence of a positive motive and the presence of negative factors gives the researcher room for comfort. I would stress that such a view may be *too* simplistic, for it would not even answer the question of why the fire and ambulance services receive false alarm calls; the perpetrators of these hoaxes do not gain material benefits or any kind of standing in the local community, they cannot broadcast their achievements and they cannot argue even a dubiously worthwhile result from their actions. Yet the world's accident and emergency services are constantly plagued by this drain on their resources and manpower. However, for the purposes of our ideal scenario we must assume that a fraudster will require a positive motive.

The two most obvious motives are fame and fortune. If the reported UFO abduction case becomes extremely famous then perhaps the satisfaction of reading about your actions for the next 40 years in a series of books published all over the world is motive enough for a fraud. We must consider therefore that our ideal hoax should result in some kind of fame, and the events related should be of a nature to produce such a result.

Fortune is by far the most obvious and easily defined motive. There is little complexity to understand behind a fraud for financial gain. In our ideal fraud, therefore, we might expect the events related to result in personal financial gain for the perpetrator. Generally speaking, the UFO field does not easily lend itself to this kind of financial reward on a regular basis as individual claims tend to be dealt with by the investigators and researchers as part of an overall work, and it is rare for scientific or pseudo-scientific publications in this field to make substantial profits. There have of course been exceptions since the 1940s.

Having narrowed down our motives to the achievement of fame and the acquisition of money, we should now examine whether or not the UFO community lends itself to fraud *at all.* The first rule of the con-man is that the job is half done if the con is perpetrated on someone who *wants to be conned.* Does this apply in the UFO community? The answer must be an emphatic 'yes'. Unfortunately this community is riddled with investigators and researchers of low standards who will accept on face value some of the most bizarre and improbable stories without corroboration. There are those who have such set belief-systems that even when cases are brought to them which do not appear to relate to their particular beliefs, they somehow seem to work the case into their predetermined conclusions. There are also those investigators and researchers who are envious of the high profile of others, and are just waiting for that one special case which will elevate them to the same status. Their search for that case can be unscientific, to say the least. One such investigator I know of 'solves' the whole UFO phenomenon each year, always with a new theory. One 'fad' included explaining *all* events — of whatever complexity — as misunderstood sightings of stars. In some cases he was prepared to reclassify as star sightings cases which occurred decades ago, even admitting that he could not name a particular star which might have caused it!

In short, if there was ever a collective group of people waiting to be conned it is the UFO community. I think it could even be argued that there is no one group of subjects *more* prone to this pitfall.

So we have our motives and we have our target audience; what then of the details?

Firstly, the timing of the fraud is all important. UFO publicity goes in waves and troughs, often unpredictably. However, some of the peaks of publicity *are* predictable; the next predictable peak from the current time will be June 1997, the fiftieth anniversary of the Kenneth Arnold sighting which heralded the modern era of UFOs. We might therefore assume that a spectacular fraud will be timed to coincide with the publicity building up to and through that period.

Secondly, in order that the fraudster can get his revelations to the public with a maximum impact (and therefore amass for himself the maximum profit) he will have to make the claim that his experiences are recent to the date of publication. To say that these things have been occurring for many years would evoke too many awkward questions about why those in the UFO community had not been approached; of course were they so approached, then there would be a danger that the story might leak out through in-house UFO publications and the impact of the revelation would be lost. We might therefore assume that the first reported event in the fraudster's calendar would be within just two or three years of the date of public release.

Before we look at the likely details of the fraud we should also examine what is likely to be the response from the UFO community, as their reaction may or may not play a significant part in the success or failure of the fraud. Quite simply, members of the UFO community will have their own axe to grind and will seek either to confirm the reports or to condemn them as fraud. What is important to note is that if the fraud is going to be exposed, it would be exposed by them and we may assume that the first act of a potential fraudster will be to seek to alienate and condemn the UFO community, and to prevent them from in-depth investigation. He will claim that their standards are inadequate, that he does not wish to be examined by them because they are not treating him with the proper care and respect. At all costs, the UFO community must be seen to be at odds with the fraudster for two reasons; firstly it will keep distance from the fraudster and prevent the likelihood of his fraud being exposed, secondly it will mean that if the fraud is exposed, he can round on the community through the media and claim he has been victimised because of the alienation between them. If he is clever he will make the antagonism appear to come from the UFO community itself; in fact this rarely ever happens because even fraudsters are a part of the UFO phenomenon, and researchers take into account the claims of fraudsters, not always because they believe them but because it is interesting to get an outside view of public perception of the phenomenon. In short, almost everybody involved in the subject is of interest for various reasons; however, our fraudster will not appreciate many of those reasons and will seek to 'hit back first'. This point should be considered with caution however; as this book has shown, 'real' abductees have good reason to be wary of the UFO community's treatment of them.

Having put together our motives, our target audience, and our broad plan of action, we must bear in mind that the ultimate aim of the fraud is to get the details to as large a percentage of the public as possible at as high a cost as possible, in order to make the maximum potential gain in both fame and fortune. Clearly, the media are available and will be targeted; newspaper articles, magazine articles, the publication of a book or books, even the production of a television series or film will be sought and ultimately perhaps — and particularly in America — a revolutionary twist which we shall come to later. We must therefore assume that our fraudster's revelation will be made in all the media forms, and in order to be so they must attract the attention in the first place not of the public but of the editors and others responsible for publication. To do this the details must be reasonably commensurate with existing knowledge, but must also be unique and revolutionary in their presentation.

Ground rules for our fraudster to follow then:

The events related should be dramatic, possibly humurous, possibly frightening, certainly never dull, and if maximum attention is sought then they should contain at least some sexual overtones. The past years of UFO reports have provided a glut of all these and so constructing a story out of known facts with one or two updates should not be difficult for an accomplished fraudster with a lively intelligent mind.

There are certain stereotypes in the UFO world which have become a 'bore' to the public and from our fraudster's point of view anything which turns off the public is going to reduce his fame and fortune. The two areas which simultaneously excite and bore the public most are the mention of UFOs themselves and of aliens, both of which are too closely associated with science fiction to be taken seriously. We might therefore assume our fraudster will not mention UFOs but will nonetheless imply their intervention in order to be a part of the UFO fraud; if this cannot be avoided then the mention of UFOs and space ships from other worlds should be reduced to an absolute minimum. The public recipient of the fraud should be left with the impression of UFOs and aliens from other planets without actually having it laboriously mentioned time and time again throughout the narrative. The second area of concern is that relating to 'alien visitors from other planets' and it would be best to avoid this at all costs. If it is quite apparent that we are in fact talking about just that subject, then again it must be inferred by implication rather than outright statement and we might expect our fraudster to refer to them by a more oblique term, perhaps entity, perhaps haunting, perhaps a vision (this may give a religious overtone which could be useful, as we shall see later), perhaps invader, etc., etc. At all costs, our fraudster will avoid the term aliens, humanoids, UFO occupants, etc.

The next ideal situation would be a dramatic series of photographs. This, however, has its dangers, as photographs enable the recipients of the story to — in effect — put themselves in the witness's place at the appropriate time and share the event. In short, here is the potential for a fraud to be exposed and, indeed, photographic evidence is some of the most controversial in the UFO field. Consider the controversy that is raging in America over the Gulf Breeze case. Also, constructing an elaborate photographic hoax involves enormous skills and/or enormous cost. It also means that others have to be involved who could later 'come clean' and give the whole game away. The fraudster will undoubtedly seek to keep the revelations solely his experience. There is also the more likely possibility that in constructing an elaborate fraud, it will be discovered by someone else. On balance therefore, it is likely that our fraudster will avoid photographic evidence entirely, possibly even covering this point by stating that he tried to take photographs but they would not come out or simply that the experience was of a nature which does not lend itself to being photographed. Since most of the media forms that we have discussed will require some kind of visual support, the fraudster will have to rely on a good artist's impression and certainly there have been many cases in UFO history where this has been considered quite acceptable.

Our fraudster will need a good anti-hero in the same way as any good fiction or plot. Presumably this will be the alien (by whatever name) and again he will have to be compatible with existing knowledge but just that bit different. This is of course not difficult for anyone with a good imagination and flair for conning (what the Irish call the gift of the blarney). Since there are no definitive forms of alien known to all, any description could be acceptable and the fraudster has an open field here to create exactly what he wants to best feed the media and public desire.

Let us assume that our fraudster is successful and achieves great fame and fortune by the publication of his fraudulent story. Where do we go from there? Undoubtedly he will find himself on a 'media circus', promoting the various forms of publication or entertainment that the story has generated. He will also find himself continually invited to different UFO congresses and conventions throughout the world, if only because the people he has alienated want to throw intellectual tomatoes at him! If our fraudster is of the highest calibre he will see the potential here for the greatest fraud of all. In outlining this we must assume that the fraud is perpetrated in America, which is not an unreasonable assumption as the vast majority of major UFO reports have come from the U.S.A. Indeed it is worth noting that all the major contactee reports had their origins in America; in fact, generally in California.

If there is one sure-fire way to print money in America in a big way, it is to *start a church.* This is not the place to discuss the different motives of those who have started 'alternative churches' in America but certainly some of them have come in for considerable criticism throughout the world, from inside and outside the theological community, and particularly where the church itself, and the main originators, have amassed enormous wealth. However, starting a new church is not necessarily an easy task. Firstly, one needs a God or, if not a God, then a God substitute. Possibly our alien (by whatever name) would do as the God substitute, not in the sense that the 'church' be designed to worship him but merely to honour him or, perhaps as a new religion, merely to join with him. In our fraud we may have the necessary elements already laid down and our fraudster may pick up on these.

Having got our God substitute we obviously have our first congregation; members of the UFO community, disillusioned and otherwise, together with the other people who have been involved in similar stories to that the fraudster has concocted. If enough money and publicity has been generated then the Message can be spread throughout America and the rest of the world, and the church could become a substantial force. It is difficult to perceive exactly how the conversion will be made from what is in effect merely another UFO abduction report to the setting up of a church, but these outlining principles are far from inconceivable and we should watch for such developments if such a fraud is to become apparent in the future. One major clue we might look for is that again the UFO community will have to be alienated and the principals of the church, mainly our fraudster, would make clear that membership of the church would be restricted to those who have the right positive attitudes towards the God-substitute. Scientific analysis is hardly likely to be considered a right attitude!

This chapter is an interesting intellectual exercise, but it also serves a purpose; as we stated at the beginning, it may help to spot a fraud developing, and it may also help to stay the hand of would be perpetrators who will be aware that there are those within the UFO community who are not perhaps so gullible and ready to be conned as others. In the end our examination and elimination of such frauds has one aim; to sift out those experiences which are genuine or perceived to be genuine, and which are legitimate areas for study in attempting to understand what may be a complex and novel human experience. Hoaxes and frauds, particularly extravagantly successful ones, make this difficult in many ways. Not only do the frauds become incorporated into the literature, where it becomes difficult to make proper comparisons of reports without occasionally stumbling across them, possibly unknowingly so, but it also feeds the public perception of events which tends to dilute and confuse the understanding of true events. Worse still, a successful fraud will encourage others, and as at least some of these are exposed, so the credibility of the subject and those involved in it is reduced.

Only if the UFO phenomenon *is* a complex mythology developing in the light of modern high-tech communications will these frauds be valid, as they will be a part of the overall 'fiction' that we seek to understand. Since the whole truth is likely to be even more complex, these frauds should be exposed and weeded out to prevent a reality *becoming* a mythology.

PART SIX

The Alternatives

The universe is not only stranger than we imagine
but stranger than we can imagine

JOHN BURDON SANDERSON HALDANE

ALIEN – BUT HOW ALIEN?

We have shown earlier that the popular, indeed overwhelmingly popular, theory that UFOs are alien spacecraft visiting the Earth seems to be fulfilling one of Man's basic needs. It was prematurely assumed; clearly even at the time of the rather routine Arnold sighting, the world was waiting for this very explanation.

Certainly, the internal logic of these claims simply does not hold water as I detailed earlier; and it is, I stress again, not sufficient to argue that 'we cannot understand or expect to understand alien logic' — the point of the assertions of many of the UFO investigators, particularly in the United States, is that they *do* claim to have understood that logic.

Fulfilling such a need does not, of course, mean that the assumption cannot be true, but an objective look at the evidence presented suggests that it is not. The direct testimonial evidence; the claims of the contactees that they met people who told them — or proved to them — that they were aliens visiting Earth, are the clearest examples of fulfilling the individual need of some people to have what Andy Warhol described as their fifteen minutes of fame; it puts them at the centre of attention, it makes them more special than their fellow Man. Perhaps they were not consciously lying, they may well have experienced something which they were trying to rationalise; but we have had thirty-five years or more since the first claims and little of the material presented has held together.

The claims of the abductees seem different, in that at face value they don't appear to be fulfilling individual needs — rather they contain the substance of the worst nightmares —

yet even that may be simplistic. To put it crudely, the difference between the contactees and the abductees may be only that some people have a need to be God, while others have a need to be whipped.

All of this leads to a *totally* psychological theory to explain UFOs, indeed to explain *away* UFOs. Such an explanation is possible, and we shall look at it shortly. However, the dominance of the standard UFO theory known as the Extraterrestrial hypothesis, and its internal absurdity, may have channelled us towards thinking that only these two quite opposite theories could explain the evidence. In fact there are a whole range of alternative possibilities to these which simply do not get exposure; some of these are detailed below.

It must be stressed that there is little in the way of hard evidence for these claims; and they are not presented here as alternative *solutions*, which would simply be to replace one wacky theory with another. They are presented merely as alternative possibilities to be considered in redressing the balance that has been lost in our dependence on this one fairly ludicrous ET theory. They have the advantage in some cases of answering legitimate arguments that have been put forward.

We have considered — ad nauseam — the standard theory; that alien humanoids travel across the galaxy, perhaps even between galaxies, in physical spaceships in a way not unlike our astronauts travel between Earth and the Moon. They visit the Earth for precisely the same reason that we visit the Moon and will one day make the journey to other planets: to examine any local flora and fauna, possibly to take from it something they want. It is the theory basically put forward by investigators in the United States; it is also the story line of many of the early 1950s and 1960s science fiction films. What, then, are the alternatives?

Firstly, consider the objection put forward by astronomers, that the distances involved are so vast that we will *never* be able to cross them, and nor will any other technology. I must say at this point that I find that almost impossible to accept and have only a limited faith in experts at the best of times; it seems to me that we have never been able to predict future changes of technology on any grand scale. Could the seafarers of earlier centuries have even conceived of space travel, could our cave dwelling ancestors be convinced of the likelihood of television and radio, etc. etc? There is certainly a basic human need to reach out across the galaxy, and possibly it exists in alien species; such a need is usually met not by advancing technology but by changing it. If we had suggested to our early seafaring ancestors that we wished to go around the world in ninety minutes they would not have suggested we use a spaceship — they would have suggested that the fastest ship could not do it, that no such ship could ever be built, therefore the premise was impossible. We did not build a faster clipper ship, we changed our technology altogether. In an example literally closer to home there were practical limits at the speed we could cook using standard ovens; any suggestion a few years ago that we would be able to cook joints of meat in a few minutes would have been ridiculed. In fact now we can — in the microwave — but this is not an advanced version of a standard oven, it is a different technology. One thing is certain, when the day comes and Man sets off between galaxies in a 'whatever-super-form-of-technology' there will be no shortage of experts and scientists to tell us how such a circumstance was, after all, only logical when you look at it (in hindsight!)

However, for the purpose of this argument let us assume that these objections are correct, or at least that the aliens who presently want to contact us have not yet reached that stage of technology. Do they give up, or do they think of a different form of contact?

Do they in fact send us some form of message? In effect, saying 'Hi there, we the people of wherever would like to introduce ourselves to you the people of Earth'. *We* have certainly done just that thing; directing radio transmissions to the stars, both deliberately and by the natural leakage of emissions from the planet. We know how we would receive those messages were they beamed at us; we would align our radio telescopes to their source and decode the transmissions. But a truly alien form may not have the same physical or technological development. Perhaps our radio transmissions would be received directly into the senses of the people themselves, possibly as a voice from afar in the way Joan of Arc and many others are commonly depicted as hearing voices. The point, to reverse the suggestion, is what if some alien species, unable or unwilling to visit Earth, is sending out its 'radio waves' and particular human receivers who happen to be 'tuned in' (a wonderful expression we can borrow from the 1960s) are hearing them.

If that is the case they why do these messages when decoded by the human receivers appear to be the plots of cheap science fiction thrillers? Three reasons explain this:

— our science fiction culture may have developed because our minds are subliminally filled with these thoughts; in short we are using their messages as the basis of our plots.

This seems relatively unlikely since it presupposes that the message sent is one of threatening invasion.

— in trying to find a common ground for communication, the aliens have decoded our television and film transmissions and are seeking to talk to us in a way that we will comprehend; talking to us at our level. This also falls short on at least two grounds; firstly because again such messages could hardly be considered friendly given the nature of much of our science fiction, and secondly because our earliest transmissions would not yet have reached very far from the Earth in astronomical terms and this would severely limit the range of potential responses. If a race from further away could get a probe to the area to listen in, then presumably it could physically fly the rest of the way and say hello in person, should it wish to do so.

— thirdly, and of these suggestions the most likely in my view, the nature of the message is simply very alien and we do not understand it; we do not know how to decode it, and what happens is that we try to fit it into the frame of reference we have. Since our culture as a species is one of violence we interpret it as a threat of sorts, and since in the First World at least we have a considerable influence of science fiction in many forms, perhaps we choose 'alien invasion' as our frame of reference. In fact the message may be quite different to anything we could suspect, but the human mind will always seek to find a translation from within itself. The contactee translations would reflect — as they did reflect — the concerns of the time about the environment and the atomic bomb, the abductee translations may reflect the individual concerns of the human receiver; kidnapping is a very basic human fear, rape is a very basic human fear, etc. And other 'translations' not held to be within our sphere — divine revelation, hauntings, poltergeist phenomena, automatic writing, etc., may be other, different translations of the same basic message according to the predisposition of the human receiver.

Such a theory has a lot going for it; it would explain why there is little consistency between *types* of UFO reports; we have radar reports and yet we rarely have an instance of a craft bent on abduction being tracked on radar; it seems that they come from a different set of data. Similarly we have craft that appear to sit by the sides of busy roads for hours on end and be seen by no-one except the abductee.

In February 1973 a case occurred that highlighted this point; a Mrs Maureen Puddy reported encounter events on the Mooraduc Road in Australia; they were investigated by Paul Norman and Judith Magee of the Victoria UFO Research Society. Norman and Magee met Mrs Puddy at the encounter location and sat with her in her car, discussing the case. Suddenly Mrs Puddy announced that the alien was *there*, walking towards them. She became visibly agitated, crying physical tears, and needed to be calmed. Norman got out of the car and stood where Mrs Puddy said the alien was; she told him that the alien had ducked back to let him pass! Norman and Magee saw nothing, yet they were equally clear that they did not think Mrs Puddy was lying. It seems she genuinely saw the alien, but in what way, at what level?

A further point; within the claims of the abductees we have very inconsistent material both between different claims and even within single claims; this is not easily explained within a physical visitation but it would be quite typical of a lot of confused people trying to sort out the meaning of this strange message they are receiving.

It would also explain why investigators do not accidentally stumble on other phenomena; why past-life investigators do not uncover UFO encounters, why UFO investigators do not uncover ghost hauntings; it would simply mean that some individuals translate this same message in this way because it is in their nature to do so; having sought out a particular type of investigator would be an indication of the structure of their thinking.

However, attractive — and possible — though this theory is, let us not be drawn into thinking this is The New Answer; this subject has regretfully abounded with the claims of people whose personal theories have been put forward as facts; I suggest this merely as another Question. Another possibility to consider.

Secondly, let us consider the above theory in a slightly new light; suppose that intelligence on Earth is not what we understand it to be — or think we understand it to be. Suppose that our own intelligence is uniquely human and that there are other intelligences, not more or less advanced than we are, but simply so different as to be alien. Not alien to the Earth, but alien to humanity.

For want of examples rather than as definitive suggestions consider the thinking processes of either ants or dolphins. In the former case we know that their society is at least as well structured as our own, if not better so. In the latter case we believe that dolphins are of high intelligence, though clearly their life style is very different from land creatures such as ants or humans, which we determine is because of the limitation placed on them by their aquatic existence. But suppose they are of this different — alien — intelligence? Might they not recognise the possibility that we too are of a dissimilar intelligence and might they not want to say hello, particularly as they share the Earth with us? What method would they use? Possibly exactly the same method as the one first described — a message that is received by different humans in different ways. In this case their problem is not that they cannot cross the gulf of Space, but rather that they are unable to cross the gulf of Mind. After that, the theory and its objections follow as before.

Thirdly, and a second alternative to the above two, is the possibility that there is a race unknown to us with which we share the Earth but which also wishes to 'say hello'. Again the same pros and cons are on offer. This suggestion has the advantage of explaining a long human history of other beings; the 'little people' of the Irish folklore, fairies, gnomes, elves etc. Perhaps they are simply a different race we have yet to properly discover, and one that is less than happy with our own social structure and our own interpretation of their message.

These above theories all have one thing in common which may seem to be flawed thinking on my part — they all assume *intention* on the part of some race. It is entirely possible that we are interpreting something not meant for us, something which does not recognise our existence. But I have ignored that for the time being, as this forms the basis of a later chapter.

Another possibility is that the messages, or even the visitations in some form, are from Earth's distant past or future. Certainly our own race, whatever it once was or one day will be, has a vested interest in what we get up to in the present time. This suggestion falls down in the main not for lack of evidence, but for lack of testimony — it probably is not the answer simply because few claim that it is.

However, there have been alien claims about their own ability to manipulate time, even a lack of understanding about what we interpret as time and although there are more prosaic explanations for this it should be considered.

A further point may well be that the one race which would want to limit our understanding of their activities might be Mankind itself from a different time; consider all those science fiction cliches about what the effect would be of killing your own grandfather in his youth or saving the Titanic, etc; to mask their activities, the 'aliens' could push out a lot of conflicting mumbo-jumbo and thereby keep us off the track. But this last point seems such an unlikely way to explain the material to hand that this 'theory' must be put on the back burner for lack of evidence.

Another quite ingenious theory that has been suggested is that the 'alien being' is in fact a form of our own existence; just as a caterpillar and a butterfly are stages of one creature's development yet quite different in all aspects, so might an early larval stage or a later development of our own species be the alien form.

This is another back-burner suggestion if only for lack of evidence once more, but there is some corroboration in the inconsistency of other material. We have already considered the link between ghost phenomena and UFO entities — and the apparent lack of links. But the message of ghost phenomena is often that the ghost is a manifestation of Man after death. Why, then, should the alien not be a similar entity, which again would explain the 'haunting' style of some UFO events and also the fact that different investigators seem to uncover their own field of study. It would simply mean that it was a question of interpretation of something not readily understood.

The list of possibilities are endless; many have been laid out in publications already and need no detailed explanation from me; John Keel's suggestion that there is a malfunctioning machine affecting our psyche; Jacques Vallee's belief that he can explain the phenomena given 'the existence of one more dimension'. Jacques Vallee even offered me a very humorous suggestion to explain the illogical inconsistency in UFO-related material but frankly it's as good as some theories I've read and probably better than the standard extra-terrestrial theory; it even has the benefit of humour. He suggested that we were the arena for a contest between two alien races — and that the contest was to see how many UFO books each could cause to get written!

Joking aside, it must be remembered that the basis of all these suggestions is that the physical evidence does not lead to sensible conclusions and if we wish to explain the material as other than purely psychological, then we must have some form of subjective response — special to the individual — which accounts for the inconsistency and the fact that the tales told seem so often to fulfil basic human needs. The truth — as always — is likely to be none of these things and, as they say, stranger than fiction; but to get to it we must be ready to open our minds to a range of possibilities. Particularly, we must step out of the mental cradle and leave the 'alien invaders' theory behind along with our other (mental) infant toys.

Later, however, we shall look at a theory which has one considerable strength, although it is allied to some of the above suggestions. All of the foregoing presupposes the existence of a different set of laws of physics to the ones we understand now, or a different understanding of Man's mental make up. That is not reason to reject them of course, we learn new concepts daily; but the suggestion we shall come to later has the merit of explaining *all* the phenomena without needing to change anything we presently understand, just to re-think our perspectives somewhat.

We shall come to this in due course.

OUT OF OUR MINDS

Any search for an explanation of the UFO phenomenon must address the question of whether or not there is, or could be, a psychological answer to the questions raised; whether or not it might simply be the product of imagination at one level or another.

This question is a crucial one, and has been addressed by many before, generally either UFO investigators and researchers or by others at their behest. My own reading of much of this work indicates that even where objective analysis is undertaken vital questions have been missed, leading to ambiguous conclusions.

Jenny Randles concludes in her book 'Abduction' that 'we do seem to have effectively disposed of the "all in the mind" school of thought'; she comments on the work of BUFORA investigator Ken Phillips and on the analysis of Dr Elizabeth Slater, a psychologist with apparently no interest in, or knowledge of, UFOs. The work of both of these people have produced interesting results, and of course in America there have been many other such studies where the 'all in the mind' school of thought is disposed of.

In the case of Ken Phillips, he worked for some years with psychologist Dr Alex Keul on a project known as Anamnesis — the study of the life profiles of close encounter (though not necessarily abduction) witnesses. Results of this work to date seem to indicate that basically such witnesses are not a 'special' set of the population with particular characteristics; indeed they seem to be a cross section of normal, healthy people. Some differences from the control population were apparent, for example, there was a higher level of ESP claims, and there was a tendency towards 'status inconsistent' life-styles; broadly speaking the witnesses tended to hold jobs or social positions in life that seemed to be inconsistent with their education or upbringing. Generally, this meant they held a job lower than might be expected; though in fact there were examples of heightened ability in some witnesses, particularly towards the arts.

In the case of Dr Slater in the United States, her involvement came about because three investigators, prominent in the field and adherents to the Extra-Terrestrial Hypothesis — Budd Hopkins, Ted Bloecher and Dr Aphrodite Clamar — wanted to put the question of a psychological answer to the test. Basic psychiatric tests were undertaken on nine abductees to determine if a common link could be established which would set them aside from the general population, and isolate the 'abduction factor'.

Again, with some slight deviations from a norm such as above-average intelligence, weak sense of personal identity, etc. — quite possibly a product of the small sample size — it was concluded that these people were healthy normal adults. Dr Slater — told of their common link after the work had been conducted — was of the opinion that their claims could not be put down to mental disorder. She found no evidence to suggest that the witnesses were 'pathological liars, paranoid schizophrenics, severely disturbed, or subject to fugue states or multiple personality shifts'. She concluded: 'There is no apparent psychological explanation for their reports'.

Although there is no reason to doubt these results, reached by qualified professional people, I have grave reservations about the conclusions ufologists further infer. It seems that, because no abnormality can be located in encounter witnesses, that they appear to be normal, healthy people, the experience cannot be psychological and probably therefore actually took place in some way or another. The absurdity of this belief was apparent to David Carpenter (pseudonym), a psychologist I discussed the question with; it presupposed that the UFO experience had to be abnormal.

There is no reason to think that this is so.

In fact, David held the view that what he understood of UFOs, contactees and abductions made them seem particular manifestations of very common needs of Man's fantasies. In short, UFO witnesses cannot be isolated from the 'normal' population because they are not abnormal, and the experience they report is normal when examined in the right context.

The first context to consider is Man's need for a God. In other words, if God didn't exist we would need to invent him. Some would argue this is precisely what we have done; while this is debatable, what is certain is that — for some people — God does not exist. Do these people therefore have to invent him? This does not mean that all abductees are atheist — some are not — nor does it mean that a need to 'invent' a God necessarily leads to an abduction crisis. Of the many millions in the world who feel they are without a saviour, some turn to materialism, some to offbeat religions, some to other forms of spiritual enlightenment; perhaps some also turn to alien contact in one form or another. This would not be a conscious process, more likely such a belief would harden fantasy impressions of the world and possibly create, in a very few, the right altered state of mind to project the abduction fantasy. Whether this is the correct solution to some cases is a matter for debate; the point is that it is a possibility and one that does not show up on personality testing since it is believed that we all share a common need for a God, which we have to satisfy in our own way. Such a need is normal.

The second context within which the psychological answer must be considered is Man's need to expand his horizons. It appears to be a normal need of Man to explore, to open new territory (shall I mischievously suggest 'to go where no man has gone before'?) This has to be for some a physical event; they become deep sea divers, astronauts, arctic explorers, mountain climbers, etc. For the majority it can be satisfied vicariously, by reading about or watching the exploits of others. The UFO phenomenon — and particularly the ETH — fulfils such a need; it seems to suggest contact with races from other worlds, perhaps even other galaxies; it makes Man part of a larger community. It means that during our lifetimes, when we will almost certainly not be able to travel between stars, we will be able to do so by meeting with those who can. Again, the UFO phenomenon seems to satisfy this need, which again most psychologists believe is a normal, healthy trait.

Thirdly, individual needs differ and for a small minority

those needs may be satisfied by the UFO phenomenon. While some people perhaps sit at their desks and dream of being James Bond, or stand at their production lines and dream of conquering Everest, a few may satisfy their fantasy needs via meetings with alien beings. For most, fantasy is a small and harmless deception of self; one experiment conducted consisted of the construction of a special mirror, a flexible version of the fairground distorted mirrors. Test subjects were placed in front of the mirror and asked to adjust it to produce the correct reflection. Virtually all subjects tested apparently believed themselves to be slightly taller and slightly thinner than they actually were! The study of fantasies has apparently been one of the most difficult for psychologists, partly because they experience difficulty in getting frank responses and partly because they cannot test the truthfulness of the responses. Also, ironically, because the *raison d'etre* for fantasy is usually private and to openly disclose it could itself be regarded as abnormal. Most fantasies remain hidden and private, some manifest harmlessly, only those which manifest violently — rape is a common one — are given close scrutiny, for obvious reasons. If someone wants to act out his fantasy by raping victims he must be stopped; for further victims to be saved he must be understood. However, if someone wants to tell the world he meets little green men there will be no psychological work carried out on the problem, as it probably causes no harm, and it will be left to those interested not in fantasies but in UFOs to do the analysis. The claims of contactees are fairly easy to understand in this context; they make the person special, he becomes one of 'the chosen few' — chosen in fact by those superior to all people on Earth; he is given a special message to impart to his fellow man, he becomes the object of attention, in some cases, he virtually achieves the status of worship. Abductees, however, seem to be less easy to understand in this way; while their selection might make them special they are treated worse than we treat some animals, with little or no respect; they are frightened and apparently harmed by their experience; they often have to keep their anonymity to avoid ridicule. Can this then be explained as a desired fantasy? The answer is 'yes', and goes back to the fact that individuals have individual needs. And for those who seek fame it may well be that the attention of a prominent UFO investigator/author/TV personality is sufficient. Although a pseudonym may be used, knowledge will leak out to those the abductee wants to know of the event, perhaps certain friends, etc. The fame may be limited, but it will be all that is required.

David suggested I should consider the fact that all people live in their fantasies, without exception. That we all see the world through glasses we 'rose tint' to our own specifications, and that even our most basic day-to-day routines are a product of our wishes as to how the world *could* be rather than our appreciation of how it actually is. For some, such a state can cause psychological problems, but this is a question of degree, of balance; it is a 'condition' in which we all share and — being normal — it does not make individuals unusual.

A further need that the UFO phenomenon might satisfy is the need for war; believed to be a natural state for Man. Not that Man has to be violent *per se*, but he needs the 'community spirit' which is most typified by war. The threat of an outside aggressor produces a whole new spirit to a people — witness Britain during the Falklands battles — and similarly the failure of a war to satisfy these needs leads to a violent social backlash — witness Vietnam, now held to have been a 'bad' war. James McCampbell, in his paper 'The significance for society if UFOs are extra-terrestrial' (an abridged version of which appeared in 'Phenomenon', edited by myself and Hilary Evans) reports on a study undertaken dealing with the potential for large scale disruption of world social order. This study was not undertaken with UFOs in mind but its conclusions were relevant: 'for the world to enjoy peace a substitute for war must be found'. In order to control the population there would need to be 'a real and immediate threat to their lives'. The UFO phenomenon might well fulfil that need, and the report quoted might even explain some of the apparent misinformation disseminated by Governments over the years.

If we were to make a case for a psychological answer then two other hurdles must be overcome. I would stress again, as I have indicated throughout this book, that I am not trying to prove or disprove particular theories, and feel strongly critical of those ufologists who have done so without proper analysis and evidence; what I want to do is to demonstrate that possibilities they believe to have been eliminated are in fact still open; that for many theories the jury is still out.

The two remaining hurdles, then, are the physical evidence and the fact that if the answer lies only in psychology, we would have to demonstrate that the UFO phenomenon could be a modern myth. For the latter case Thomas Bullard, a folklorist in the United States, deeply involved in the study of UFO phenomena, believes he has demonstrated that UFOs do not conform to a developing mythology. I believe I can show that this analysis may have overlooked a key factor.

For the physical evidence, what forms do they take? At this juncture we must be prepared to ignore hoaxes; because of their very nature they are likely to offer the best physical evidence but form no part of this study. Maurizio Verga points out that — hoaxes aside — physical evidence can be 'found' in two ways; either by physical evidence triggering a memory, or a later memory of the event taking the witness back to the site to search for physical proof. He points out that both can be unreliable since they tend to reinforce each other though no connection is necessarily established.

There are radar contacts with UFOs, though few that have pin-pointed craft claimed to be involved in abductions. In the Betty and Barney Hill case, the craft they reported was in fact tracked by Air Force radar, but what does this prove? Only that the object was probably physical, and we have never had reason to doubt that the Hills' encounter was at least triggered by some real event. The radar trace corroborates the sighting, not the abduction.

In the Hill case there were two other main physical effects; Barney developed a ring of warts on his groin which were in the area that he recalled the aliens placing an instrument on him. The warts appeared in 1962 though hypnotic regression did not reveal the story until later, when they became inflamed again. Secondly, there were circular marks on the boot of their car the day following the incident.

For the first point, the ring of warts, Barney himself realised they could be psychosomatic, a physical manifestation of his fears. The fears may well have been buried below conscious level; that they were, might well explain the manner of their manifestation. It has been suggested that the warts were a radiation effect of the equipment used on him by the aliens; if so then why should they become inflamed during regression sessions years later? Does this not in fact strengthen the belief that they were a reaction to his mind, not his body?

In the case of the circular patches on the car boot, no-one has yet put forward a definitive explanation; they appear to have upset a compass passed over them, and to be 'polished' areas of the metalwork. The point, however, is that they have never even been positively associated with the UFO by the Hills's conscious or other memory.

All that has happened is that two strange events have been linked, each apparently giving strength to the validity of the other. No actual cause and effect has been shown. Whatever happened to the car could have happened some time before, we shall never know for certain, but the fears about the night of the encounter certainly made Betty examine more closely that which perhaps she would not have otherwise.

Other cases have produced other evidence; in the Kathie Davis case there was an area of ground damage in the garden where the UFO was alleged to have landed and flown away from; Kathie Davis herself on one occasion had blood on her night clothing after alleged abductions, and she, like many other abductees, exhibits scars on her body she could not account for from memories.

I shall not try to give definitive alternative answers to these points, because I do not have them. I would again ask though that their strength be considered in relation to the claims being made for them. In the case of the ground damage there must be some possibility that natural soil damage by fungus, for example, can produce similar effects; Phillip Klass has suggested that bird droppings from a nearby bird feeder could have done so. Blood on the nightclothes probably means that, for example, there was a probe pushed into the nose during the night, to produce this physical effect. That probe could very easily have been the witness's own finger if during sleep the nose was agitated, or even if a peculiar dream manifested. I have watched both my daughters do just this and in the case of one of them, trigger off a series of messy nosebleeds that drenched parts of their nightclothes. This does not have to have happened to Kathie Davis, perhaps an alien did probe into her nose, but the physical evidence is not a strong corroboration so long as it could have a prosaic cause. To be objective in this study, a sense of proportion and balance must be maintained, or certainly real answers will be overlooked.

For the scars found on so many witness's bodies I would comment only that almost everyone I have spoken to agrees that they have scars of which they cannot recall the origin. I have myself; but as a normal healthy boy I would have climbed trees, run through woods and fallen and cut myself without realising it would scar. Such an event is quickly forgotten; years later the scar is a mystery. I see no reason to believe that a few marks on the body should make me fear I am an abduction witness. And I earlier pointed out that in earlier centuries witchfinders would use similar techniques to 'prove' a person was a witch; we now know what it proved was that if you want evidence for a pet theory you can always find it.

Photographs are another type of physical evidence to consider. In abduction cases, there are no photographs of merit; photographs in contactee cases have been called into serious question; the most probably 'genuine' photographs belong to the lights and discs in the sky era, and they prove only that — like the Hills' radar trace — something real was there. They do not prove an extra-terrestrial origin. I am mindful of the comments made to me by top film special effects expert Martin Bower when he deliberately faked a close encounter for me as an experiment for the book 'Phenomenon'; he said then, when I asked how real a fake could be particularly if there was significant money to be made, 'You don't have to fake as such. Give me a few days and a reasonable budget and I'll build the full size one hundred foot craft. And I'll get it in the air for you, without wires.' The point made here is agreed upon by most ufologists; photographs are worth nothing alone and are only a source of corroboration. They have not yet performed even this task in the case of abductions.

There is other evidence; one contactee — Menger — was given the ability to build the power unit of a flying saucer, which he did. But it did nothing, and therefore proved nothing. Cars have been subjected to what seem to be electromagnetic effects. Kenneth Behrendt, an engineering consultant in the United States has shown these could be the accidental backlash of the operating mechanism of the alien craft, yet again we have to ask ourselves about the motives of the aliens; they seem to want to hide their activities from us, yet they affect passing cars in this way, while at the same time they frequently 'buzz' airplanes which do not exhibit the same effects. Either we have our thinking wrong, or the aliens are playing a very subtle game, in which case we certainly have our conclusions wrong.

I have not confined my research to UFO evidence and the UFO witnesses. A large part of my work has been to study UFO investigators and their methods and motives. I believe that I have learned a lot about the phenomenon in this way, particularly how it has developed. One physical trace that reveals much about the UFO-ETH-devotees' motives is the so-called 'landing nests' or cornfield circles. Probably more garbage has been written about this subject than any other physical trace; with some desperate attempts made to fit it into UFO mythology.

To summarise these circles; they typically appear in England in the summer, though not exclusively so. They are known as cornfield circles since they appear frequently in fields of such crops, but they also occur in other crop locations. They are often very symmetrical patterns, sometimes a large central circle, with perhaps four smaller circles at points north, south, east and west of the main circle. The circles tend to be areas where the crop is flattened in a spiral fashion. To devoted extra-terrestrialists they are held to be the landing sites of UFOs and such 'investigators' have put a great deal of effort into proving so.

BUFORA felt that it was necessary to investigate these circles because the media continuously associated them with UFOs, although in fact no reliable case has ever been found which places a circle at the site of a UFO sighting. BUFORA's work took several years, and many theories were examined; Paul Fuller, who headed up the investigation, consulted — amongst others — the National Farmers Union and the

Tornado and Storm Research Organisation. A definitive answer is not available simply because no one has yet watched a circle form with independent corroboration, though one countryman reported his watching a circle form in a field over the short duration he watched it. With this caveat aside, it is now almost certain that the circles are a curious but nonetheless natural weather phenomenon; the result of hurricane vortices forming in the lower atmosphere and touching ground level at certain places. Some vortices are quite predictable, around the bases of large buildings for example, and have been filmed there, showing the curious patterns that can occur, though no one has yet manufactured a multi-circle pattern or predicted with accuracy where in the open fields such a phenomenon would occur.

Despite this work, there are a great number of unscientific and sloppy researchers who cling to the UFO theory for only two reasons; the circles are round (and so are 'flying saucers') and they are a mystery (and so are 'flying saucers'). Several researchers recently went for the Grand Slam on circles, when they made a UFO case out of a combination of a circle in a field, a troubled Harrier aircraft which flew after its pilot ejected, and Stonehenge, though no UFO was ever reported! Such a pity the flight path of the Harrier was limited or they might have worked in the Yeti and the Bermuda Triangle, too!

But if we accept the theory, how else does the evidence match up. As Maurizio Verga has stated in his paper 'Traces of UFO landings?' where we can match up the occasional UFO report with a circle, the object might be oval but the circle is always a circle.

And where we have a pattern it is presumed that the central large circle is the body of the craft and the four out-circles are the depressions of the landing legs. The pattern would then be similar to that left by the landing legs of the Apollo lunar module. But the out-circles also exhibit flattening of crops in a spiral fashion; as we have no reports at all of UFOs where the landing legs have each been spinning we are left with only one (extra-terrestrial) conclusion; that the aliens employ a special UFO for landing in cornfields so as to leave more distinctive marks than they otherwise would. Of course that objection could be overcome if we assumed that a large UFO, spinning, landed in a cornfield, and its own presence caused the vortices that formed the out-circles. But that would mean admitting the existence of vortex phenomena, and if that was admitted then the central UFO would not be needed!

There are a host of other logical objections to connecting extra-terrestrials with cornfield circles; they are not an important enough phenomenon to go into further here. But it tells us something of how UFO myths have been perpetrated, and it is a cautionary tale.

This leads us to a last set of criteria that must be considered if we are to leave the psychological possibilities open. We know that UFO stories have continued unabated for forty years; that there has been a development in activity which may or may not represent our own increasing knowledge in what 'they' are doing. There is a great deal of literature on the subject, increasing daily. For the phenomenon to be wholly psychological, all of this would have to be a developing mythology. Can this be shown to be the case, or at least a viable possibility?

The most careful study of this was conducted by Thomas Bullard, a folklorist in the United States who compared the UFO 'myth' with known, accepted myths to see if they followed the same patterns. One comparison he made was to the story of Cinderella.

Cinderella is a tale that exists all over the world, but each country, or area, has its own version of the story. Some versions differ quite considerably from others, yet the basic story is so similar that the connection is clear. Bullard points out that the UFO stories do not follow the same pattern as these folk tales; there is considerable consistency of detail, where he expected changes across time and location as the tale was 're-worked' in its development. The consistency of detail, he believes, means that there is a real, common event behind them. Over time, Bullard would expect modern UFO stories to be more alike than earlier stories, but finds this is not the case. Bullard summarises: 'If abductions are stories then the accounts should branch off into a different national version for each geographical area, but they do not. If abductions are stories the investigator should be able to impose an individual style on them... If abductions are stories they should change according to an expected pattern over time, but their history is steady instead, even to the point of opposing external influences.'

I would not necessarily agree with all these conclusions, in that I think there *are* some national characteristics for some stories — the little alien with the large head and the wrap around eyes seems commonly American in reports received, I think some investigators *do* impose an individual style, all too obviously in some cases, but I would certainly agree that there is a consistency over time that seems to defy the usual folklore development.

But does it, in fact?

Cinderella, Robin Hood, etc., are folk tales from centuries ago. They were passed on largely by word of mouth, over a great passage of time; they were influenced by social and cultural changes which also took place over time (in the usual telling of Little Red Riding Hood the wolf eats the girl's grandmother and lies in wait to trap and eat the girl, to be interrupted by a team of woodcutters who slit him open to release the still living grandmother; in a recent version my daughter received in this modern, 'aware' age the wolf locks Granny up in the cupboard and hides in wait to steal the girl's sandwiches, the woodcutters interrupt only to let granny out of the cupboard and tell the wolf not to be so naughty!).

The UFO phenomenon does not fit this picture, but I do not believe that proves it is not a continuing myth. What seems to have been overlooked is the possibility that it may be the first myth to develop in the modern, high-tech, instant global communication world. The myth does not have a chance to distort as it spreads quickly round the world, and furthermore the state of technology has meant that people have become more standardised than previously, more 'citizens of Earth' than of individual countries. While this might not be true of less technologically advanced races in, say, undeveloped Africa, it must be remembered that while they might *have* the experiences, it tends to be 'Western Man' that investigates them, reports on them and writes books about them. If the subject is, as I fear is possible, investigator-driven, then the standardisation across national boundaries becomes expected rather than surprising.

And it is also certain that folklore fulfils a human need; we start with Santa Claus, which is most children's early introduction to 'accepted untruths'; he is discarded early, though a myth such as the Pied Piper may last longer towards adulthood as a valid possibility. But do adults ever grow out of the need for such myths? Special effects expert Martin Bower attributes the success of his work in major science fiction films to what he calls 'kidult' mentality; in effect that we never really grow out of our childhood but merely superimpose our adult needs over it. Could UFOs be the adult Santa Claus or the adult Pied Piper?

Because of the speed of development of the UFO phenomenon, because of the type of world in which it has developed, I think we must leave the door open for the possibility that it is no more than a modern myth. Because it seems to fulfil basic human needs I think we must also leave the door open for an explanation that needs only psychology as its basis. This does not necessarily mean that I believe this has to be the answer, in fact I don't, but I feel a need to redress the balance lost by so many 'definitive' answers.

In the end I fall back on the old adage; if UFOs are extraterrestrial then that will be possibly the most important and significant event ever to have occurred to Mankind, affecting his society, his religion, his concepts of his race. We have no right to suggest this as a certainty until we have evidence of equal intensity. And we do not yet have that degree of evidence.

A SOLUTION THAT WORKS – THE MOTH PROPOSAL

What has been missing in the subject of UFOs is a possible answer that reconciles all of the contradictory evidence, but does not require exotic changes to the world we know; new physics, other dimensions, parallel universes, and the like. Further, all theories to date are based on the assumption that whatever the UFO phenomenon is, it is designed with us in mind, targeted towards us. This is contrary to the fact that most interaction between animals on Earth is accidental; that actions of one species which affect others, far from being premeditated, are often not even intended to be noticed by other species. The man who removes a wasp's nest from his loft and destroys it does not do so because of some reason concerning the wasps, he does it for his home's sake; the man who walks through an ant's nest and scatters it may not even know it was ever there.

With that in mind, this chapter sets out a possible alternative answer taking account of these points. As before, I don't seek to replace one unproven theory with another; merely to offer a new perspective to consider, not least to try to reconcile some of the contradictory evidence which denies the extra-terrestrial hypothesis, yet to acknowledge that the significant number of people in the world reporting the UFO experience must be undergoing *some* experience. As such therefore any evidence in support of this concept is tenuous and insubstantial, but it should be remembered that there is no stronger evidence supporting the ETH.

Man, and all creatures, must analyse and understand the world through their own senses, and it is doubtful that any species is in a position to totally understand the possible limitations of that perspective.

This conditioning applies to the 'basic' senses and the physical world in the first instance; at the 1988 International UFO Conference in Brussels, Dr Jacques Vallee showed a slide of a cat that had been fitted throughout its life with special 'glasses' which only allowed a horizontal perspective of the world. That cat could jump onto a flat table surface as easily as any other cat, but it could not negotiate the uprights, it would bump into the table's legs, for instance, because it could not comprehend them. Similarly a cat fitted in a similar way with glasses allowing only a vertical perspective would have no trouble with the table legs, but would be unable to leap onto the horizontal surface.

In the BBC programme 'The Mind Machine', study and analysis of the connection between the physical body and the development of the brain was examined. The presenter, Colin Blakemore, related a story from within his own family. His daughter, Sarah, had suffered from long sight in one eye but it had gone unnoticed for many years. Blakemore pointed out that corrective lenses did not seem to help the condition; that in fact the physical defect in her eye had prevented the necessary connections from developing in the brain so that she simply could not be made to see 'correctly'. Nerve impulses from the eyes had permanently altered the *physical* structure of her brain in development. In the same programme the neurobiologist Hendrick van der Loos explained his experiment with the whiskers of a mouse. He discovered that each whisker acts, as he put it, like a blind man's cane, giving the animal tactile awareness, and each whisker has a group of nerve cells in the brain exclusively devoted to it. If the whiskers were removed shortly after birth, the nerve cells in the brain do not develop. After a certain time, six days in the case of mice, removing the whiskers has no such effect; the brain is now committed to its perception of the world. Blakemore pointed out this is both an advantage and a disadvantage; the brain loses flexibility to develop, but on the other hand it gains stability.

Obviously it is vital to understand this if we are to comprehend how we perceive the world around us. But the implications are far wider in the study of the understanding of Man as a species. If the inputs to our senses affect the development of the brain then what of the images it receives. Are we brought up in a world where we can only 'see' those things that fit into our understanding of the world. There is much evidence to suggest this. We know, for example, that people describe the things they see in the terminology of the time, or the place. The old film cliche of the primitive tribe referring to an airplane as a 'great silver bird' is an interpretation of this. But do the tribe see an airplane and describe it as if by comparison; or do they in fact see a bird. If they have never been exposed to technology *can* they see it as such? In the early days of the settlement of America, when the railroads were being laid across that continent, the native population were described not as failing to understand the 'iron horse', but of failing to see it at all. It did not fit into their comprehension. They must have seen something — after all the trains occupied physical space in front of their eyes. But *what* did they see?

This is clearly very important in our understanding of the study of UFOs. It is held that if UFOs are in fact physical 'nuts and bolts' craft then we would all see the same thing, whereas UFO reports seem to suggest we do not. But perhaps because the object is outside the comprehension of our development, we cannot 'see' it as it is. In fact, though, whether UFOs are physical, or only partly so, it is clear that *if we are not conditioned to see them then we shall not perceive them correctly.*

Vladimir Rubtsov, a Soviet researcher, stated in his paper to the 1988 Brussels UFO conference that there are three elements to a scheme of scientific observation; sensors, a channel and a researcher. In the case of ufology, these instruments are usually all human, and all are 'characterised by so large variability of their parameters, that it is impossible to relate uniquely the "output" of the observation to its "input".'

Rubtsov points out, with perception: 'the image of the phenomenon, created in the mind of the witness, is not equal to a photograph. It comes into being as a result of the interaction between the sensory data and "anticipating patterns" that are kept deep in human memory. Seeing a completely new object means building promptly a new pattern to assimilate the non-standard sensory information. Such a pattern is usually constructed by association, which does not always warrant its conformity to the real structure of the observed phenomenon and may lead to various illusions.'

It is worth at this stage suggesting an alternative possibility to the somewhat unlikely one that alien astronauts are visiting the Earth with a rather bizarre campaign of genetic study in mind: Let us consider that the UFOs, and the 'aliens', are in fact just a natural part of our world, but one which humans have lost — or never developed — association with, and are not conditioned to understand. Dr Jacques Vallee has made similar suggestions; he pointed out, at the Brussels Conference, that he only needed confirmation of one more dimension to allow his theory to gain the strength it needed. The core of this proposal is that it does not need a world different from the one we know we live in.

Could it be that for all of Man's time on Earth, believing himself to be the dominant intelligence of the planet, he has misunderstood the truth? And could it be that all creatures, without exception, believe themselves to be the highest form of intelligence, and that all — to some degree — are right to make that claim?

Before explaining the proposal, let me make an analogy.

The moth is a common insect found throughout the world; over two thousand species are found in the British Isles alone. They are clearly physical, as are humans; they are mortal, and as such can be considered to be comparable to humans.

Let us consider a family of moths living near a motorway. They would be able to see some of Man's achievements; they would frequently see cars and coaches and lorries, they would occasionally see Man himself, usually walking from a broken down vehicle to an emergency telephone, they would sometimes encounter the vehicles as they fly near the motorway; they might be blown off course, and some will die in collisions with windscreens. They will see and possibly touch telegraph poles near the motorway, they will see the motorway lighting which will — at night — attract and even kill some of their number.

Yet what would they really understand of human society from their observations?

Can Man's society be understood from seeing him walking down the hard shoulder from a stationary vehicle, or relieving himself behind a bush? Yet that family of moths would see nothing more.

Can the purpose of vehicles be understood by the moths? Indeed, would moths regard the humans or the vehicles as the dominant or intelligent life form?

Would moths assume that when they encounter our vehicles, even die on the windscreens, that this is part of a human plot to abduct their numbers; that the 'visitations' of our vehicles are for a specific purpose relating to moths? Certainly when UFOs and aliens act in a way which affects humans, we assume that we are the target of their actions rather than simply caught up in something that may not even concern us.

Is it therefore possible for moths to understand that most of us pass closely by their home, even perhaps disturb it, without the slightest interest or concern, let alone premeditation?

From their interaction with telegraph poles, could they ever understand the telephone?

Would they assume that the motorway lighting, switched on when the moths are most active, are a device for luring and killing them? From their perspective, could they ever understand the true meaning of the lights, could they comprehend that when we constructed them, we never even thought of moths?

And would our family of moths, talking to members of another family that lived, say, in the loft of a house in a big city, even recognise that there was a link between the humans and vehicles seen by each. The activities of the humans, their attitudes, even their dress, would appear so different to each colony, and the speeds and uses of the vehicles so dissimilar, that it might not even cross their minds to consider comparing them.

Even if some super intelligent, Einstein-moth could put together each and every clue available to the moth world regarding human society, could it even then begin to conceive of the works of Shakespeare, of Da Vinci, of opera and art and literature. Could they understand the deeds of Genghis Khan and Adolf Hitler, or those of Mother Theresa, Gandhi, and others.

What does this mean in the quest to understand Man's relationship with the UFO phenomenon?

The question is, is it possible that Mankind shares this planet with one or more species that are as geographically spread as we are, that are as rich in number as we are, that are as physical and mortal as we are but which are so different in their culture that we completely fail to understand what we see or perceive? The logical answer seems to be *no* — after all we closely monitor the whole planet, we understand so much science, what could possibly escape our notice?

The *answer* lies in the very many things Man does not understand, including UFOs.

Could UFO sightings — so inconsistent, varied and seemingly illogical — be a manifestation of a culture with which we share the Earth and yet don't understand? Could alien abductions be our quite wrong interpretation of some activity of theirs that doesn't even involve us? Could ghosts be some other manifestation of another activity of theirs that we totally fail to understand?

And if there is deliberate interaction with us, would we understand? Could our failure to do so explain the mysteries of much paranormal activity. Could poltergeist activity, telekinesis, visions, apparitions, etc., all be forms of their activity, even perhaps an attempt at communication with us that we have not understood?

Let us consider the UFOs as a product of their technology, but *not* vehicles of any kind; rather let us consider them a mental device for carrying messages, which we 'intercept'. Because of the influence of science fiction on our culture, perhaps, we interpret what we see as spaceships. In the next chapter we shall look at how we perceive situations and impressions through models in the mind; the only real model we have of the UFO phenomenon comes from science fiction, so perhaps for that reason we perceive the phenomenon in that way; possibly quite wrongly if our model is incorrect.

What we think of as alien abductions could be messages or activities designed to show that they understand our minds and bodies house intelligence, but they are incapable of expressing this properly.

In the past three chapters we have considered alternatives to the unsupportable theory that UFOs are alien spacecraft, visiting the Earth for prosaic reasons that owe more to anthropomorphic thinking than to the evidence. They offer solutions to the contradictions inherent in the material as we see it, but they are unlikely to be right in more than a general sense. If it is true that anthropomorphic thinking is an *essential* part of human thinking, and it seems to be, then perhaps it would be impossible to comprehend, let alone express, the truth until such time as we have become conditioned to perceive the true answers. Perhaps that other race, from wherever, is doing its best to build that bridge of understanding.

If there is anything to the paranormal outside of human psychology then we must try to be flexible enough to see the signals they are sending for what they are, not what we want them to be.

PART SEVEN

The Future

I doubt not but that time who is still the father of new truths, and hath revealed unto us many things which our ancestors were ignorant of, will also manifest to our posterity that which we now desire but cannot know

JOHN WILKINS

IN CONCLUSION — TOWARDS 2047

After the Kenneth Arnold sighting of June 1947 the media believed they would have concrete answers to the questions it raised within one day. In June 1987, the slogan of the MUFON congress in America was 'Forty Years is Long Enough'. What will be the slogan of the congresses of June 2047, the centenary of the modern era of UFOs? Impossible to predict; one thing is certain — by then the phenomenon will have undergone as many changes again as it has already.

The history of abductions has been a continuing development in the unfolding of the UFO phenomenon; in that it is also part of a continuing mythology — *to some extent.*

The phenomenon has affected much of our modern society, our culture, our fiction, areas of our religion and much more. It has done *this without proof of reality*; people's perception of the world has changed because of the existence of the literature, whether or not there is a basis in reality. This will continue into the future whether there is a foundation in reality or not, so long as people believe *something.*

The future will therefore hold two realities; one based on what people believe, the other based on what actually is. Both will, as ever, interact.

The problem with the UFO phenomenon is that it may be some form of occurrence that does not fit into human perception; *about which we do not have the right perspectives.* In analysing any situation or object, we do so by comparing it to 'models' held within our mind, built up from our experiences. *And we do not have the model of the UFO phenomenon.*

To give an example of this; a model of the world is what allows us to plan journeys, and therefore our immediate future. From experience we build a model and to make plans we 'run' the model at high speed in our imagination, to see if our plans fit what we know of the situation. Suppose we wish to plan a car journey from London to Edinburgh; firstly we buy a pre-planned model — a map. Then we decide when we need to be in Edinburgh. We work our the distance, the average expected speed of travel, the stops we are likely to have to make on the journey. Back calculation gives us the time we have to leave. We can then run the plan forward to see if it has any flaws. Once we have finalised it we have a journey time and route with known likely events planned for. We are in effect predicting our future when we run the model as a test.

If we had no model such a journey would be impossible. If we had no conception of distance, or speed, or time then we could not plan the journey. We rely on these models in our mind absolutely in such circumstances.

I tested this point with one of my daughters. Aged five at the time, she had the normal child's lack of perspective about the world (due to the lack of opportunity to build such models by that age; in fact since she could read much of a newspaper before her fourth birthday she is likely to start this sort of model building earlier than average). I decided to try to explain the relative size of the world to her, with amusing results.

I started by showing her a map of southern England, pointing out places she knew of; our home, our former home, her grandparents home, and Streatham where John and Jane, friends of ours, lived. She seems to take this in so I then showed her a map of the United Kingdom, first pointing out the area that matched the previous map, showing her on the second map the same places I had shown her on the first, then adding information about her relatives in Scotland, whom she had visited several times. I went through this procedure again taking in all of Europe and pointing out places where we had been on holiday, or where she knew I had been, or places such as Sweden where she knows several of her friends come from. Intelligently she nodded her understanding and finally we moved on to a map of the world. I pointed out Europe and its place, then indicated Australia. We have friends there with whom we regularly correspond and she knows them from our discussions and their photographs. I asked her where she thought this country was and who lived there, telling her it was the farthest point from our home in the world. She thought about it for a while and answered, 'John and Jane; its Streatham isn't it?'

A good example, I thought, of not having a model to work from.

In an earlier chapter I referred to an experiment Jacques Vallee had lectured on at the Brussels 1988 conference; where a cat had been conditioned from birth to see only the horizontal; setting up a totally false image of the world which prevented it from proper analysis of its situation.

So we may conclude that we can only understand the world through our models, and that perhaps the lack of understanding of the UFO phenomenon is a result of having no model to work from. Considering the experiment with the cat, if our understanding of what we think we know of the phenomenon is at fault, then the model we are building from experience may be equally faulty.

What we need, therefore, is a precise recording instrument. Since the UFO experience appears to be one of human interaction, then the recording device will have to be a person. To be precise, that person will have to be brought up from birth with the right model of the phenomenon in his mental make up, so that he can learn from it, understand it, and interact properly with it.

As this is presently impossible, we might have arrived at the core problem which has prevented us — *and may always prevent us* — from understanding this phenomenon, unpalatable though such a thought will be to many.

It is a three point problem:

— If the UFO phenomenon is a set of objects and activities which are a natural part of the human world then we should have developed the right model long ago, since the problem will have evolved within the same framework as our own minds. Since we appear not to have done so, despite considerable effort in this direction, then it is reasonable to consider that the answer lies elsewhere.

— If the UFO phenomenon is purely psychological, and the product of developing mythology, then it is not an answerable problem as such. To try to find an 'answer' to it would be as inappropriate as trying to 'answer' Love, the story of Cinderella, or other abstracts which do not beg an answer. Further, it would be impossible to ever pin down the phenomenon to a stable condition since it would develop along with human thinking, changing as we begin to understand and interact with it. In short, like so many aspects of our higher abstract life, it would be like a firework display for us to watch and experience, constantly changing, constantly forcing us to think and re-think, changing as we did so. It would not be a problem that required solving. Since the phenomenon exhibits these characteristics and appears to have developed over time as we seek to understand it, then this possibility must be considered.

— If the UFO phenomenon is truly alien to humanity, be it terrestrial or extra-terrestrial, then we may never be able to build the correct model. It may be, in fact, that we are incapable of building models about anything that is outside human perspective. To accept this requires the acceptance of something outside our ability to understand, as discussed in the chapter 'A solution that works'. We can accept that no amount of self-education would allow our moth colony of that chapter to understand Man's social structures; is it so terrible to consider that we might be to some form of life as moths are to us? In that event it may even be impossible for 'them' to educate us; could we ever teach a moth all it needed to know to fully appreciate human art and sciences?

The awful truth in these circumstances, which may be the only option on offer, is that we might have to consider the UFO phenomenon is a 'question' that will never be 'answered'. Indeed, that cannot be answered.

If it can be answered, then it will certainly require an immense change in our perspectives.

REFERENCES AND BACKGROUND MATERIAL

Books

The Interrupted Journey
John G Fuller
Souvenir Press 1966

Intruders
Budd Hopkins
Random House 1987

Missing Time
Budd Hopkins
Richard Merrick 1981

UFO Abductions — A Dangerous Game
Philip J Klass
Prometheus 1988

The UFO Abductors
Brad Steiger
Berkley 1988

Alien Abductions
D Scott Rogo
Signet 1980

Abduction
Jenny Randles
Robert Hale 1988

Dimensions
Jacques Vallee
Souvenir Press 1988

Visions, Apparitions, Alien Visitors
Hilary Evans
Aquarian Press 1984

The Evidence for Alien Abductions
John Rimmer
Aquarian Press 1984

Communion
Whitley Strieber
Century Hutchinson 1987

Flying Saucers : A Modern Myth of Things Seen in the Skies
C G Yung
Arc 1987 (First published 1959)

Passport to Magonia
Jacques Vallee
Spearman 1970

The Invisible College
Jacques Vallee
Dutton 1975

The Andreasson Affair
R Fowler
Prentice-Hall 1979

Close Encounters of an Australian Kind
K Basterfield
Reed 1981

UFOs: The Public Deceived
Philip Klass
Prometheus 1983

UFO
Robert Chapman
Granada 1968

UFO Exist!
Paris Flammonde
Ballantine 1976

Flying Saucers Have Landed
Desmond Leslie and George Adamski
Futura 1977 (First published 1953)

Project Blue Book
Brad Steiger (Ed.)
Ballantine 1976

UFOs Past, Present and Future
Robert Emenegger
Ballantine 1974

Aliens from Space
Major Donald E Keyhoe
Panther 1975

UFO Trek
Warren Smith
Sphere 1977

Strange Creatures from Time and Space
John Keel
Sphere 1976

The Cosmic Question
John A Keel
Panther 1978

Visitors from Space
John A Keel
Panther 1976 (First published as The Mothman Prophecies)

The Evidence for UFOs
Hilary Evans
The Aquarian Press 1983

Beyond Earth
Ralph and Judy Blum
Corgi 1974

Flying Saucers from Outer Space
Donald E Keyhoe
Tandem 1969

The Humanoids
Charles Bowen (Ed.)
Futura 1974

Ancient Astronauts: A Time Reversal?
Robin Collyns
Sphere 1978

The Gold of the Gods
Erich von Daniken
Souvenir Press 1972

Return to the Stars
Erich von Daniken
Souvenir Press 1970

Chariots of the Gods?
Erich von Daniken
Souvenir Press 1969

Colony : Earth
Richard Mooney
Granada Publishing 1975

Gods of Air and Darkness
Richard Mooney
Panther 1977

Temple of the Stars
Brinsley Le Poer Trench
Fontana 1973

Operation Earth
Brinsley Le Poer Trench
Tandem 1974

Mysterious Visitors
Brinsley Le Poer Trench
Pan Books 1975

Gods and Spacemen in the Ancient East
W Raymond Drake
Sphere 1973

Operation Trojan Horse
John Keel
Putman 1970

Secret of the Saucers
Orfeo Angelucci
Amherst Press 1955

Aboard a Flying Saucer
Truman Bethurum
De Vorss 1954

From Outer Space to You
Howard Menger
Saucerian 1959

The White Sands Incident
Daniel W Fry
New Age 1954

When Prophecy Fails
Festinger/Reichen/Schacker
Harper & Row 1964

The Hynek UFO Report
Dr J Allen Hynek
Sphere 1978

The Tungus Event
Rupert Furneaux
Panther 1977

Encounter Cases from Flying Saucer Review
Charles Bowen (Ed.)
Signet 1977

The UFOnauts
Professor Hans Holzer, PhD
Panther 1979

Other Worlds
Carl Sagan
Bantam 1975

UFO Study
Jenny Randles
Robert Hale 1981

The Roswell Incident
Charles Berlitz and William Moore
Granada Publishing 1980

Above Top Secret
Timothy Good
Sidgwick and Jackson 1987

UFOs 1947–1987
Hilary Evans with John Spencer (Eds.)
Fortean Tomes 1987
(Contributors: V J Ballester Olmos, Ken Behrendt, Michel Bougard, Bill Chalker, David Clarke, Hilary Evans, Robert Girard, Richard Haines, Kim Hansen, Cynthia Hind, Peter Hough, John Keel, Alex Keul, Anders Liljegren, Claude Mauge, James McCampbell, Kevin McClure, Bertram Meheust, Michel Monnerie, Mark Moravec, Grenville Oldroyd, Ken Philips, John Prytz, Jenny Randles, John Rimmer, Andy Roberts, Chris Rutkowski, Bronislaw Rzepecki, Martin Shough, Willy Smith, John Spencer, Dennis Stacy, Leonard Stringfield, Clas Svahn, Jacques Vallee, Maurizio Verga, Enrique Vicente, Nigel Watson, Rob Westrum).

Phenomenon
John Spencer and Hilary Evans (Eds.)
MacDonald 1988
(Contributors: Lionel Beer, Pierre Lagrange, Nigel Watson, Anders Liljegren, Clas Svahn, Bronislaw Rzepecki, Kim Hansen, Paul Norman, Martin Shough, Andy Roberts, Peter Hough, Dennis Stacy (a particularly useful source of reference for contactee material), Budd Hopkins, Jenny Randles, John Rimmer, John A Keel, Maurizio Verga, Gerald Mosbleck, John Shaw, Stephen Gamble, Michael Wootten, J Danby, Dr Willy Smith, Bertil Kuhlemann, Bill Chalker, Dr Allen Tough, John Prytz, Kenneth W Behrendt, Chris Rutkowski, David Clarke, Paul Devereux, Mark Moravec, James McCampbell, Cynthia Hind, Kevin McClure, Hilary Evans, John Spencer).

Parapsychology and the UFO
Manford Cassierer
(Private Publication 1988)

The Invasion of the Moon 1969
Peter Ryan
Penguin Books 1969

The Right Stuff
Tom Wolfe
Jonathan Cape 1980

The Boston Strangler (for regression hypnosis material)
Gerald Frank
Pan Books 1967

The Search for Bridey Murphy
Morey Bernstein
Doubleday 1956

A Pictorial History of Science Fiction Films
Jeff Rovin
Citadel Press 1975

Witch Hunt
Isabel Adam
MacMillan 1978

Natural and Supernatural
Brian Inglis
Hodder & Stoughton 1977

Psychic Powers
Time-Life Editors
Time-Life 1988

Deeper into the Occult
Peter Underwood
Harrap 1975

Fairy Faith in Celtic Counties
W Evans-Wentz
Oxford University Press 1911

The Naked Ape
Desmond Morris
Tryad Grafton 1977

Magazines and Periodicals

BUFORA Journal and Bulletin
(from 1968 to 1988)
(Various Editors: current Editor Michael Wootten)

The Journal of Transient Aerial Phenomena
(1980–1988)
(Various Editors: current Editor-in-Chief S J Gamble)

MUFON UFO Journal
(July 1987–November 1988)
(Editor Dennis Stacy)

UFO Brigantia
(November 1987–October 1988)
(Editor Andy Roberts)

SOBEPS News
(January 1976–September 1977)
(Editor Michel Bougard)

OVNI Presence (1988)
(Editor Yves Bosson)

Cuadernos de Ufologia
(1987–1988)
(Editors Julio Arcas and Jose Ruesga)

Anomaly (1987–1988)
(Editor Alan Cleaver)

Fortean Times (1987)
(Editors Robert Rickard and Paul R A De G Sieveking)

Italian UFO Reporter
(1988)
(Editors Gian Grassino, Eduardo Russo, Paolo Toselli and Maurizio Verga)

UFO-IFO
Scufori-Probe Production
(Editor Ian Mrzygrod)

UFOAFRI News (1988)
(Editor Cynthia Hind)

Mystery of the Circles
BUFORA Publications
(Compiled by Paul Fuller and Jenny Randles)

A sample survey of the incidents of geometrically shaped crop damage
(1988)
(Commissioned by BUFORA and The Tornado and Storm Research Organisation) by C P Fuller

also:

The BBC television programme: 'The Mind Machine'.

Various privately published papers by Dr Willy Smith, William Moore, James McCampbell

INDEX